Eat Your Heart Out
Volume One

PRESS

AN ONI PRESS PUBLICATION

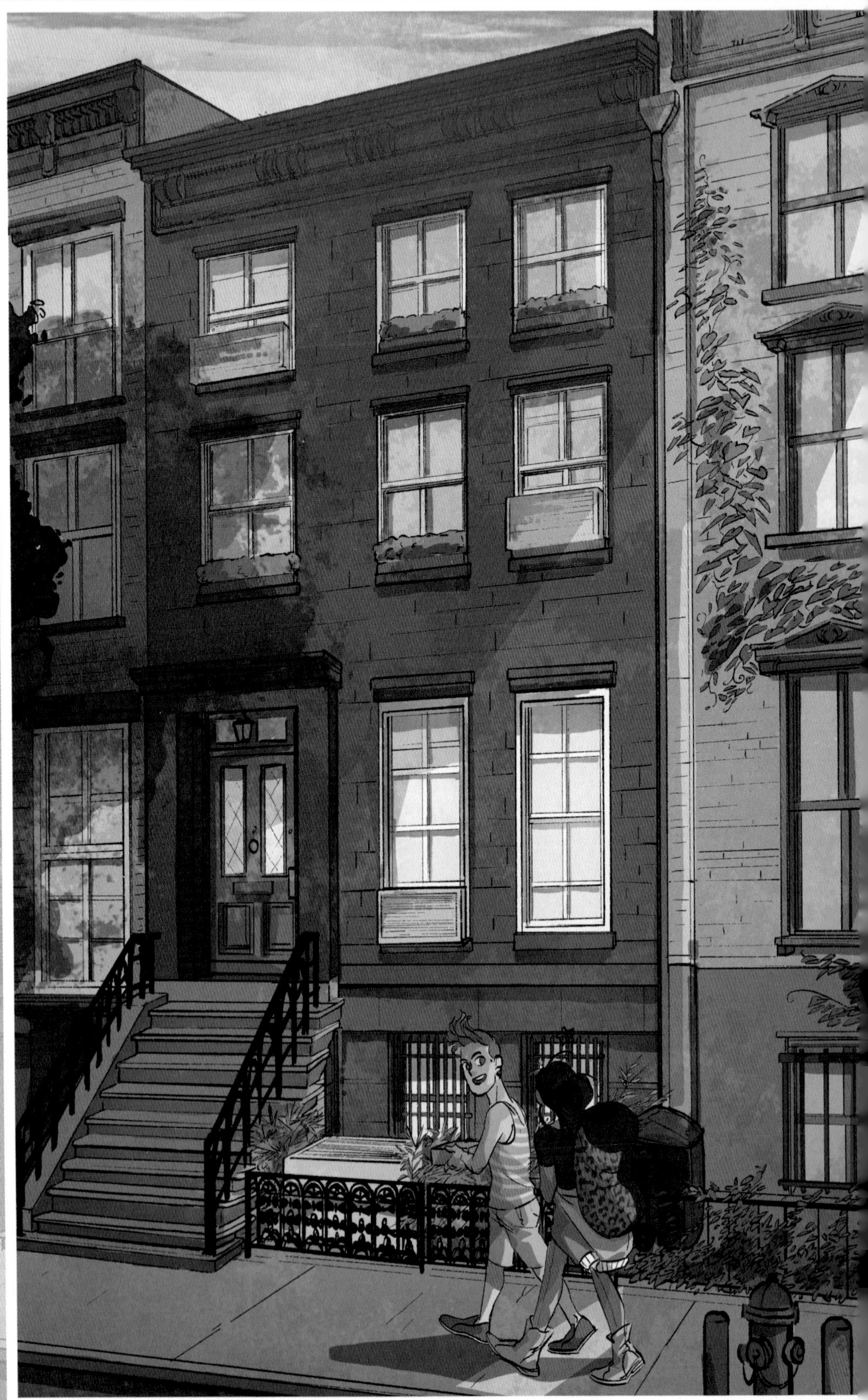

Eat Your Heart Out
Volume One

CREATED and CO-WRITTEN BY
TERRY BLAS **and** MATTY NEWTON

ART BY
LYDIA ANSLOW

COLORS BY
CLAUDIA AGUIRRE

LETTERS BY
JIM CAMPBELL

FLATS BY
GABRIEL FISCHER

DESIGNED BY
CAREY SOUCY

EDITED BY
DESIREE RODRIGUEZ, GRACE SCHEIPETER,
GABRIEL GANILLO, ROBIN HERRERA,
AND SHANNON WATTERS

ONI PRESS

PUBLISHED BY ONI-LION FORGE PUBLISHING GROUP, LLC.
Hunter Gorinson, president & publisher • Sierra Hahn, editor in chief Troy Look, vp of publishing services • Spencer Simpson, vp of sales Angie Knowles, director of design & production • Katie Sainz, director of marketing • Jeremy Colfer, director of development • Chris Cerasi, managing editor • Bess Pallares, senior editor • Grace Scheipeter, senior editor • Karl Bollers, editor • Megan Brown, editor • Gabriel Granillo, editor Jung Hu Lee, assistant editor • Michael Torma, senior sales manager • Andy McElliott, operations manager • Sarah Rockwell, senior graphic designer Carey Soucy, senior graphic designer • Winston Gambro, graphic designer • Matt Harding, digital prepress technician • Sara Harding, executive coordinator • Kaia Rokke, marketing & communications coordinator • Joe Nozemack, publisher emeritus

onipress.com facebook.com/onipress
twitter.com/onipress instagram.com/onipress
thatnormdude.com | louiejoyce.com

First Edition: August 2024 | ISBN: 978-1-63715-454-0
eISBN: 978-1-63715-455-7 | Printed in: China | LCCN: 2023947287
1 2 3 4 5 6 7 8 9 10

Eat Your Heart Out Volume One, July 2024. Published by Oni-Lion Forge Publishing Group, LLC., 216 SE Martin Luther King Jr. Blvd., Suite 216, Portland, OR 97214.

FOR CRYSTAL, WHOSE FRIENDSHIP AND KINDNESS ENCOURAGED ME AND SAVED ME. AND STILL DOES. —TB

TO ADELA, FOR YOUR GIFTS AND GUIDANCE. —MN

DEDICATED TO MY OWN EMILE, MY BEST HOMIE, LARISSA, AND MY MOM AND DAD, WHO ALL THANKFULLY SUPPORTED ME THROUGH EVERYTHING. —LA

Chapter One

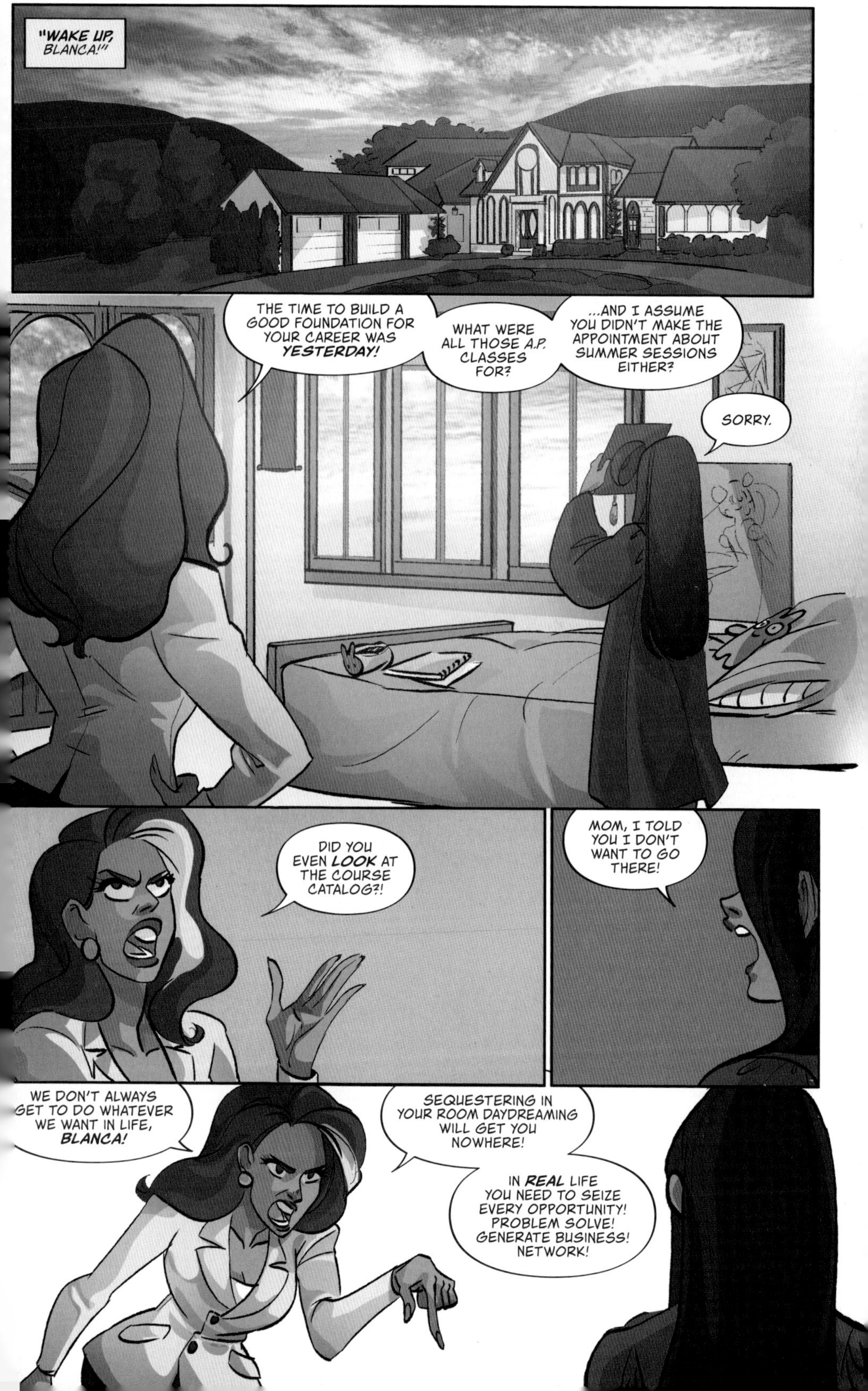
"WAKE UP, BLANCA!"
THE TIME TO BUILD A GOOD FOUNDATION FOR YOUR CAREER WAS YESTERDAY!
WHAT WERE ALL THOSE A.P. CLASSES FOR?
...AND I ASSUME YOU DIDN'T MAKE THE APPOINTMENT ABOUT SUMMER SESSIONS EITHER?
SORRY.
DID YOU EVEN LOOK AT THE COURSE CATALOG?!
MOM, I TOLD YOU I DON'T WANT TO GO THERE!
WE DON'T ALWAYS GET TO DO WHATEVER WE WANT IN LIFE, BLANCA!
SEQUESTERING IN YOUR ROOM DAYDREAMING WILL GET YOU NOWHERE!
IN REAL LIFE YOU NEED TO SEIZE EVERY OPPORTUNITY! PROBLEM SOLVE! GENERATE BUSINESS! NETWORK!

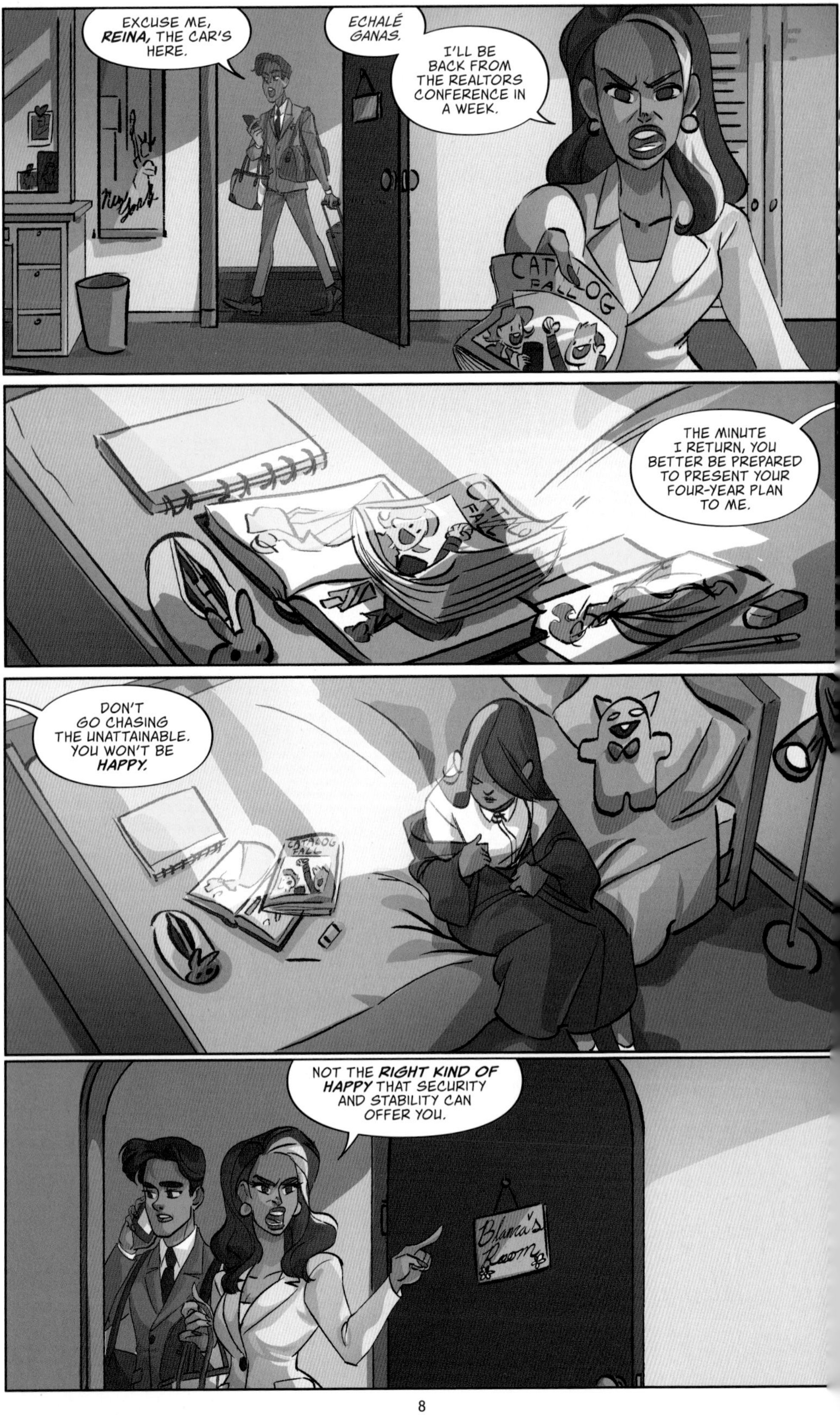
EXCUSE ME, REINA, THE CAR'S HERE.
ECHALÉ GANAS.
I'LL BE BACK FROM THE REALTORS CONFERENCE IN A WEEK.
CATALOG FALL
THE MINUTE I RETURN, YOU BETTER BE PREPARED TO PRESENT YOUR FOUR-YEAR PLAN TO ME.
DON'T GO CHASING THE UNATTAINABLE. YOU WON'T BE HAPPY.
CATALOG FALL
NOT THE RIGHT KIND OF HAPPY THAT SECURITY AND STABILITY CAN OFFER YOU.
Blanca's Room

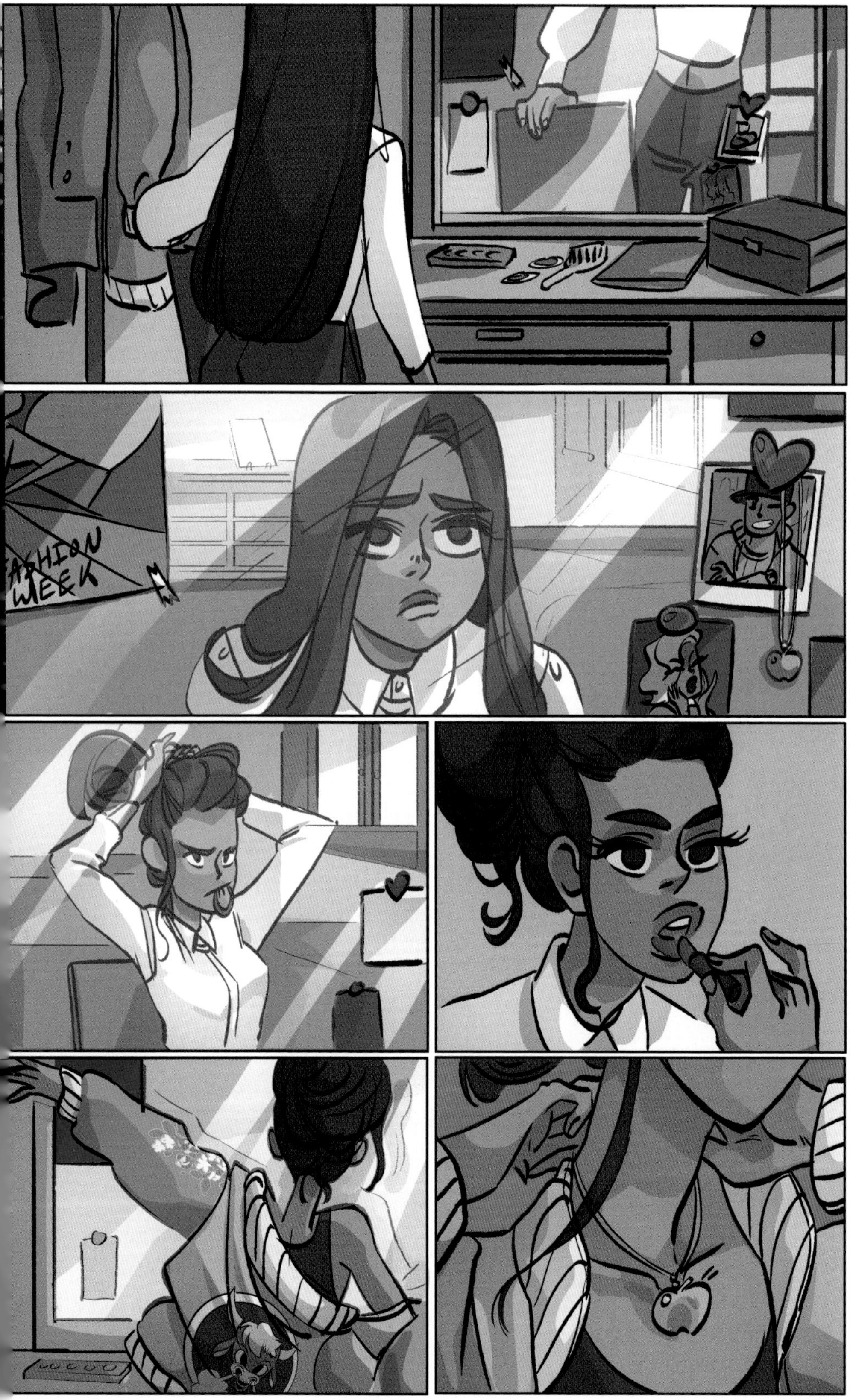
FASHION
WEEK

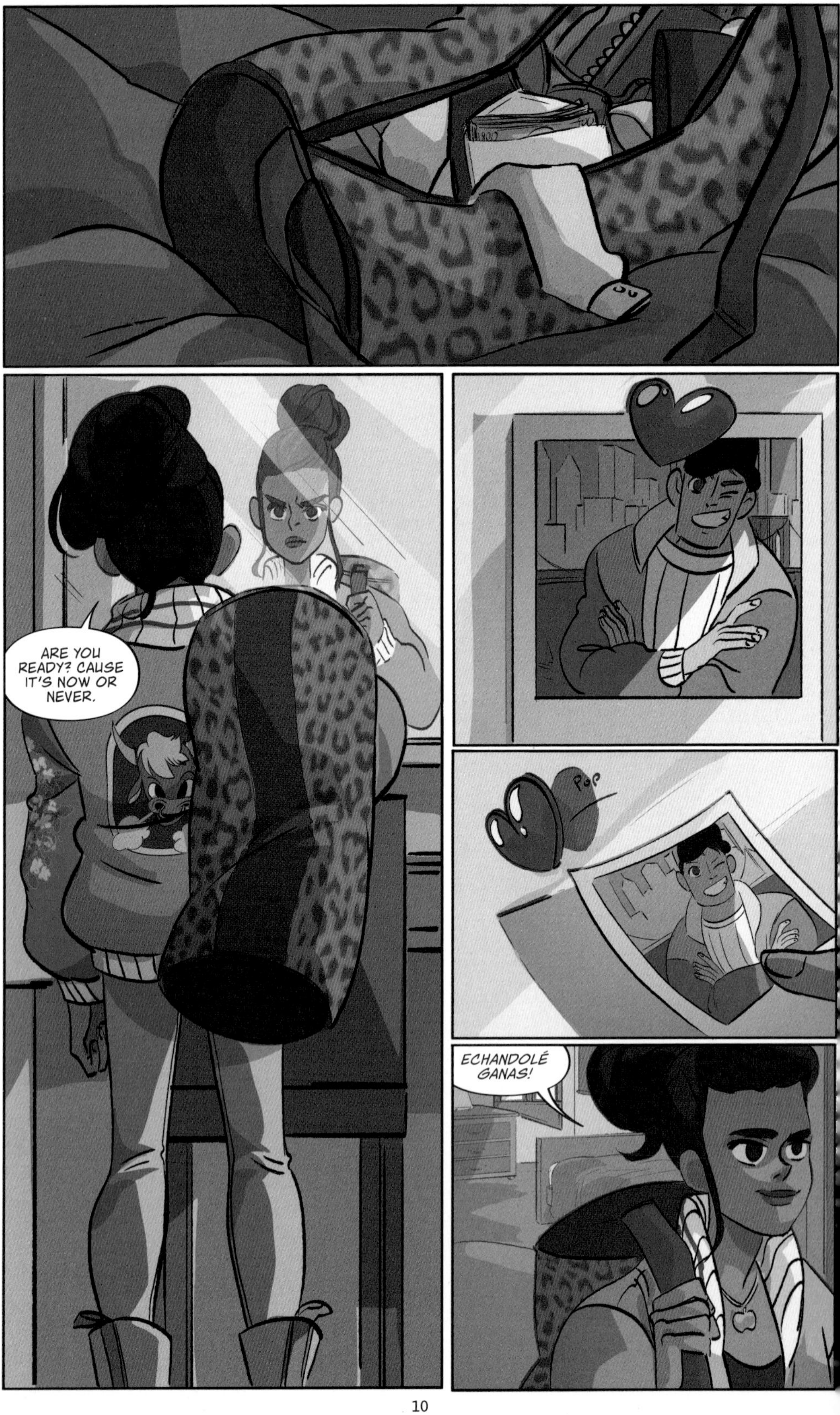
ARE YOU READY? CAUSE IT'S NOW OR NEVER.
POP
ECHANDOLÉ GANAS!

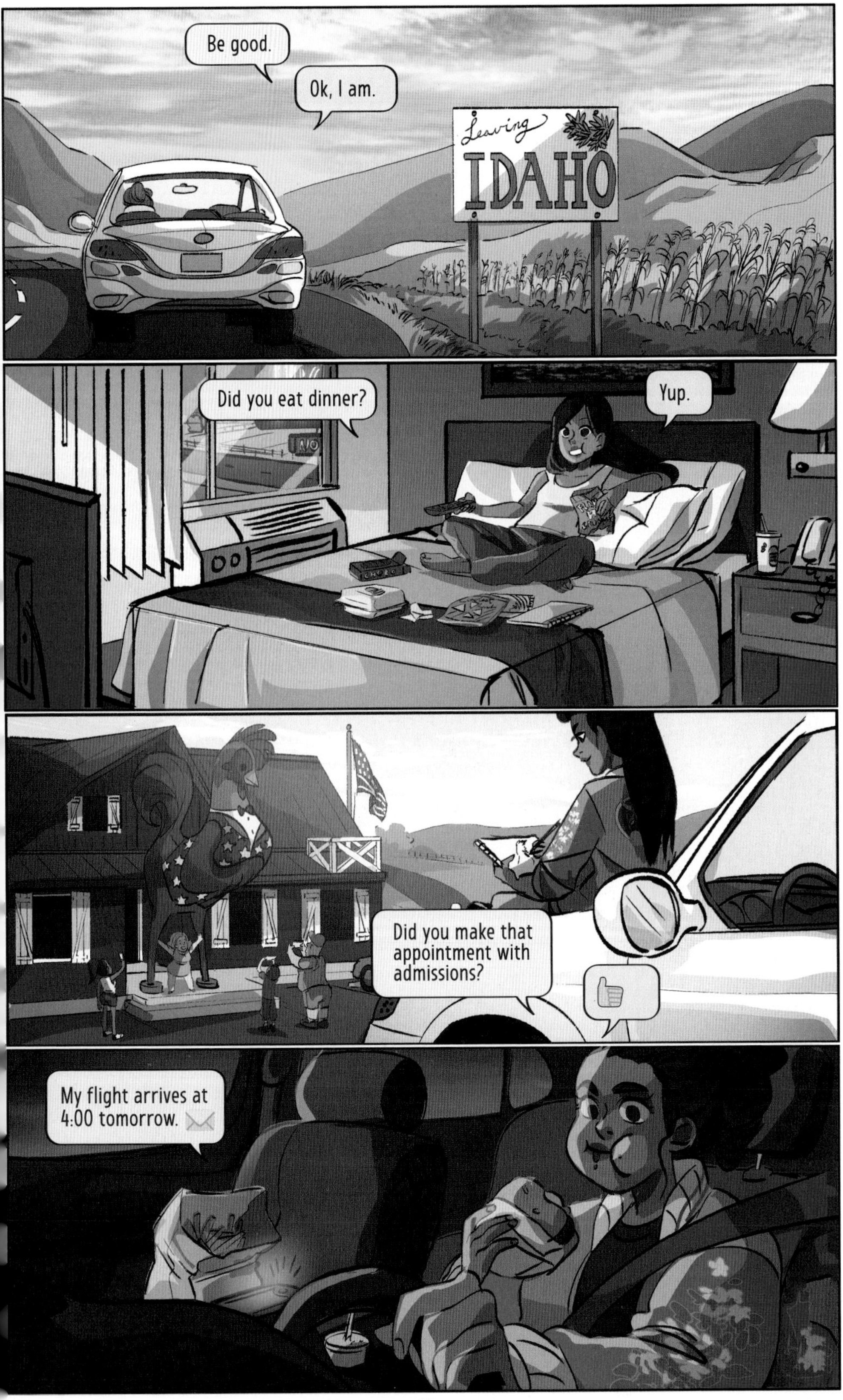
Be good.
Ok, I am.
Leaving IDAHO
Did you eat dinner?
Yup.
Did you make that appointment with admissions?
My flight arrives at 4:00 tomorrow.

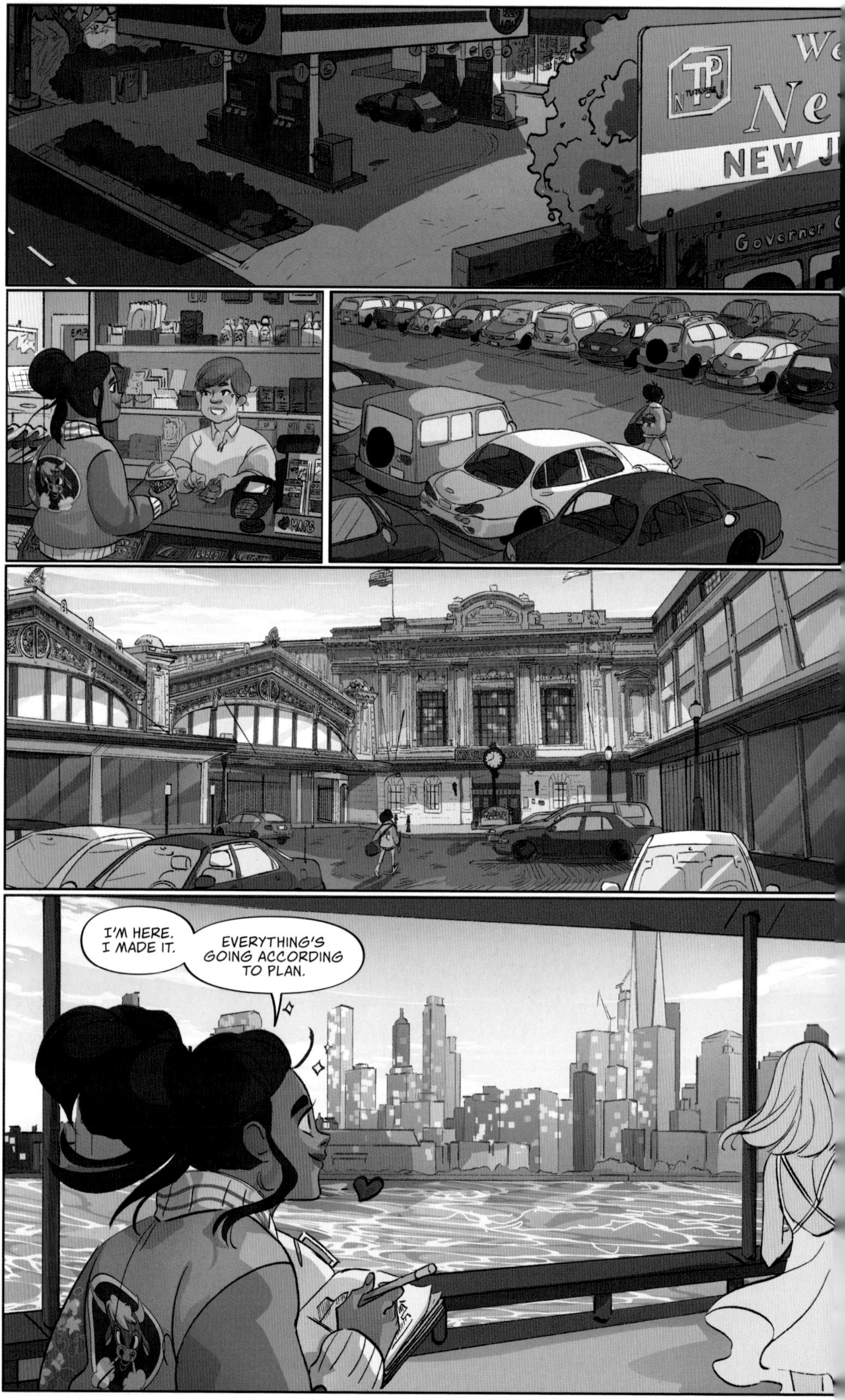
I'M HERE. I MADE IT.
EVERYTHING'S GOING ACCORDING TO PLAN.

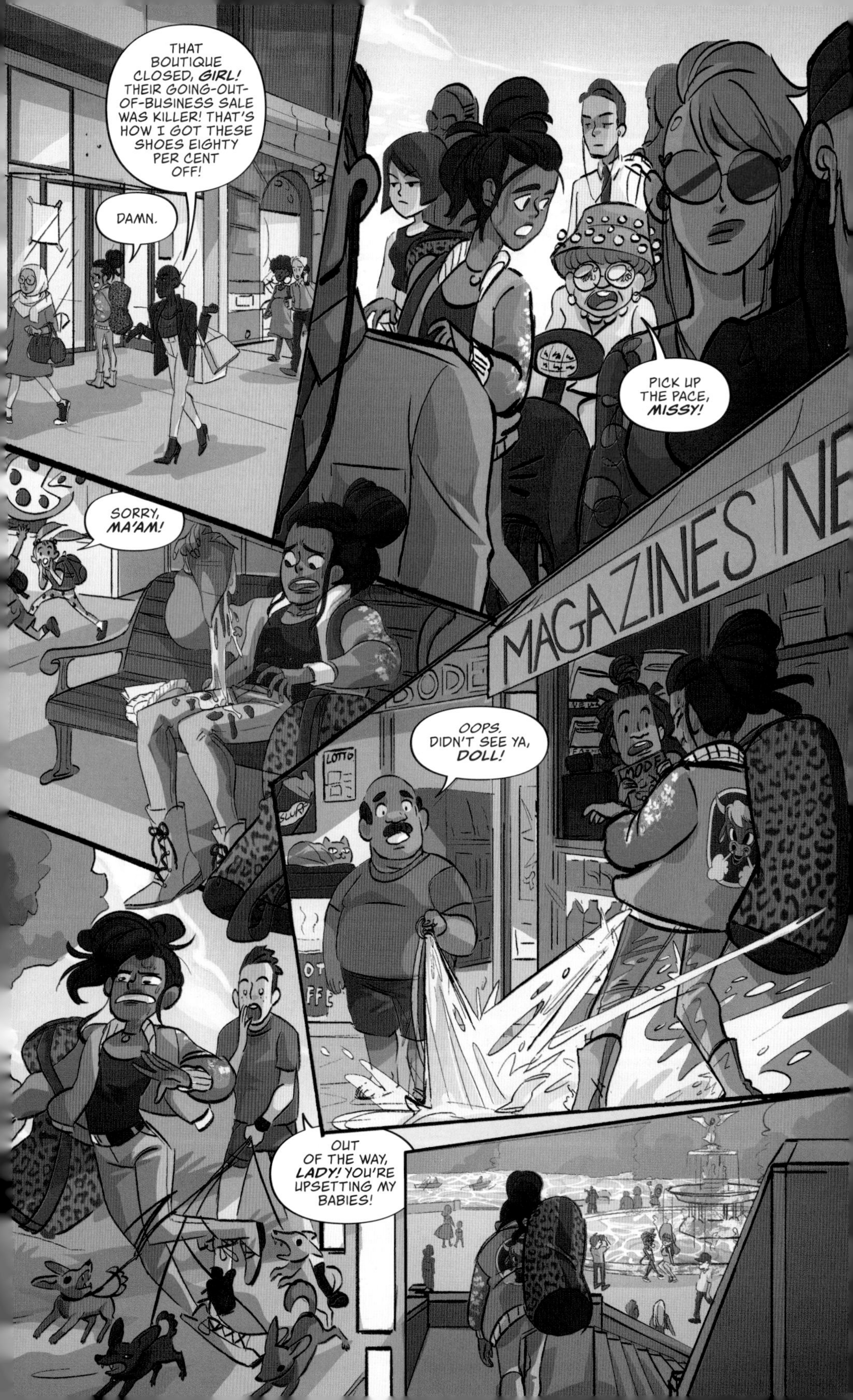
THAT BOUTIQUE CLOSED, GIRL! THEIR GOING-OUT-OF-BUSINESS SALE WAS KILLER! THAT'S HOW I GOT THESE SHOES EIGHTY PER CENT OFF!
DAMN.
PICK UP THE PACE, MISSY!
SORRY, MA'AM!
MAGAZINES NE
OOPS. DIDN'T SEE YA, DOLL!
LOTTO
OUT OF THE WAY, LADY! YOU'RE UPSETTING MY BABIES!

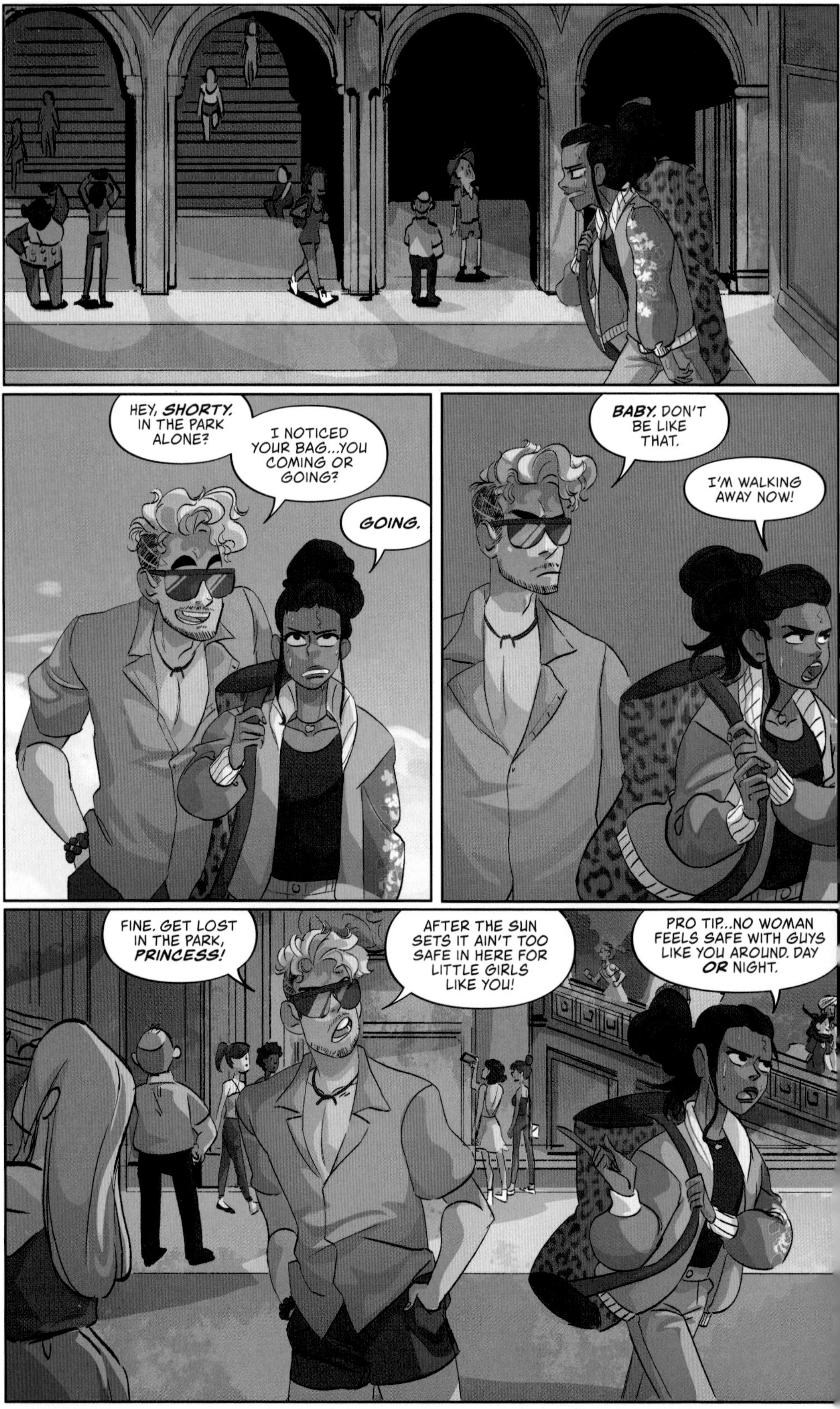
HEY, SHORTY. IN THE PARK ALONE?
I NOTICED YOUR BAG...YOU COMING OR GOING?
GOING.
BABY. DON'T BE LIKE THAT.
I'M WALKING AWAY NOW!
FINE. GET LOST IN THE PARK, PRINCESS!
AFTER THE SUN SETS IT AIN'T TOO SAFE IN HERE FOR LITTLE GIRLS LIKE YOU!
PRO TIP...NO WOMAN FEELS SAFE WITH GUYS LIKE YOU AROUND. DAY OR NIGHT.

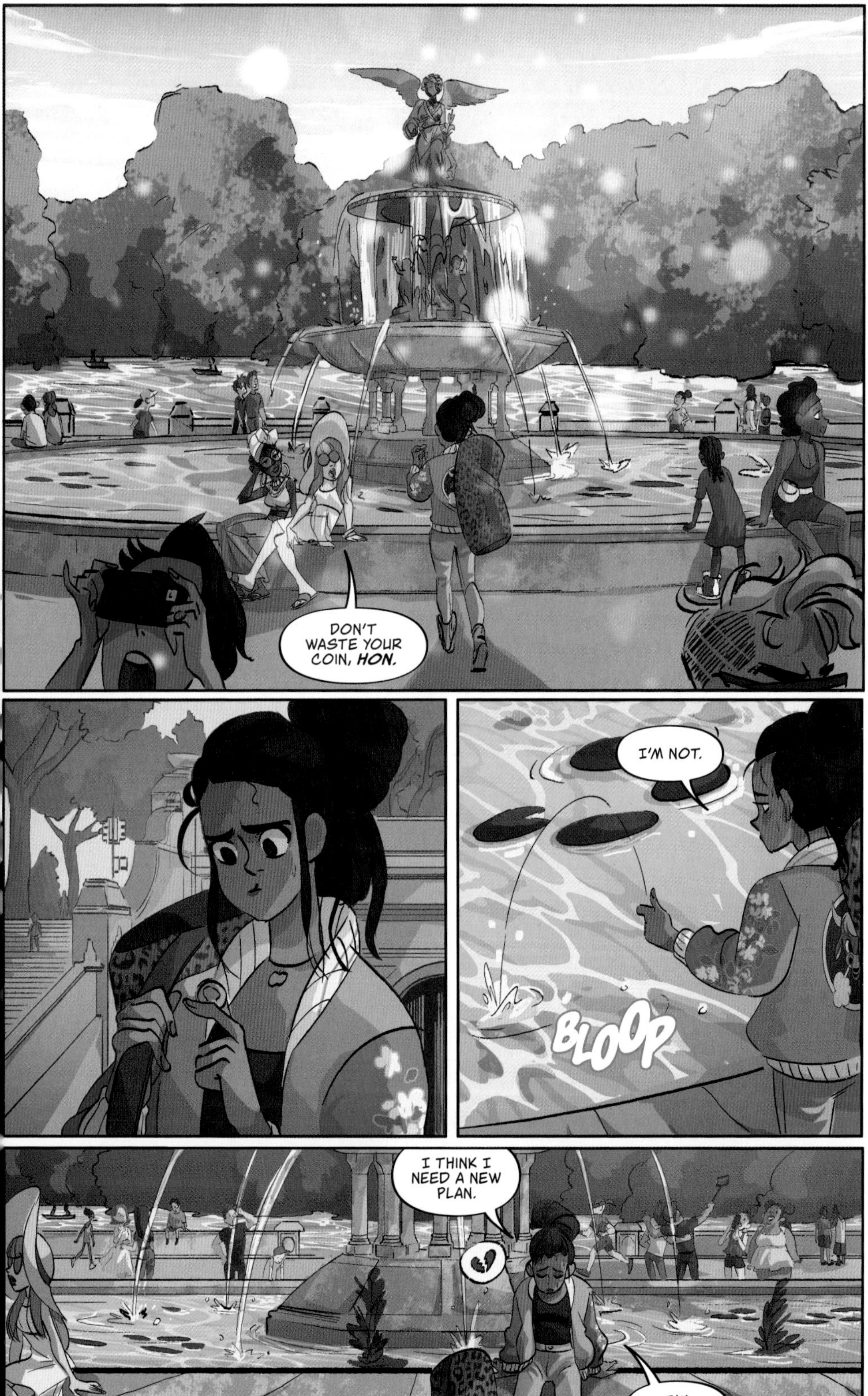
DON'T WASTE YOUR COIN, HON.
I'M NOT.
BLOOP
I THINK I NEED A NEW PLAN.
I'M HUNGRY.

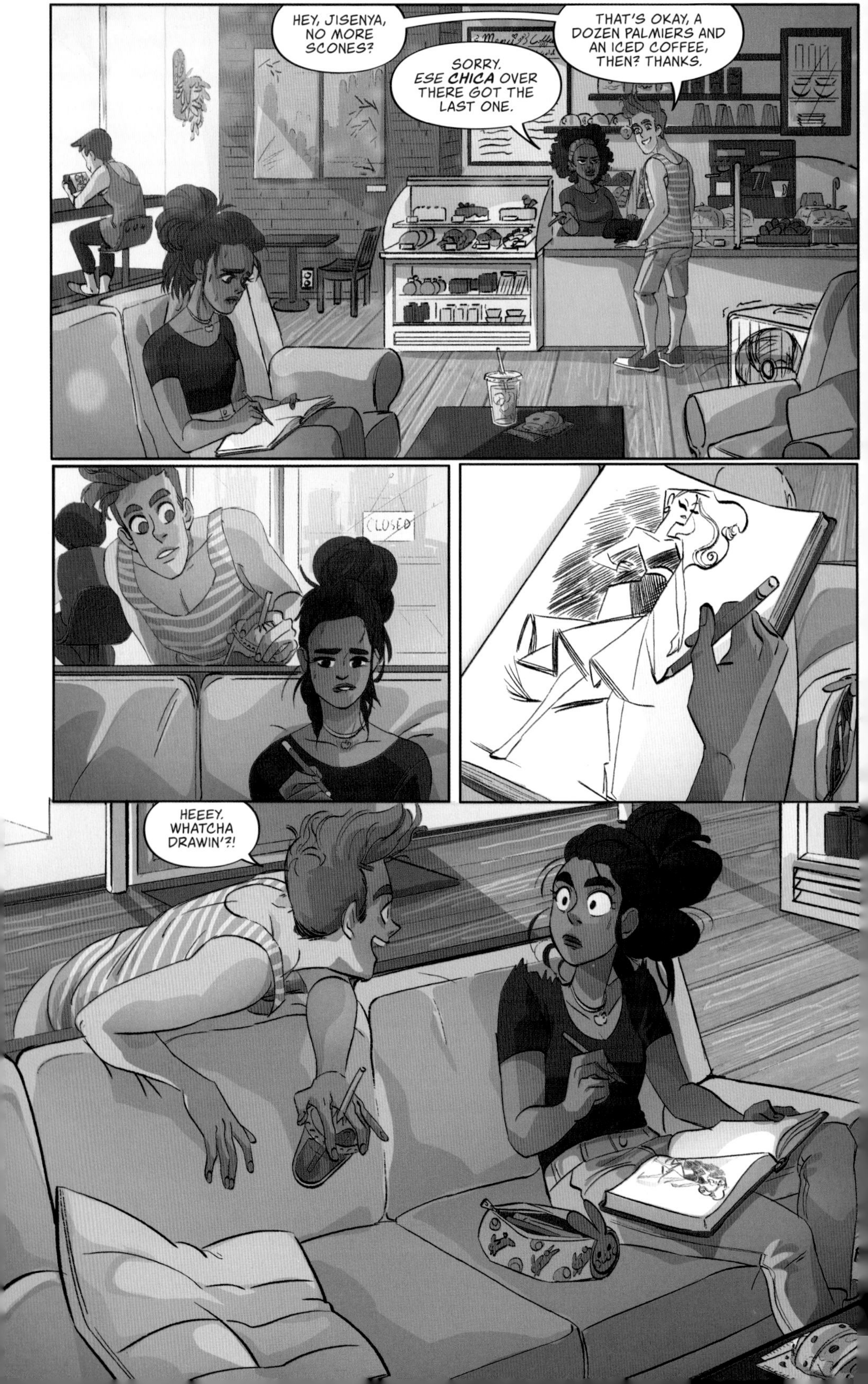
HEY, JISENYA, NO MORE SCONES?
SORRY. ESE **CHICA** OVER THERE GOT THE LAST ONE.
THAT'S OKAY, A DOZEN PALMIERS AND AN ICED COFFEE, THEN? THANKS.
CLOSED
HEEEY. WHATCHA DRAWIN'?!

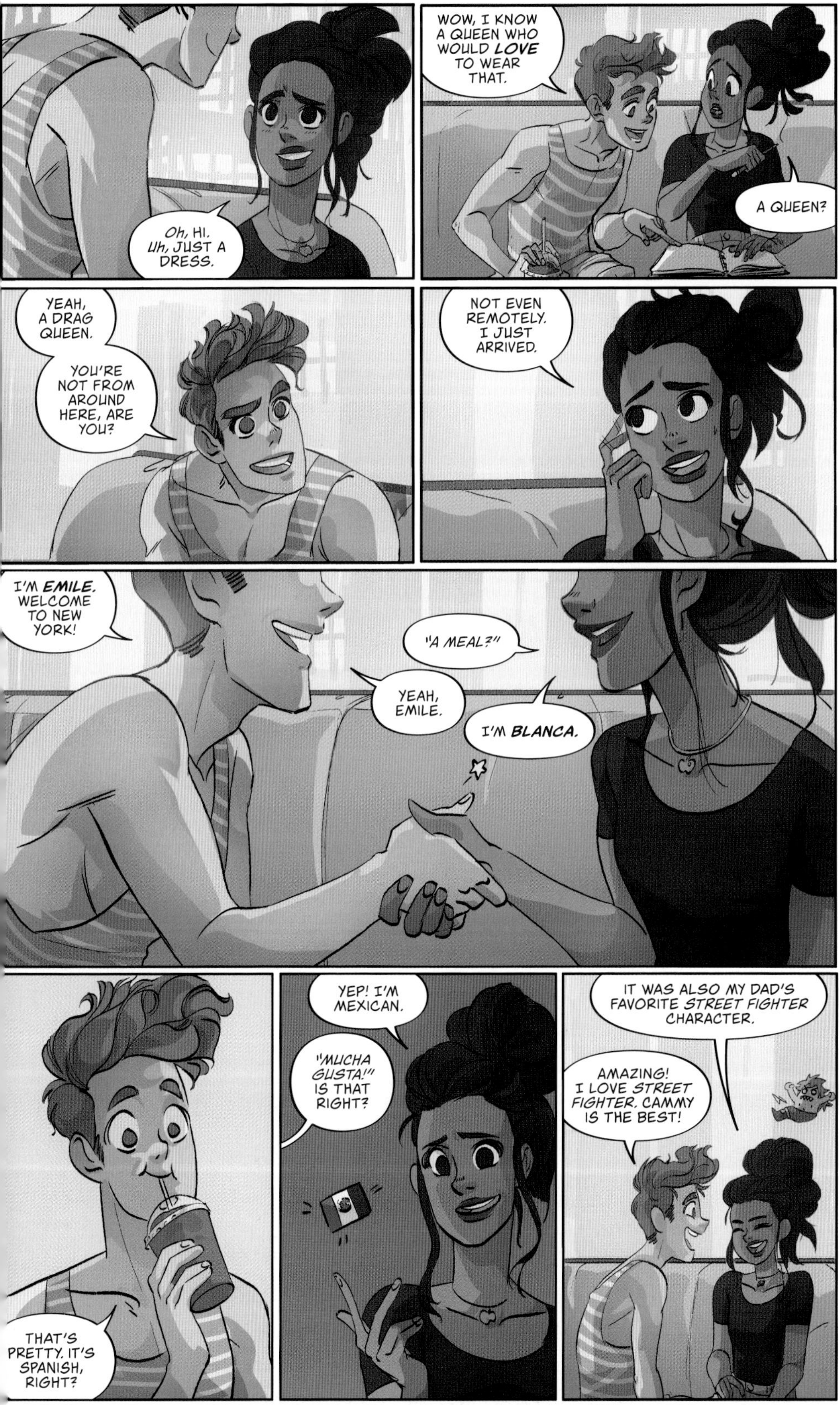
Oh, HI. Uh, JUST A DRESS.
WOW, I KNOW A QUEEN WHO WOULD LOVE TO WEAR THAT.
A QUEEN?
YEAH, A DRAG QUEEN.
YOU'RE NOT FROM AROUND HERE, ARE YOU?
NOT EVEN REMOTELY. I JUST ARRIVED.
I'M EMILE. WELCOME TO NEW YORK!
"A MEAL?"
YEAH, EMILE.
I'M BLANCA.
THAT'S PRETTY. IT'S SPANISH, RIGHT?
YEP! I'M MEXICAN.
"MUCHA GUSTA!" IS THAT RIGHT?
IT WAS ALSO MY DAD'S FAVORITE STREET FIGHTER CHARACTER.
AMAZING! I LOVE STREET FIGHTER. CAMMY IS THE BEST!

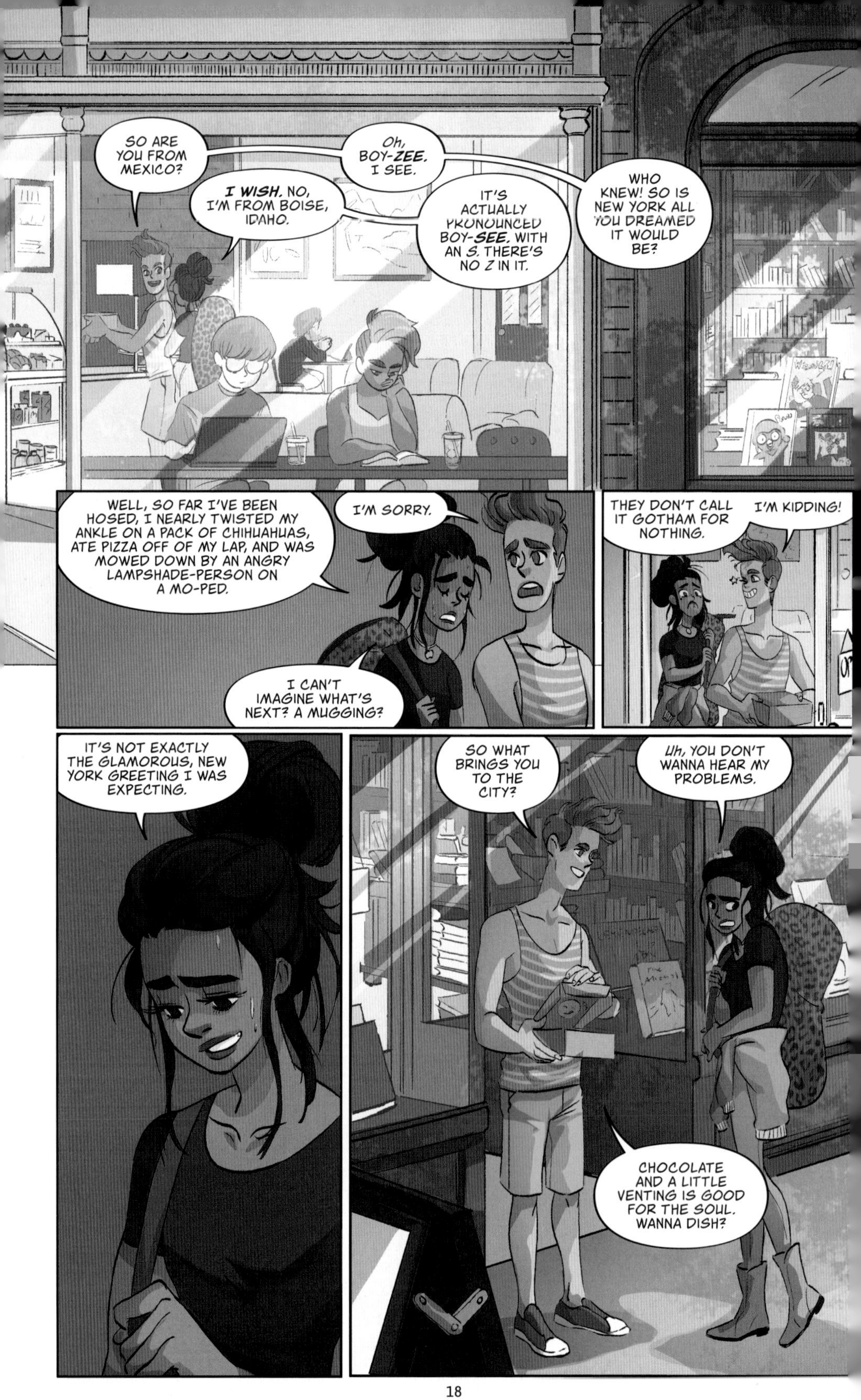
SO ARE YOU FROM MEXICO?
I WISH. NO, I'M FROM BOISE, IDAHO.
Oh, BOY-ZEE. I SEE.
IT'S ACTUALLY PRONOUNCED BOY-SEE. WITH AN S. THERE'S NO Z IN IT.
WHO KNEW! SO IS NEW YORK ALL YOU DREAMED IT WOULD BE?
WELL, SO FAR I'VE BEEN HOSED, I NEARLY TWISTED MY ANKLE ON A PACK OF CHIHUAHUAS, ATE PIZZA OFF OF MY LAP, AND WAS MOWED DOWN BY AN ANGRY LAMPSHADE-PERSON ON A MO-PED.
I'M SORRY.
I CAN'T IMAGINE WHAT'S NEXT? A MUGGING?
THEY DON'T CALL IT GOTHAM FOR NOTHING.
I'M KIDDING!
IT'S NOT EXACTLY THE GLAMOROUS, NEW YORK GREETING I WAS EXPECTING.
SO WHAT BRINGS YOU TO THE CITY?
Uh, YOU DON'T WANNA HEAR MY PROBLEMS.
CHOCOLATE AND A LITTLE VENTING IS GOOD FOR THE SOUL. WANNA DISH?

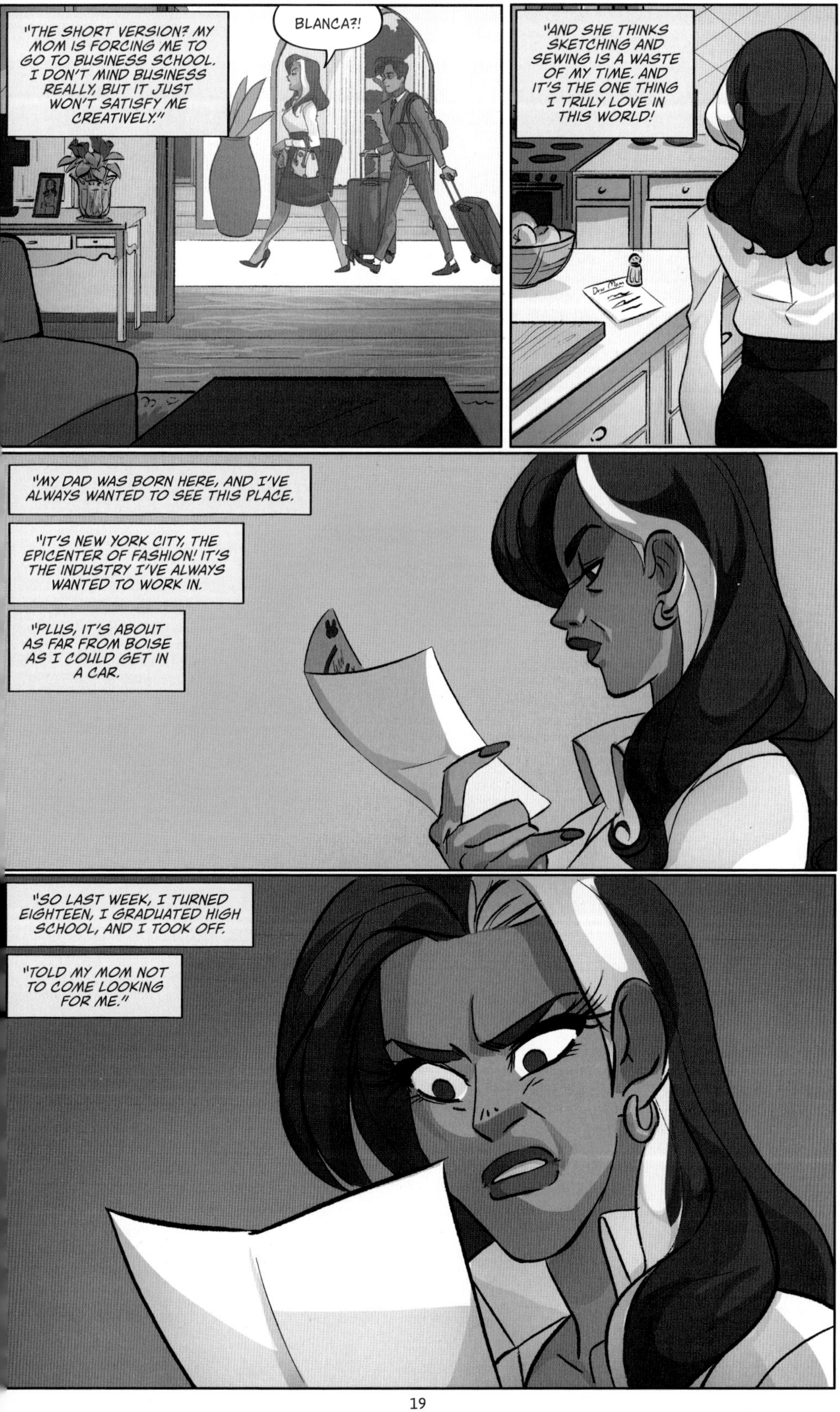
"THE SHORT VERSION? MY MOM IS FORCING ME TO GO TO BUSINESS SCHOOL. I DON'T MIND BUSINESS REALLY, BUT IT JUST WON'T SATISFY ME CREATIVELY."
BLANCA?!
"AND SHE THINKS SKETCHING AND SEWING IS A WASTE OF MY TIME. AND IT'S THE ONE THING I TRULY LOVE IN THIS WORLD!
Dear Mom
"MY DAD WAS BORN HERE, AND I'VE ALWAYS WANTED TO SEE THIS PLACE.
"IT'S NEW YORK CITY, THE EPICENTER OF FASHION! IT'S THE INDUSTRY I'VE ALWAYS WANTED TO WORK IN.
"PLUS, IT'S ABOUT AS FAR FROM BOISE AS I COULD GET IN A CAR.
"SO LAST WEEK, I TURNED EIGHTEEN, I GRADUATED HIGH SCHOOL, AND I TOOK OFF.
"TOLD MY MOM NOT TO COME LOOKING FOR ME."

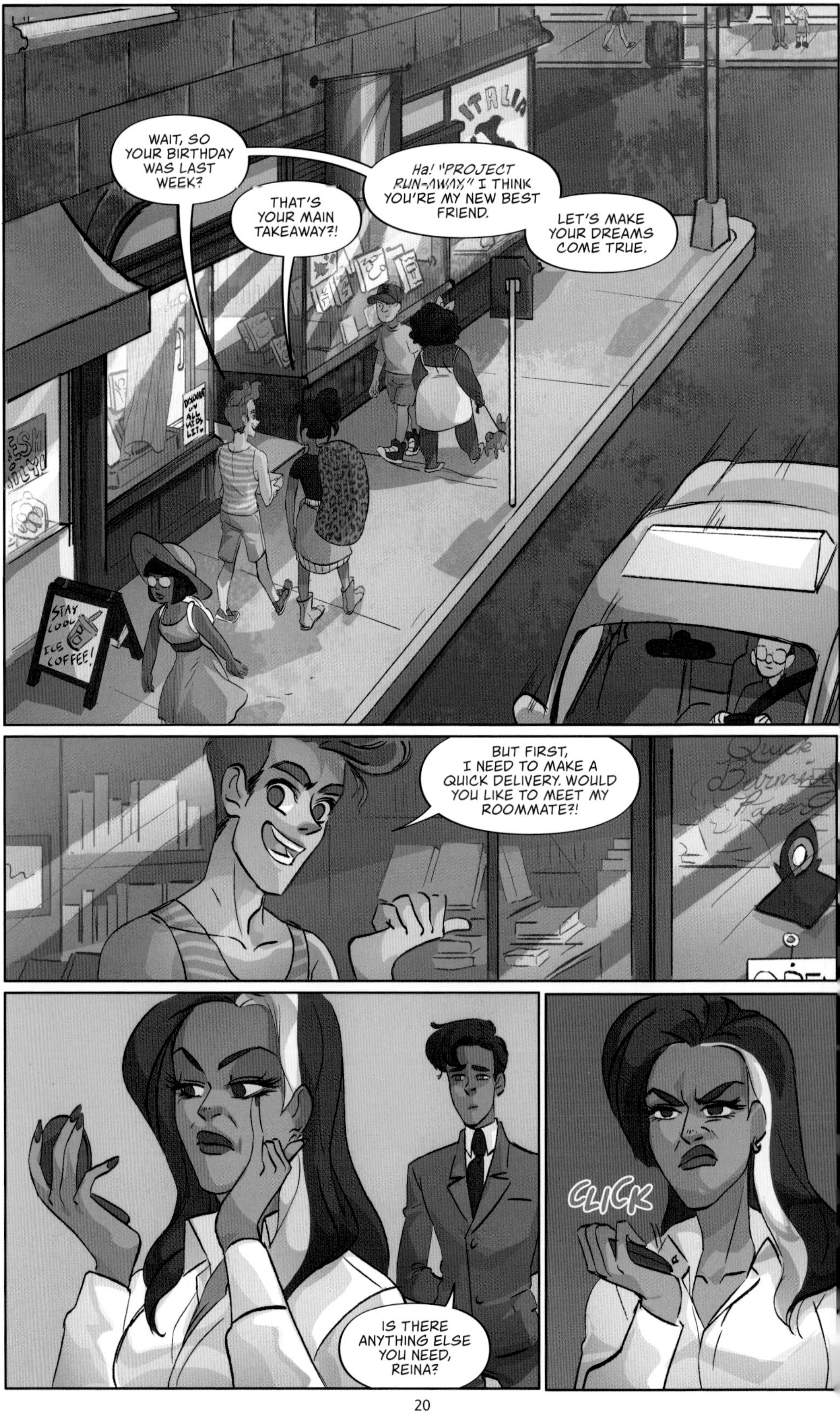
WAIT, SO YOUR BIRTHDAY WAS LAST WEEK?
THAT'S YOUR MAIN TAKEAWAY?!
Ha! "PROJECT RUN-AWAY," I THINK YOU'RE MY NEW BEST FRIEND.
LET'S MAKE YOUR DREAMS COME TRUE.
ITALIA
STAY COOL ICE COFFEE!
BUT FIRST, I NEED TO MAKE A QUICK DELIVERY. WOULD YOU LIKE TO MEET MY ROOMMATE?!
IS THERE ANYTHING ELSE YOU NEED, REINA?
CLICK

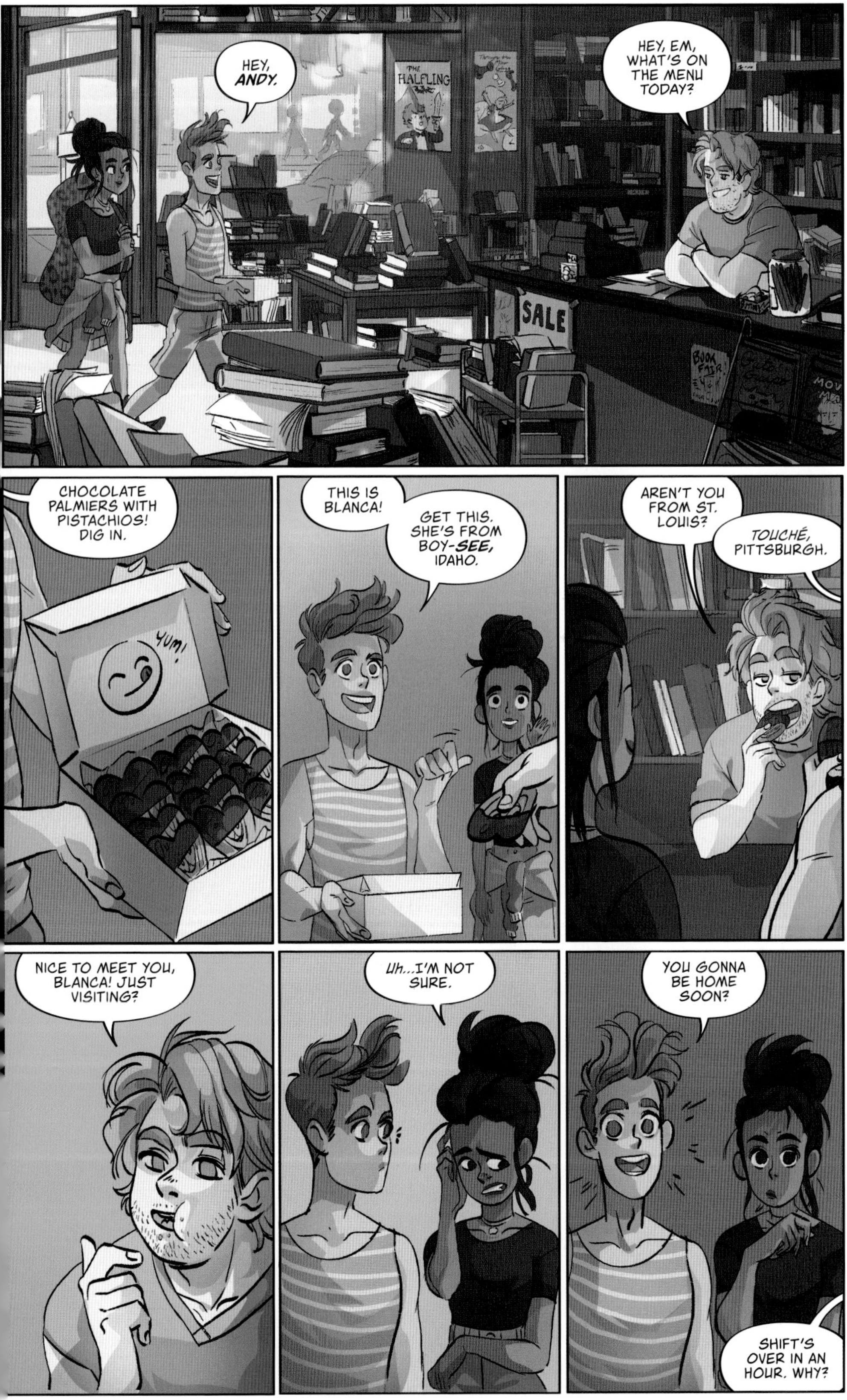
HEY, ANDY.
HEY, EM, WHAT'S ON THE MENU TODAY?
THE HALFLING
SALE
CHOCOLATE PALMIERS WITH PISTACHIOS! DIG IN.
YUM!
THIS IS BLANCA!
GET THIS. SHE'S FROM BOY-SEE, IDAHO.
AREN'T YOU FROM ST. LOUIS?
TOUCHÉ, PITTSBURGH.
NICE TO MEET YOU, BLANCA! JUST VISITING?
UH...I'M NOT SURE.
YOU GONNA BE HOME SOON?
SHIFT'S OVER IN AN HOUR. WHY?

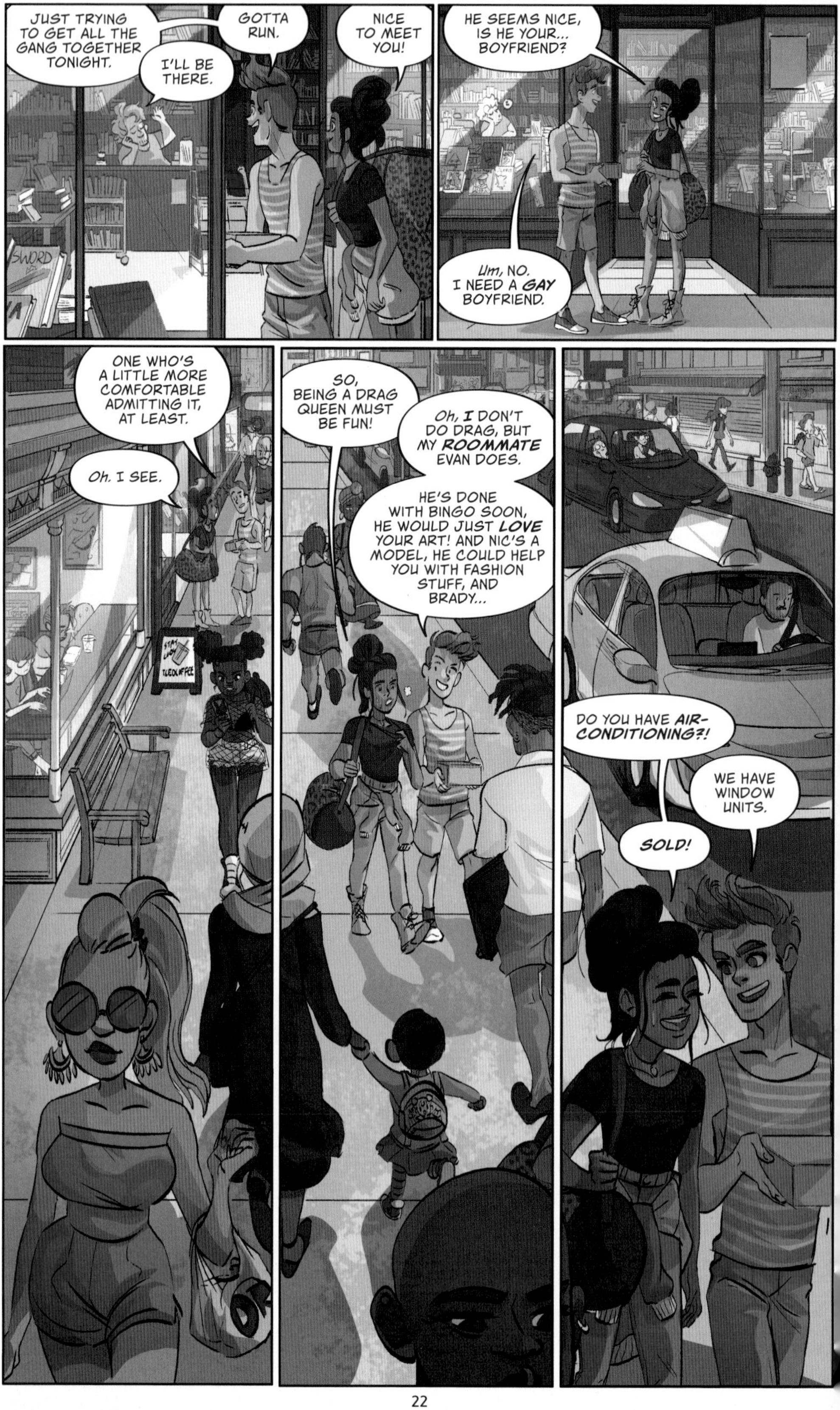
JUST TRYING TO GET ALL THE GANG TOGETHER TONIGHT.
GOTTA RUN.
I'LL BE THERE.
NICE TO MEET YOU!
HE SEEMS NICE, IS HE YOUR... BOYFRIEND?
Um, NO. I NEED A GAY BOYFRIEND.
ONE WHO'S A LITTLE MORE COMFORTABLE ADMITTING IT, AT LEAST.
Oh. I SEE.
SO, BEING A DRAG QUEEN MUST BE FUN!
Oh, I DON'T DO DRAG, BUT MY ROOMMATE EVAN DOES.
HE'S DONE WITH BINGO SOON, HE WOULD JUST LOVE YOUR ART! AND NIC'S A MODEL, HE COULD HELP YOU WITH FASHION STUFF, AND BRADY...
DO YOU HAVE AIR-CONDITIONING?!
WE HAVE WINDOW UNITS.
SOLD!

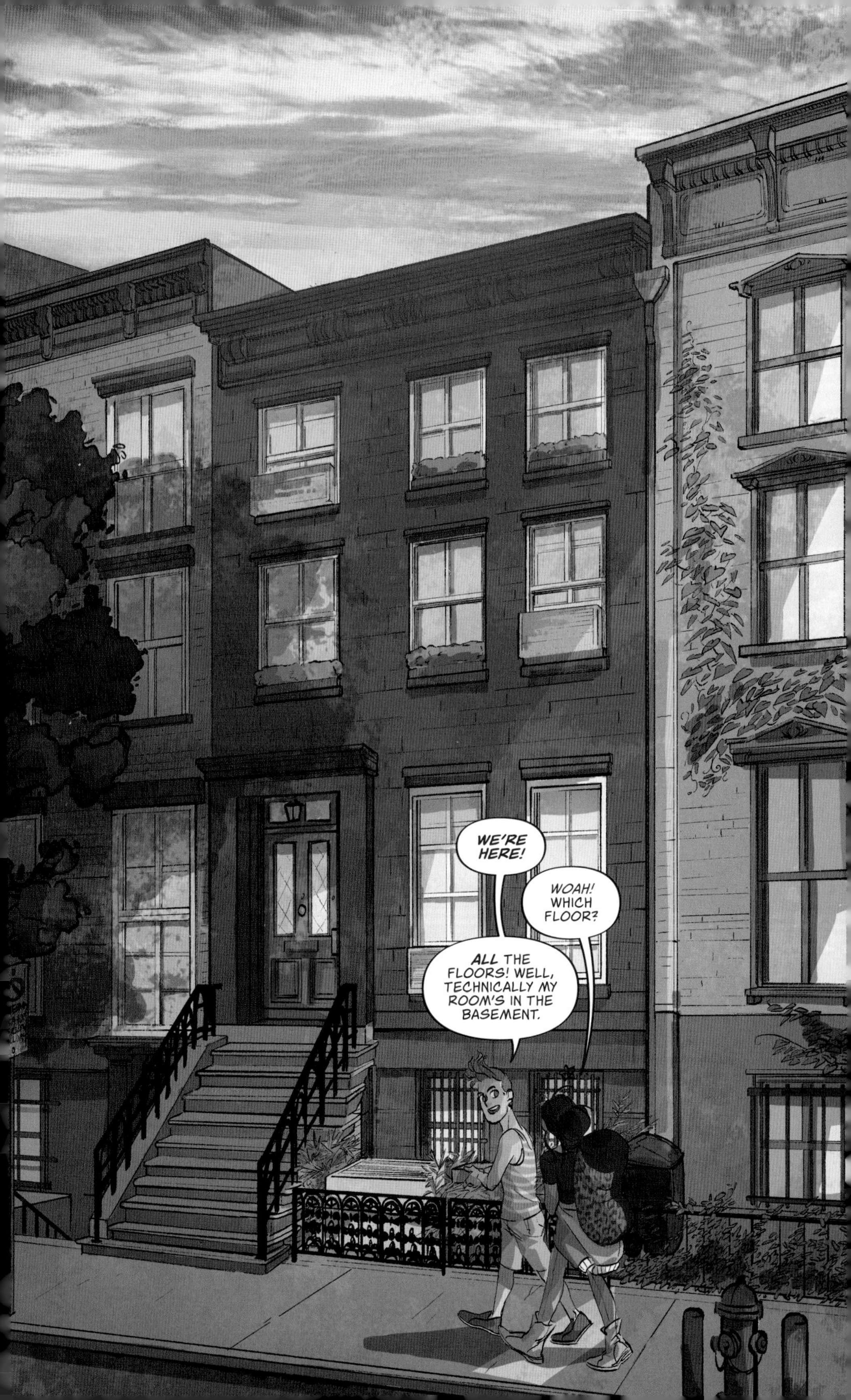
WE'RE HERE!
WOAH! WHICH FLOOR?
ALL THE FLOORS! WELL, TECHNICALLY MY ROOM'S IN THE BASEMENT.

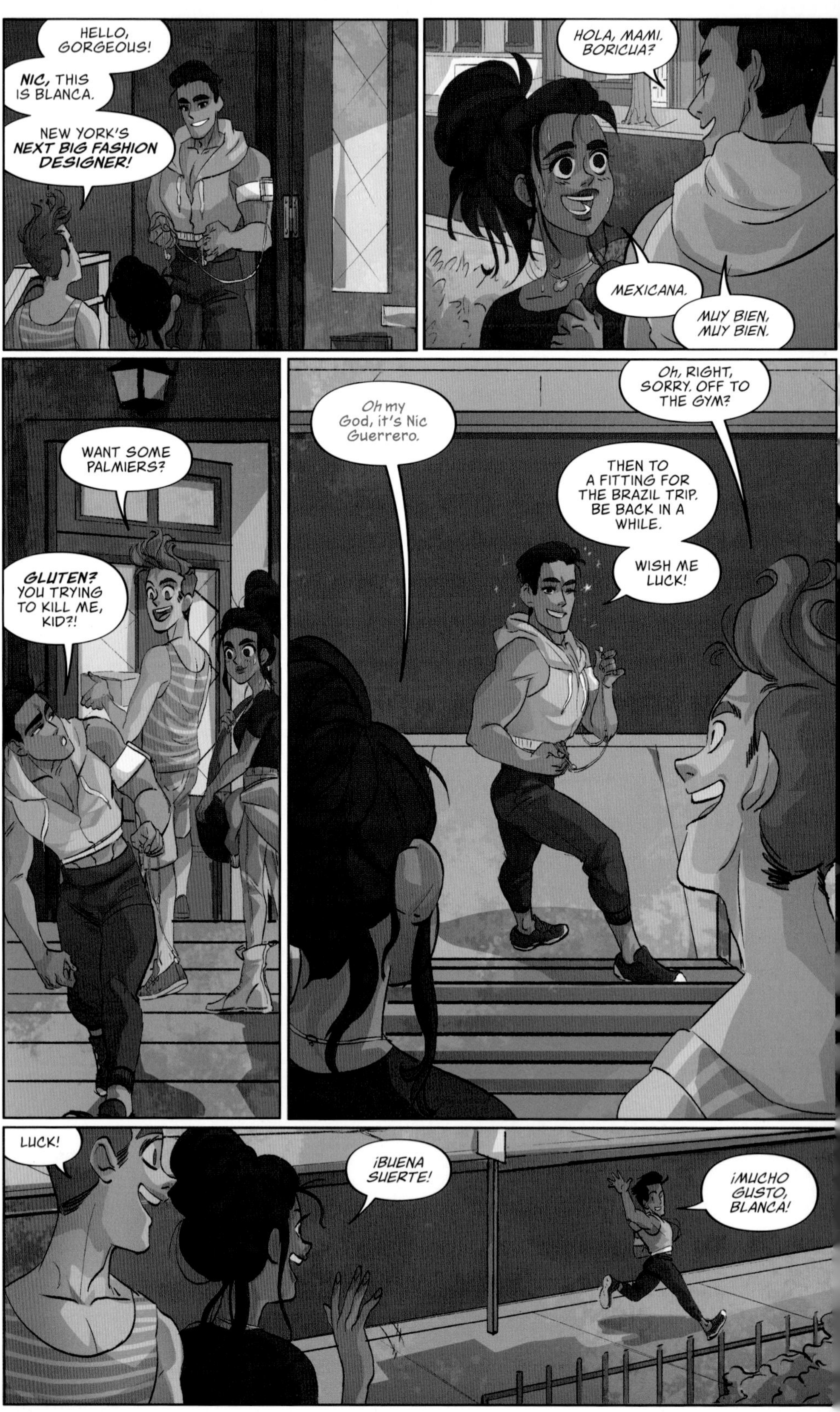
HELLO, GORGEOUS!
NIC, THIS IS BLANCA.
NEW YORK'S NEXT BIG FASHION DESIGNER!
HOLA, MAMI. BORICUA?
MEXICANA.
MUY BIEN, MUY BIEN.
WANT SOME PALMIERS?
GLUTEN? YOU TRYING TO KILL ME, KID?!
Oh my God, it's Nic Guerrero.
Oh, RIGHT, SORRY. OFF TO THE GYM?
THEN TO A FITTING FOR THE BRAZIL TRIP. BE BACK IN A WHILE.
WISH ME LUCK!
LUCK!
¡BUENA SUERTE!
¡MUCHO GUSTO, BLANCA!

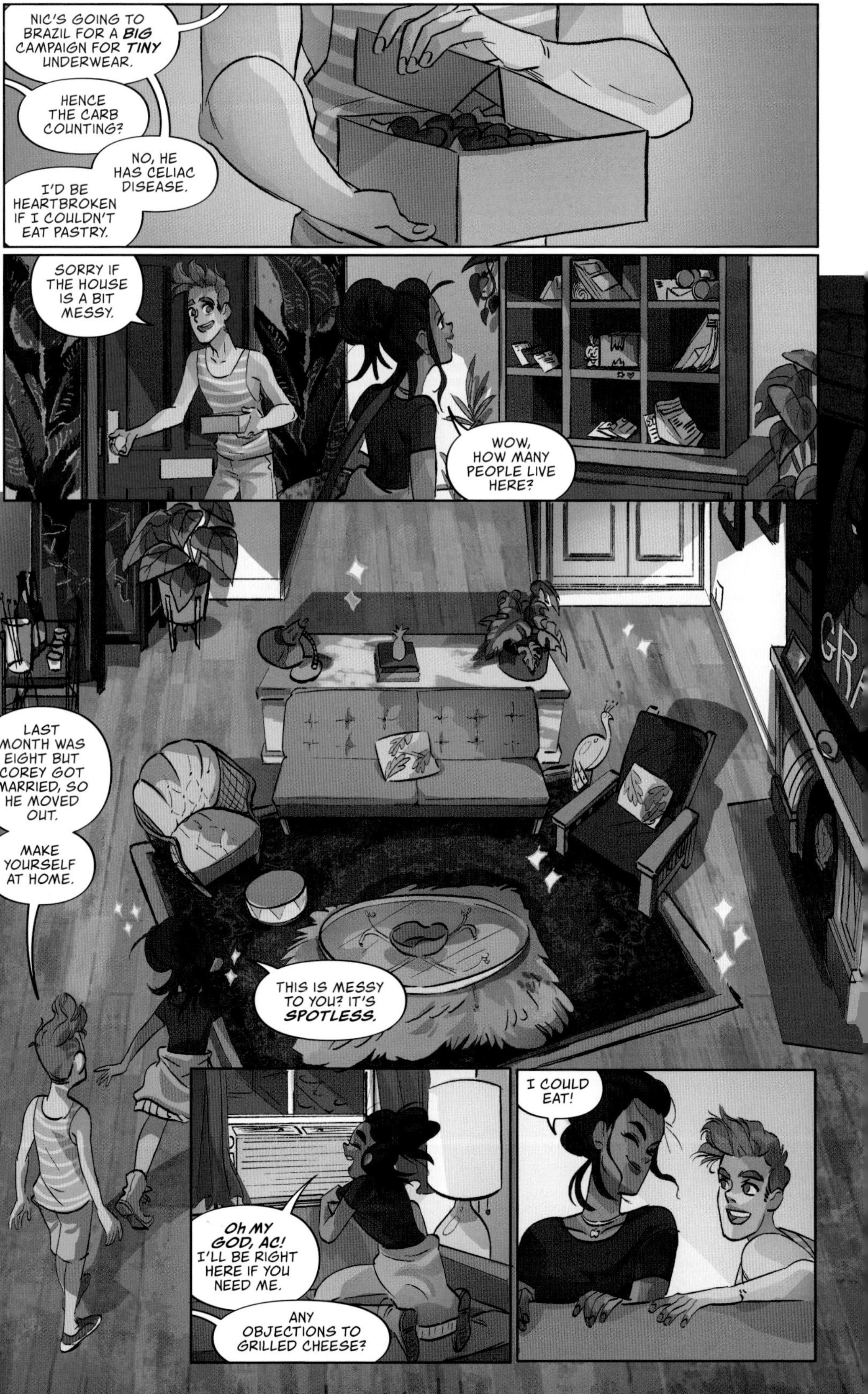
NIC'S GOING TO BRAZIL FOR A BIG CAMPAIGN FOR TINY UNDERWEAR.
HENCE THE CARB COUNTING?
NO, HE HAS CELIAC DISEASE.
I'D BE HEARTBROKEN IF I COULDN'T EAT PASTRY.
SORRY IF THE HOUSE IS A BIT MESSY.
WOW, HOW MANY PEOPLE LIVE HERE?
LAST MONTH WAS EIGHT BUT COREY GOT MARRIED, SO HE MOVED OUT.
MAKE YOURSELF AT HOME.
THIS IS MESSY TO YOU? IT'S SPOTLESS.
Oh MY GOD, AC! I'LL BE RIGHT HERE IF YOU NEED ME.
ANY OBJECTIONS TO GRILLED CHEESE?
I COULD EAT!

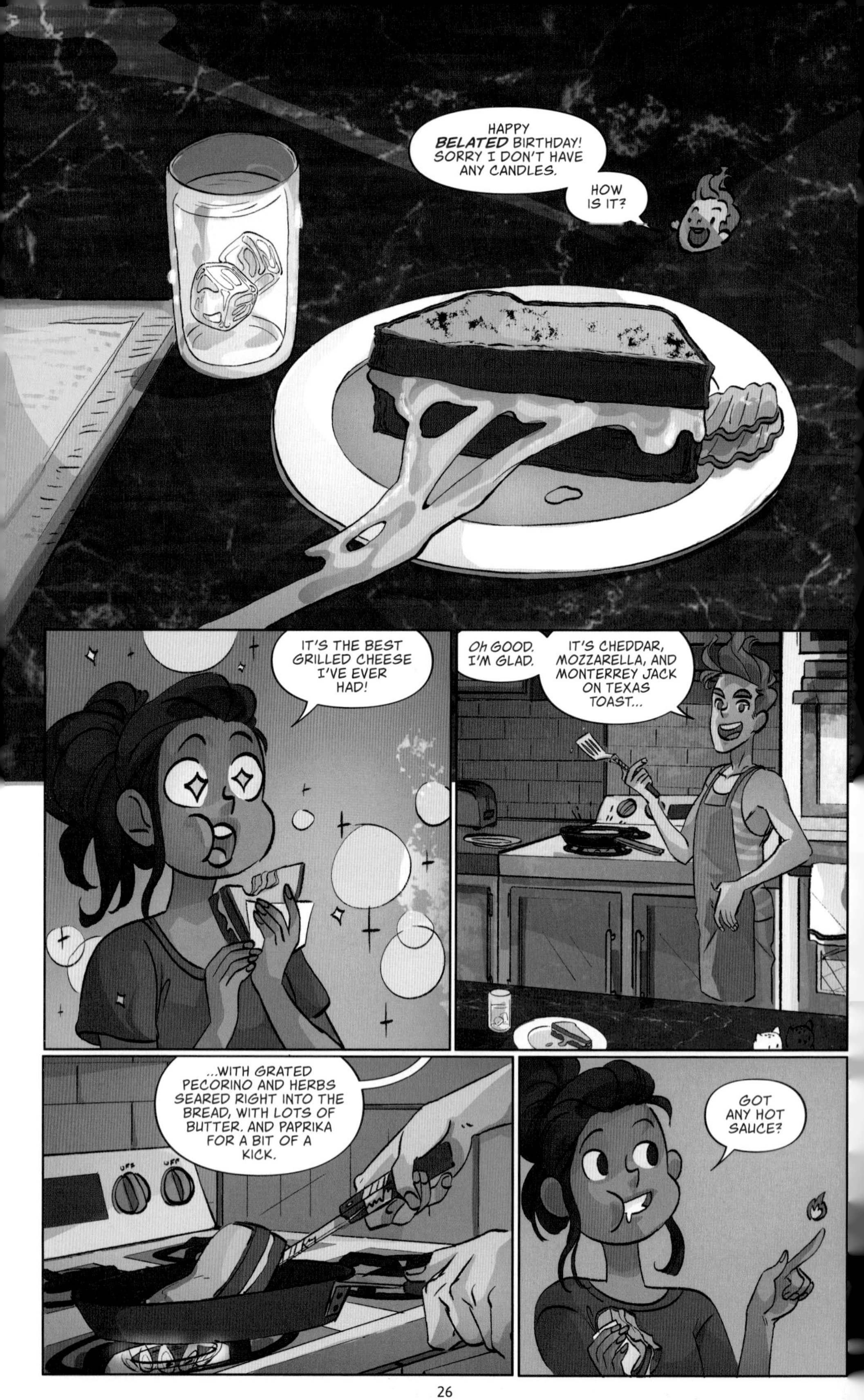

HAPPY *BELATED* BIRTHDAY! SORRY I DON'T HAVE ANY CANDLES.
HOW IS IT?
IT'S THE BEST GRILLED CHEESE I'VE EVER HAD!
Oh GOOD. I'M GLAD.
IT'S CHEDDAR, MOZZARELLA, AND MONTERREY JACK ON TEXAS TOAST...
...WITH GRATED PECORINO AND HERBS SEARED RIGHT INTO THE BREAD, WITH LOTS OF BUTTER. AND PAPRIKA FOR A BIT OF A KICK.
GOT ANY HOT SAUCE?

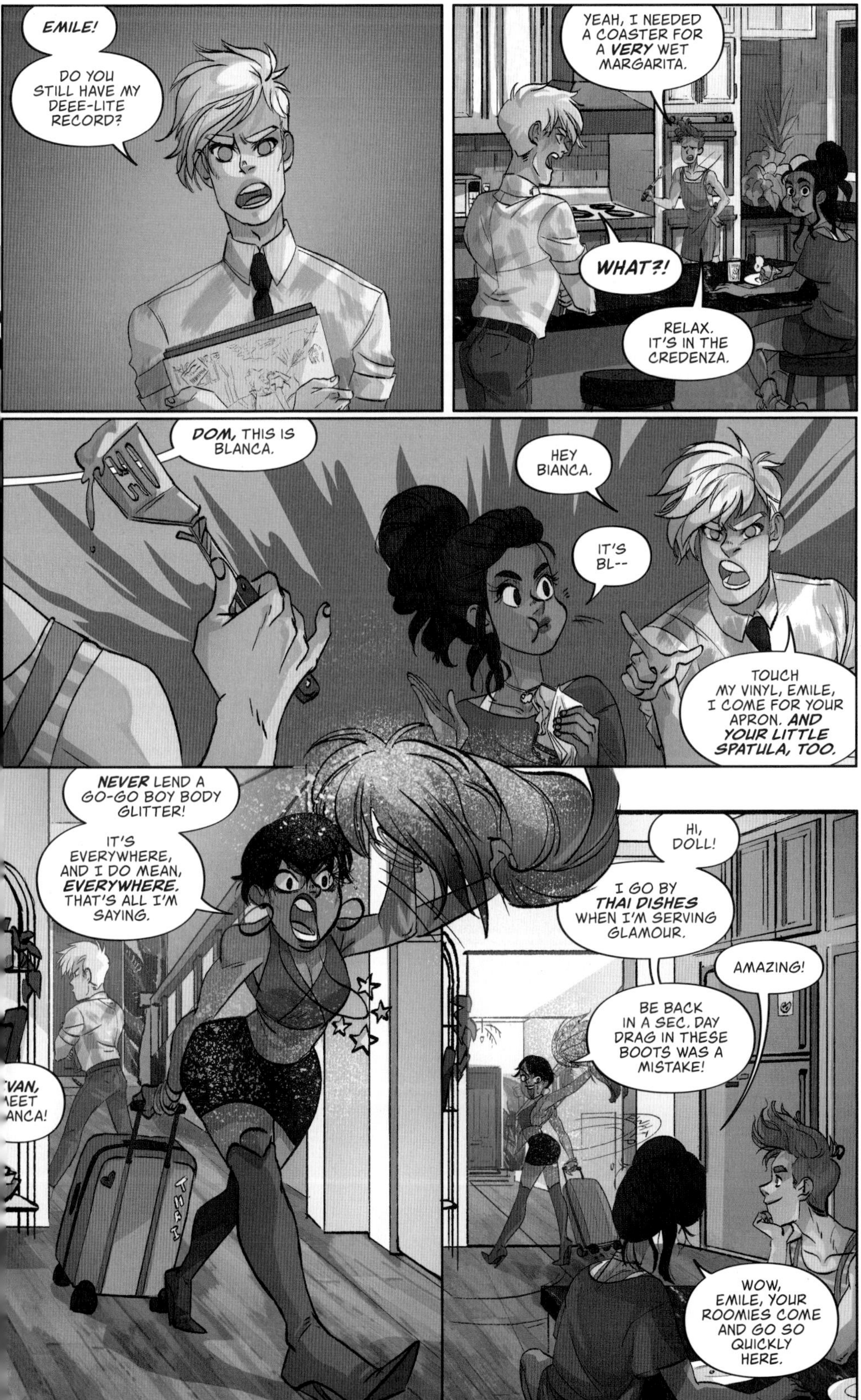
EMILE!
DO YOU STILL HAVE MY DEEE-LITE RECORD?
YEAH, I NEEDED A COASTER FOR A VERY WET MARGARITA.
WHAT?!
RELAX. IT'S IN THE CREDENZA.
DOM, THIS IS BLANCA.
HEY BIANCA.
IT'S BL--
TOUCH MY VINYL, EMILE, I COME FOR YOUR APRON. AND YOUR LITTLE SPATULA, TOO.
NEVER LEND A GO-GO BOY BODY GLITTER!
IT'S EVERYWHERE, AND I DO MEAN, EVERYWHERE. THAT'S ALL I'M SAYING.
HI, DOLL!
I GO BY THAI DISHES WHEN I'M SERVING GLAMOUR.
AMAZING!
BE BACK IN A SEC. DAY DRAG IN THESE BOOTS WAS A MISTAKE!
WOW, EMILE, YOUR ROOMIES COME AND GO SO QUICKLY HERE.

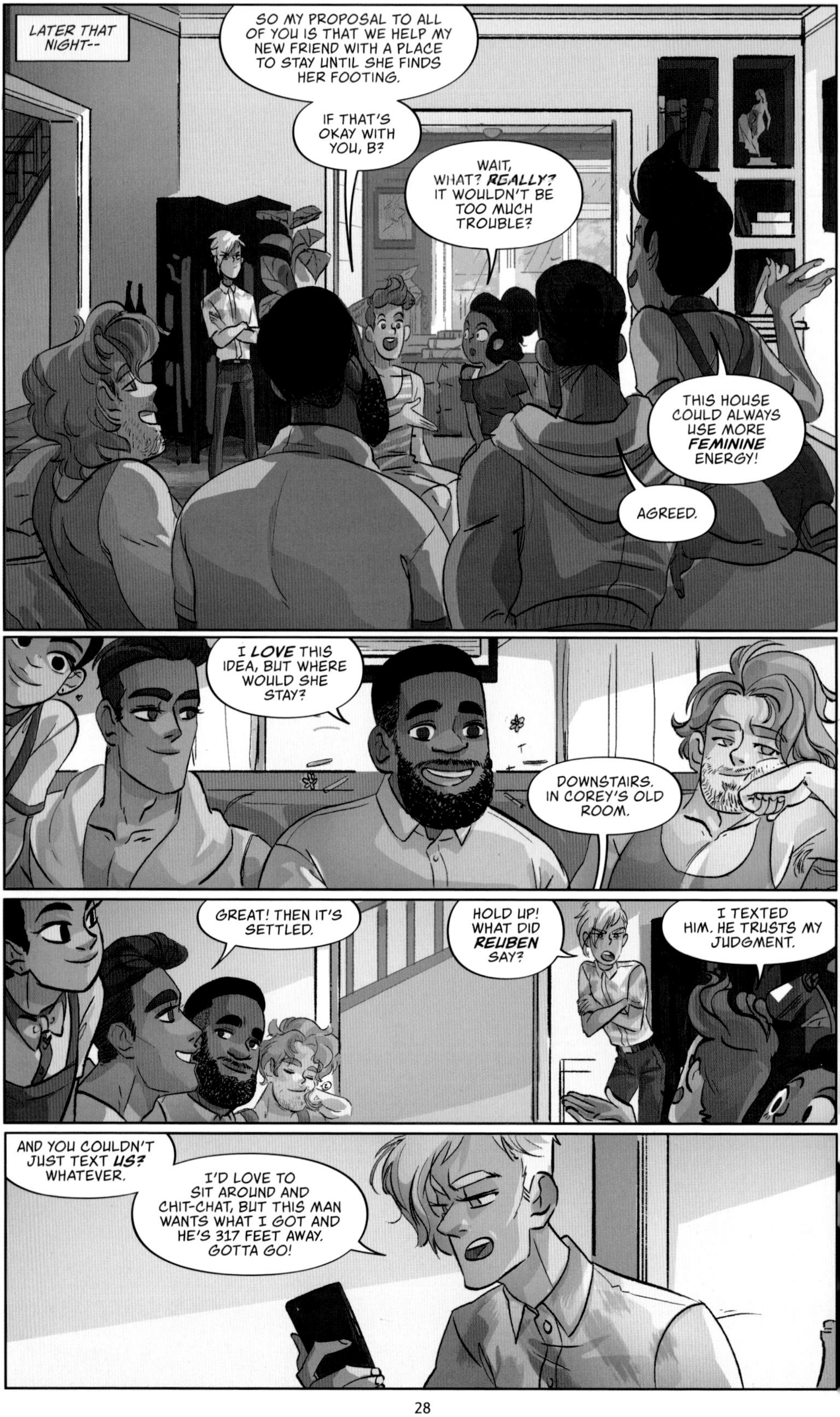
LATER THAT NIGHT--
SO MY PROPOSAL TO ALL OF YOU IS THAT WE HELP MY NEW FRIEND WITH A PLACE TO STAY UNTIL SHE FINDS HER FOOTING.
IF THAT'S OKAY WITH YOU, B?
WAIT, WHAT? REALLY? IT WOULDN'T BE TOO MUCH TROUBLE?
THIS HOUSE COULD ALWAYS USE MORE FEMININE ENERGY!
AGREED.
I LOVE THIS IDEA, BUT WHERE WOULD SHE STAY?
DOWNSTAIRS. IN COREY'S OLD ROOM.
GREAT! THEN IT'S SETTLED.
HOLD UP! WHAT DID REUBEN SAY?
I TEXTED HIM. HE TRUSTS MY JUDGMENT.
AND YOU COULDN'T JUST TEXT US? WHATEVER.
I'D LOVE TO SIT AROUND AND CHIT-CHAT, BUT THIS MAN WANTS WHAT I GOT AND HE'S 317 FEET AWAY. GOTTA GO!

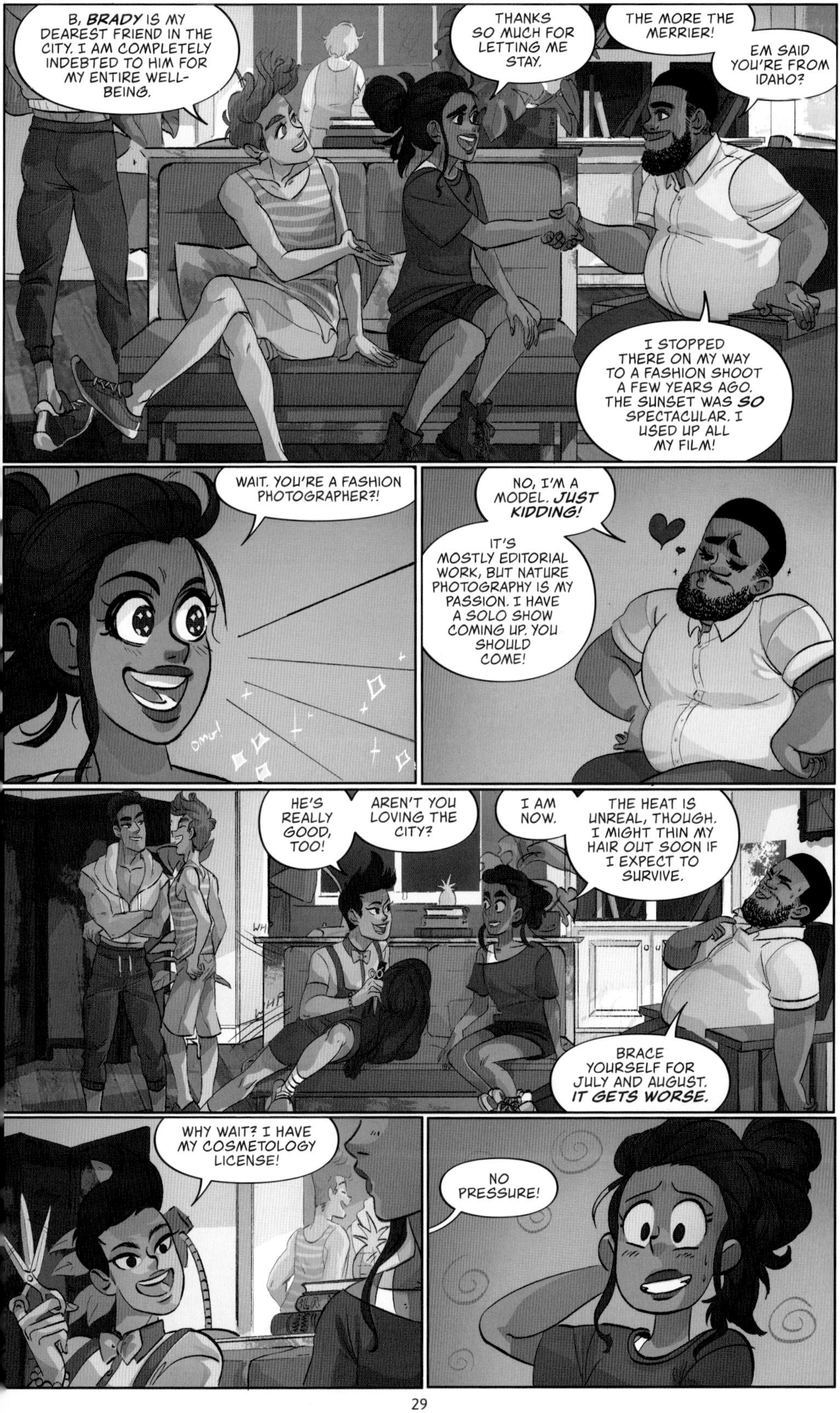
B, BRADY IS MY DEAREST FRIEND IN THE CITY. I AM COMPLETELY INDEBTED TO HIM FOR MY ENTIRE WELL-BEING.
THANKS SO MUCH FOR LETTING ME STAY.
THE MORE THE MERRIER!
EM SAID YOU'RE FROM IDAHO?
I STOPPED THERE ON MY WAY TO A FASHION SHOOT A FEW YEARS AGO. THE SUNSET WAS SO SPECTACULAR. I USED UP ALL MY FILM!
WAIT. YOU'RE A FASHION PHOTOGRAPHER?!
NO, I'M A MODEL. JUST KIDDING!
IT'S MOSTLY EDITORIAL WORK, BUT NATURE PHOTOGRAPHY IS MY PASSION. I HAVE A SOLO SHOW COMING UP. YOU SHOULD COME!
HE'S REALLY GOOD, TOO!
AREN'T YOU LOVING THE CITY?
I AM NOW.
THE HEAT IS UNREAL, THOUGH. I MIGHT THIN MY HAIR OUT SOON IF I EXPECT TO SURVIVE.
BRACE YOURSELF FOR JULY AND AUGUST. IT GETS WORSE.
WHP
WHP
WHY WAIT? I HAVE MY COSMETOLOGY LICENSE!
NO PRESSURE!

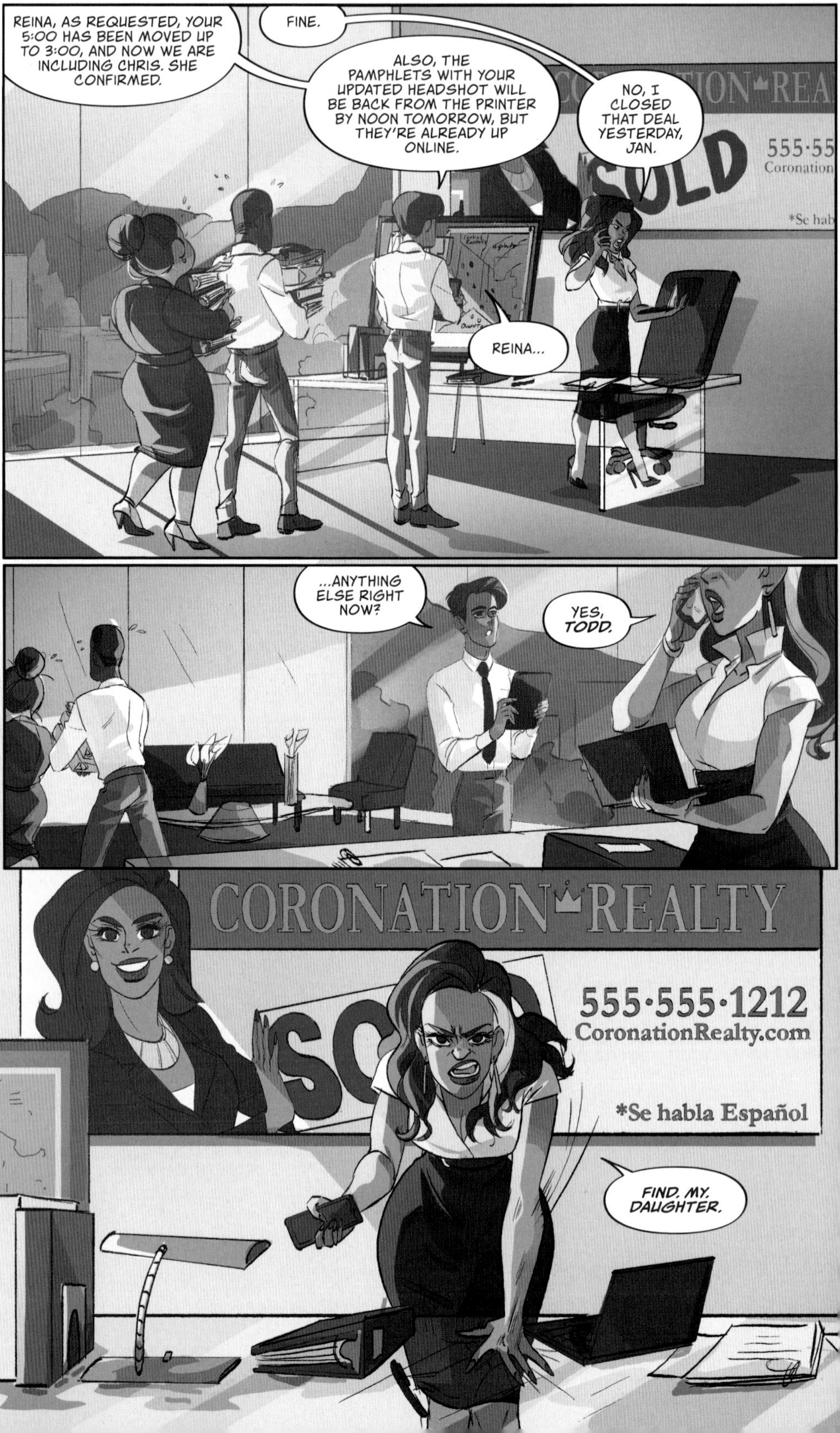
REINA, AS REQUESTED, YOUR 5:00 HAS BEEN MOVED UP TO 3:00, AND NOW WE ARE INCLUDING CHRIS. SHE CONFIRMED.
FINE.
ALSO, THE PAMPHLETS WITH YOUR UPDATED HEADSHOT WILL BE BACK FROM THE PRINTER BY NOON TOMORROW, BUT THEY'RE ALREADY UP ONLINE.
NO, I CLOSED THAT DEAL YESTERDAY, JAN.
SOLD
555·55
Coronation
*Se hab
REINA...
...ANYTHING ELSE RIGHT NOW?
YES, *TODD.*
CORONATION REALTY
555·555·1212
CoronationRealty.com
*Se habla Español
FIND. MY. DAUGHTER.

Chapter Two

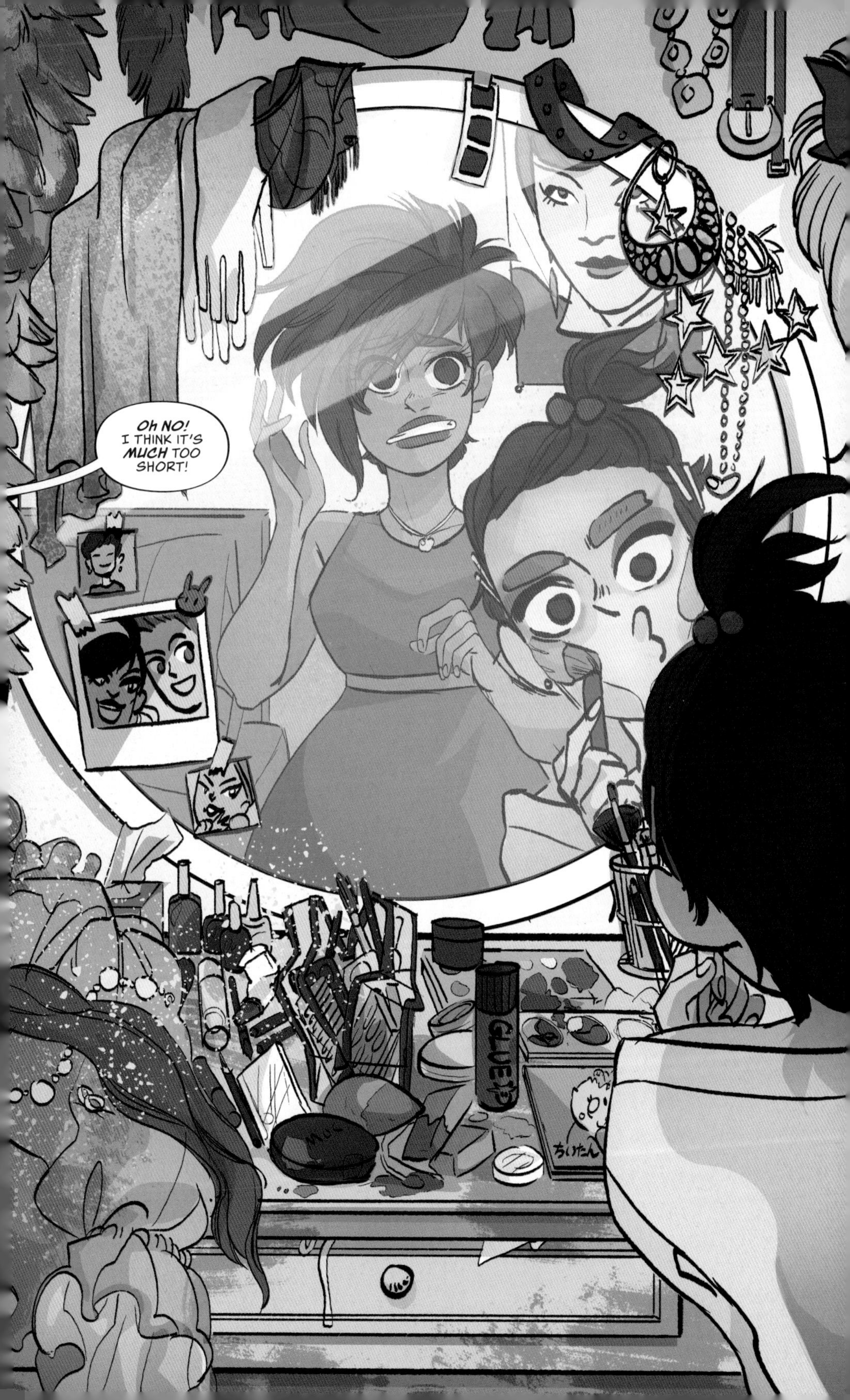
Oh NO! I THINK IT'S MUCH TOO SHORT!
GLUE

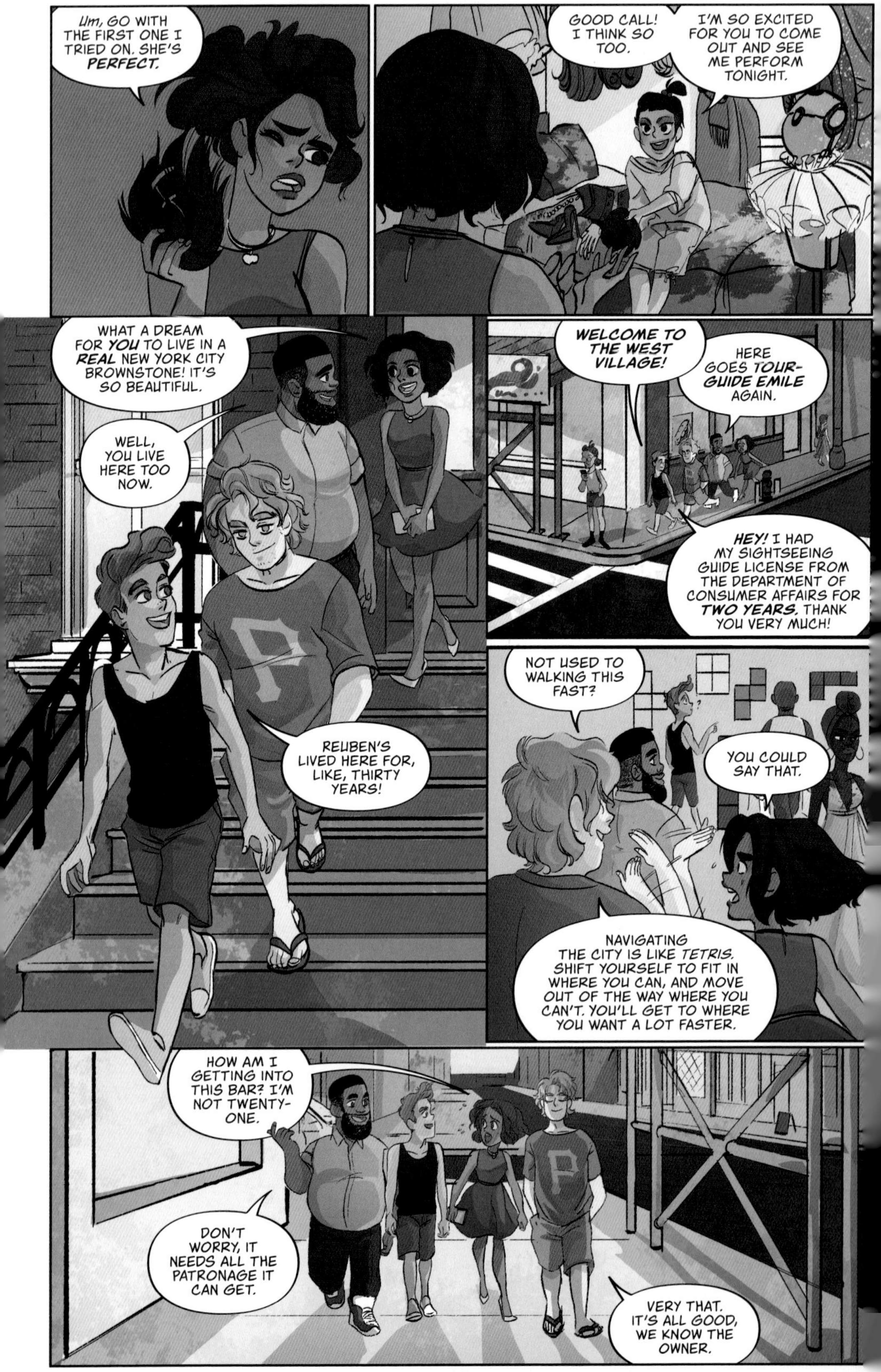
Um, GO WITH THE FIRST ONE I TRIED ON. SHE'S PERFECT.
GOOD CALL! I THINK SO TOO.
I'M SO EXCITED FOR YOU TO COME OUT AND SEE ME PERFORM TONIGHT.
WHAT A DREAM FOR YOU TO LIVE IN A REAL NEW YORK CITY BROWNSTONE! IT'S SO BEAUTIFUL.
WELL, YOU LIVE HERE TOO NOW.
REUBEN'S LIVED HERE FOR, LIKE, THIRTY YEARS!
WELCOME TO THE WEST VILLAGE!
HERE GOES TOUR-GUIDE EMILE AGAIN.
HEY! I HAD MY SIGHTSEEING GUIDE LICENSE FROM THE DEPARTMENT OF CONSUMER AFFAIRS FOR TWO YEARS. THANK YOU VERY MUCH!
NOT USED TO WALKING THIS FAST?
YOU COULD SAY THAT.
NAVIGATING THE CITY IS LIKE TETRIS. SHIFT YOURSELF TO FIT IN WHERE YOU CAN, AND MOVE OUT OF THE WAY WHERE YOU CAN'T. YOU'LL GET TO WHERE YOU WANT A LOT FASTER.
HOW AM I GETTING INTO THIS BAR? I'M NOT TWENTY-ONE.
DON'T WORRY, IT NEEDS ALL THE PATRONAGE IT CAN GET.
VERY THAT. IT'S ALL GOOD, WE KNOW THE OWNER.

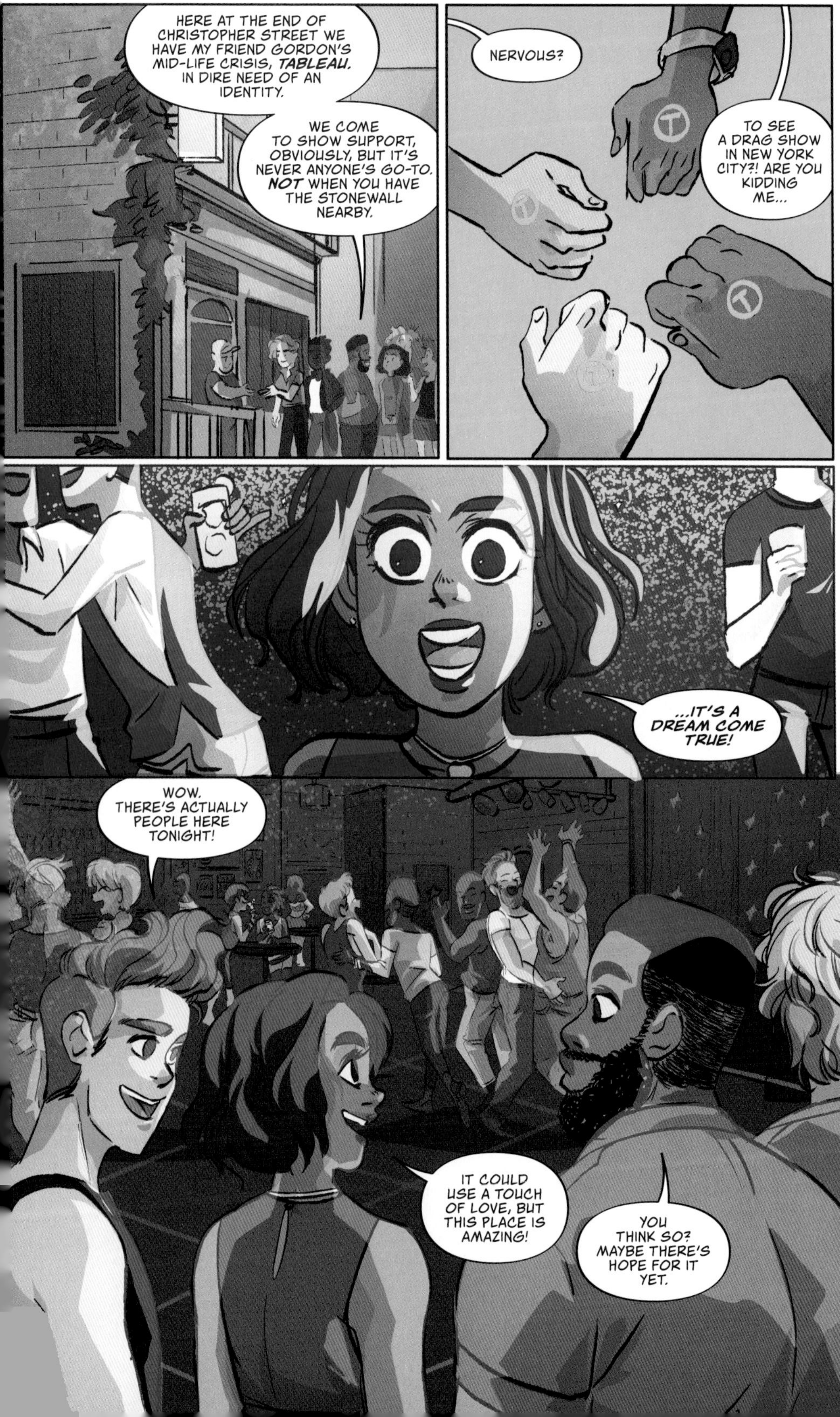
HERE AT THE END OF CHRISTOPHER STREET WE HAVE MY FRIEND GORDON'S MID-LIFE CRISIS, TABLEAU, IN DIRE NEED OF AN IDENTITY.
WE COME TO SHOW SUPPORT, OBVIOUSLY, BUT IT'S NEVER ANYONE'S GO-TO. NOT WHEN YOU HAVE THE STONEWALL NEARBY.
NERVOUS?
TO SEE A DRAG SHOW IN NEW YORK CITY?! ARE YOU KIDDING ME...
...IT'S A DREAM COME TRUE!
WOW. THERE'S ACTUALLY PEOPLE HERE TONIGHT!
IT COULD USE A TOUCH OF LOVE, BUT THIS PLACE IS AMAZING!
YOU THINK SO? MAYBE THERE'S HOPE FOR IT YET.

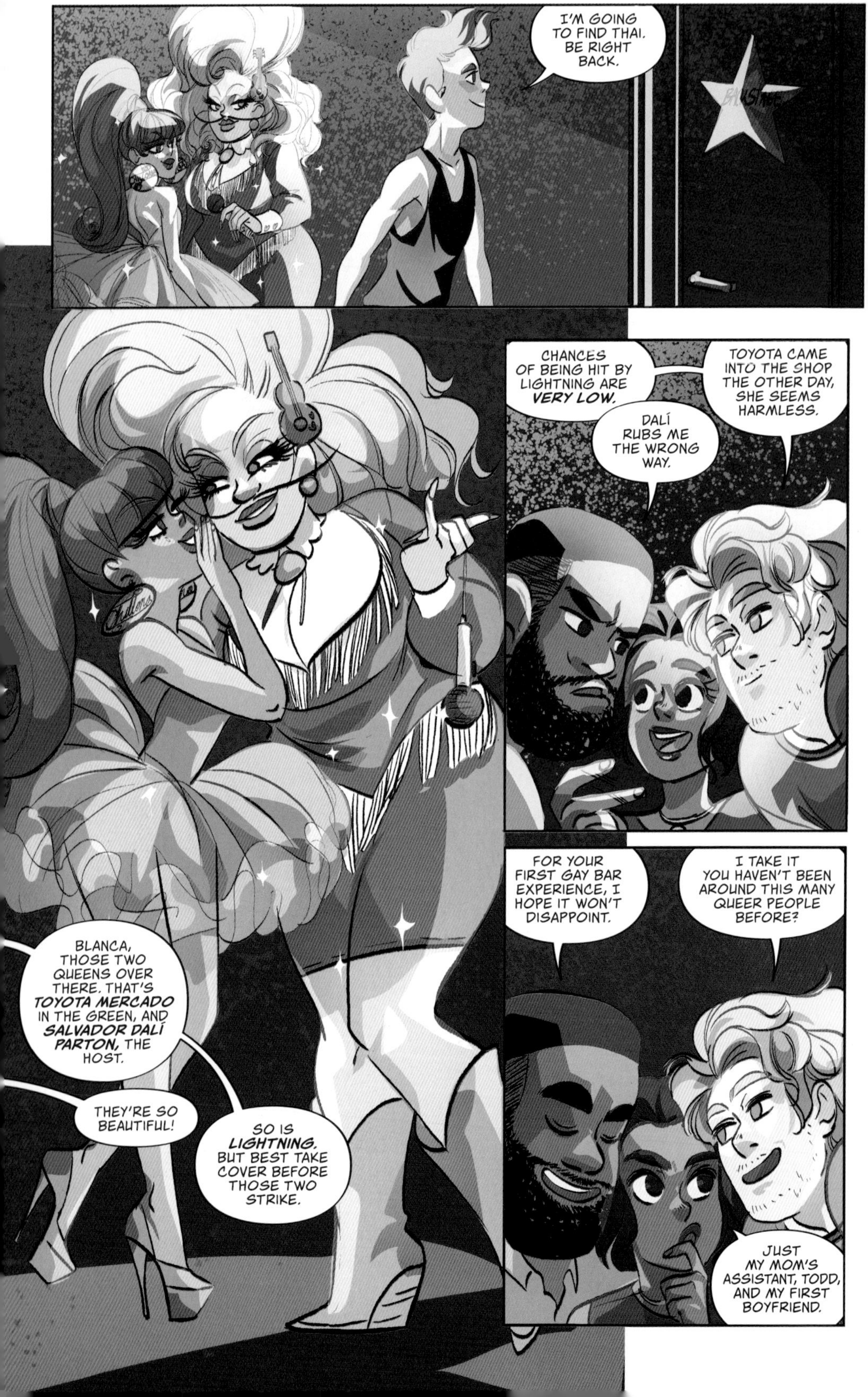
I'M GOING TO FIND THAI. BE RIGHT BACK.
BLANCA, THOSE TWO QUEENS OVER THERE. THAT'S TOYOTA MERCADO IN THE GREEN, AND SALVADOR DALÍ PARTON, THE HOST.
THEY'RE SO BEAUTIFUL!
SO IS LIGHTNING, BUT BEST TAKE COVER BEFORE THOSE TWO STRIKE.
CHANCES OF BEING HIT BY LIGHTNING ARE VERY LOW.
DALÍ RUBS ME THE WRONG WAY.
TOYOTA CAME INTO THE SHOP THE OTHER DAY, SHE SEEMS HARMLESS.
FOR YOUR FIRST GAY BAR EXPERIENCE, I HOPE IT WON'T DISAPPOINT.
I TAKE IT YOU HAVEN'T BEEN AROUND THIS MANY QUEER PEOPLE BEFORE?
JUST MY MOM'S ASSISTANT, TODD, AND MY FIRST BOYFRIEND.

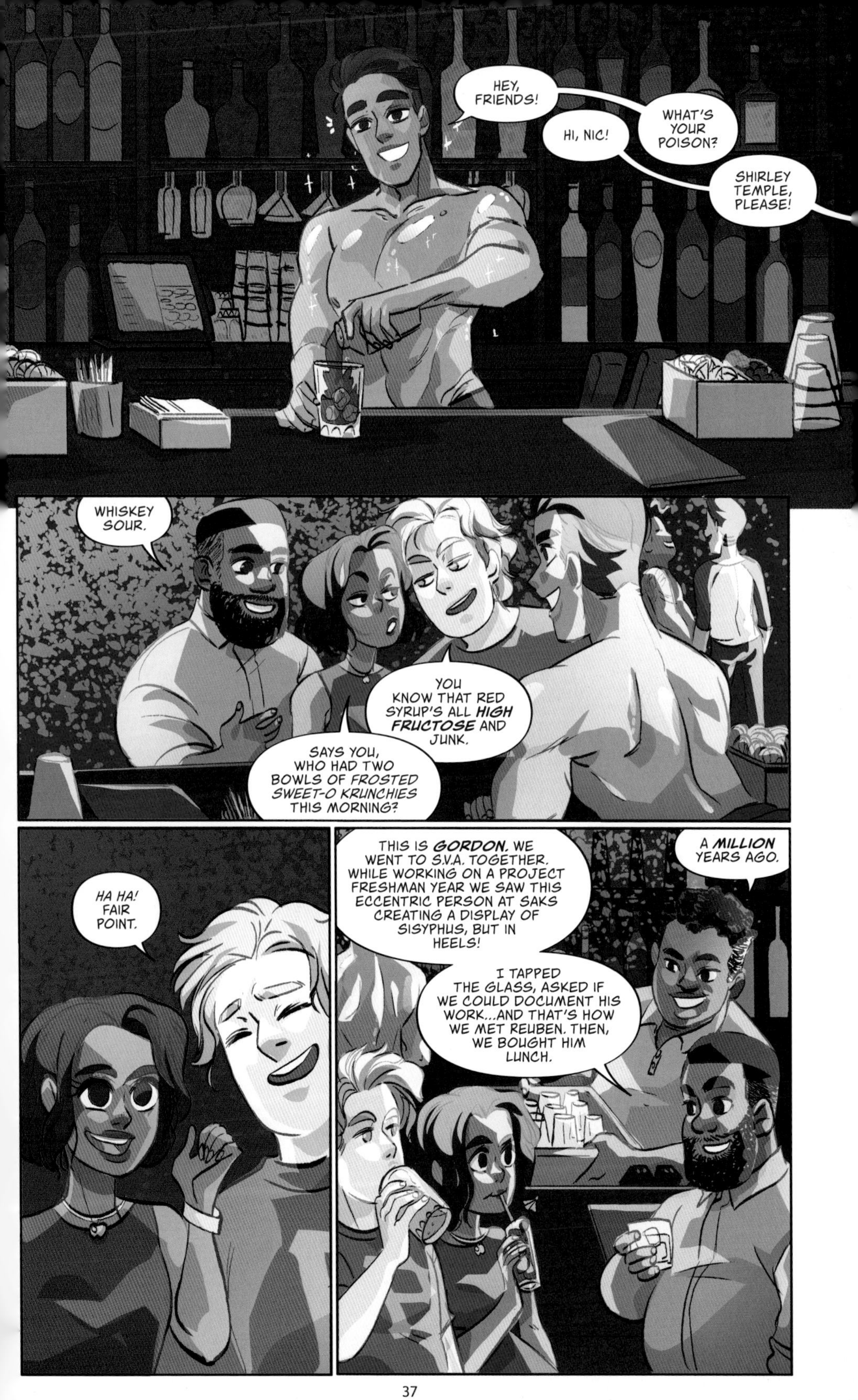

HEY, FRIENDS!
HI, NIC!
WHAT'S YOUR POISON?
SHIRLEY TEMPLE, PLEASE!
WHISKEY SOUR.
YOU KNOW THAT RED SYRUP'S ALL HIGH FRUCTOSE AND JUNK.
SAYS YOU, WHO HAD TWO BOWLS OF FROSTED SWEET-O KRUNCHIES THIS MORNING?
HA HA! FAIR POINT.
THIS IS GORDON. WE WENT TO S.V.A. TOGETHER. WHILE WORKING ON A PROJECT FRESHMAN YEAR WE SAW THIS ECCENTRIC PERSON AT SAKS CREATING A DISPLAY OF SISYPHUS, BUT IN HEELS!
I TAPPED THE GLASS, ASKED IF WE COULD DOCUMENT HIS WORK...AND THAT'S HOW WE MET REUBEN. THEN, WE BOUGHT HIM LUNCH.
A MILLION YEARS AGO.

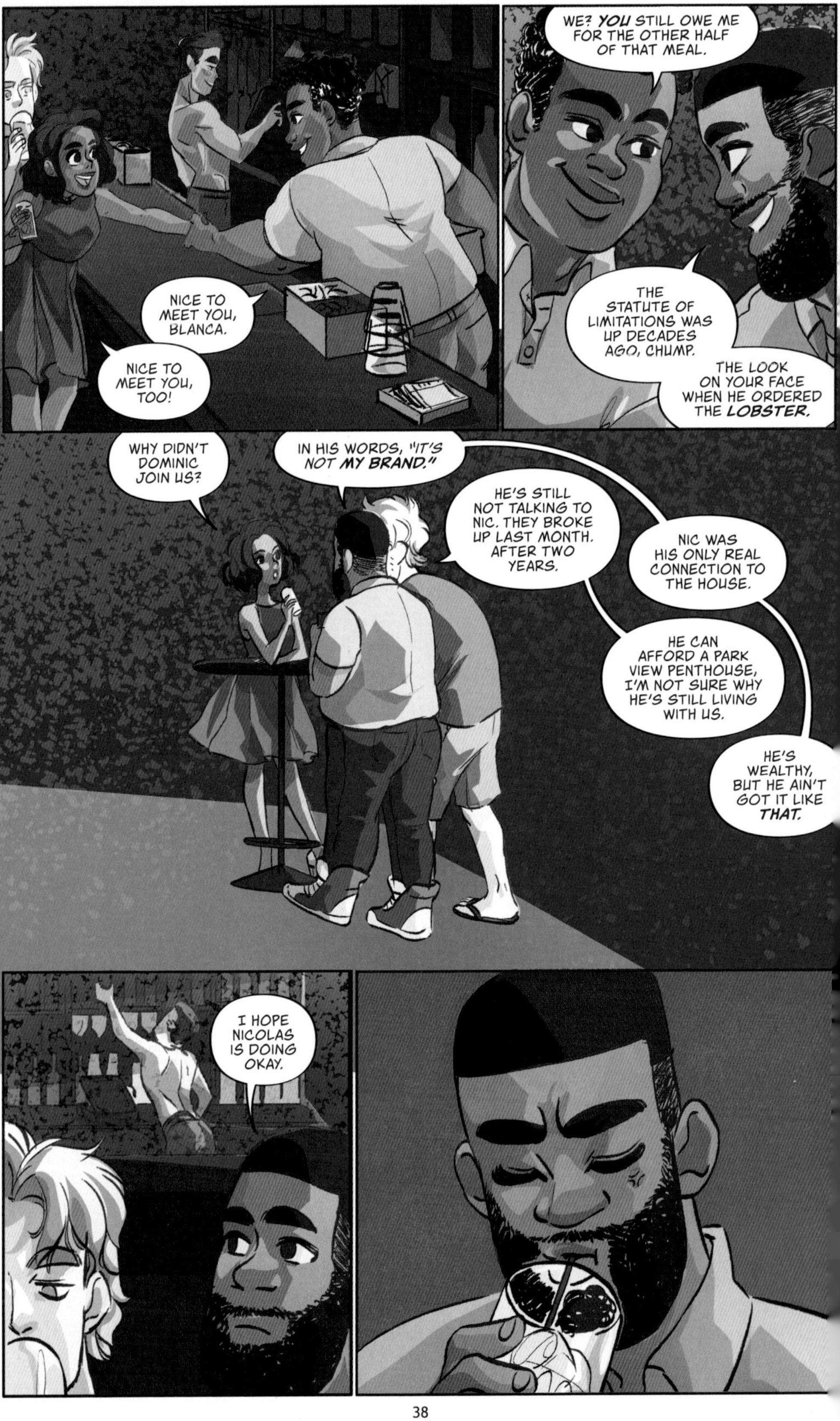
NICE TO MEET YOU, BLANCA.
NICE TO MEET YOU, TOO!
WE? YOU STILL OWE ME FOR THE OTHER HALF OF THAT MEAL.
THE STATUTE OF LIMITATIONS WAS UP DECADES AGO, CHUMP.
THE LOOK ON YOUR FACE WHEN HE ORDERED THE LOBSTER.
WHY DIDN'T DOMINIC JOIN US?
IN HIS WORDS, "IT'S NOT MY BRAND."
HE'S STILL NOT TALKING TO NIC. THEY BROKE UP LAST MONTH. AFTER TWO YEARS.
NIC WAS HIS ONLY REAL CONNECTION TO THE HOUSE.
HE CAN AFFORD A PARK VIEW PENTHOUSE, I'M NOT SURE WHY HE'S STILL LIVING WITH US.
HE'S WEALTHY, BUT HE AIN'T GOT IT LIKE THAT.
I HOPE NICOLAS IS DOING OKAY.

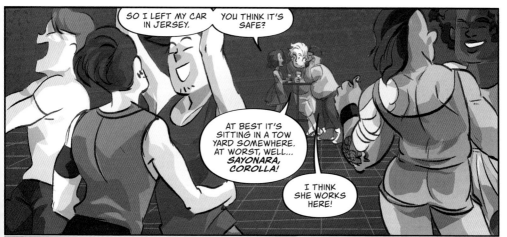

SO I LEFT MY CAR IN JERSEY.

YOU THINK IT'S SAFE?

AT BEST IT'S SITTING IN A TOW YARD SOMEWHERE. AT WORST, WELL... *SAYONARA, COROLLA!*

I THINK SHE WORKS HERE!

DO YOU HAVE ANY JOB OPENINGS AT THE BOOK-STORE?

NO. *QUICK-BURNING PAPER* IS CLOSING NEXT MONTH. FOR GOOD.

IT'S SAD. I SEE HOW IMPORTANT IT IS, ESPECIALLY TO OUR OLDER CUSTOMERS.

IT'S GREAT FOR QUEER VISIBILITY, BUT OUR GENERATION JUST CONSUMES MEDIA IN A DIFFERENT WAY.

I'M GOING TO PRINT MY RÉSUMÉ TOMORROW. WANNA JOIN ME? WE CAN PRINT YOURS, TOO?

SURE! I'LL WALK WITH YOU, *TETRIS-STYLE!*

TETRIS-STYLE!

BLANCA! COME QUICK, SOMETHING'S WRONG WITH THAI!

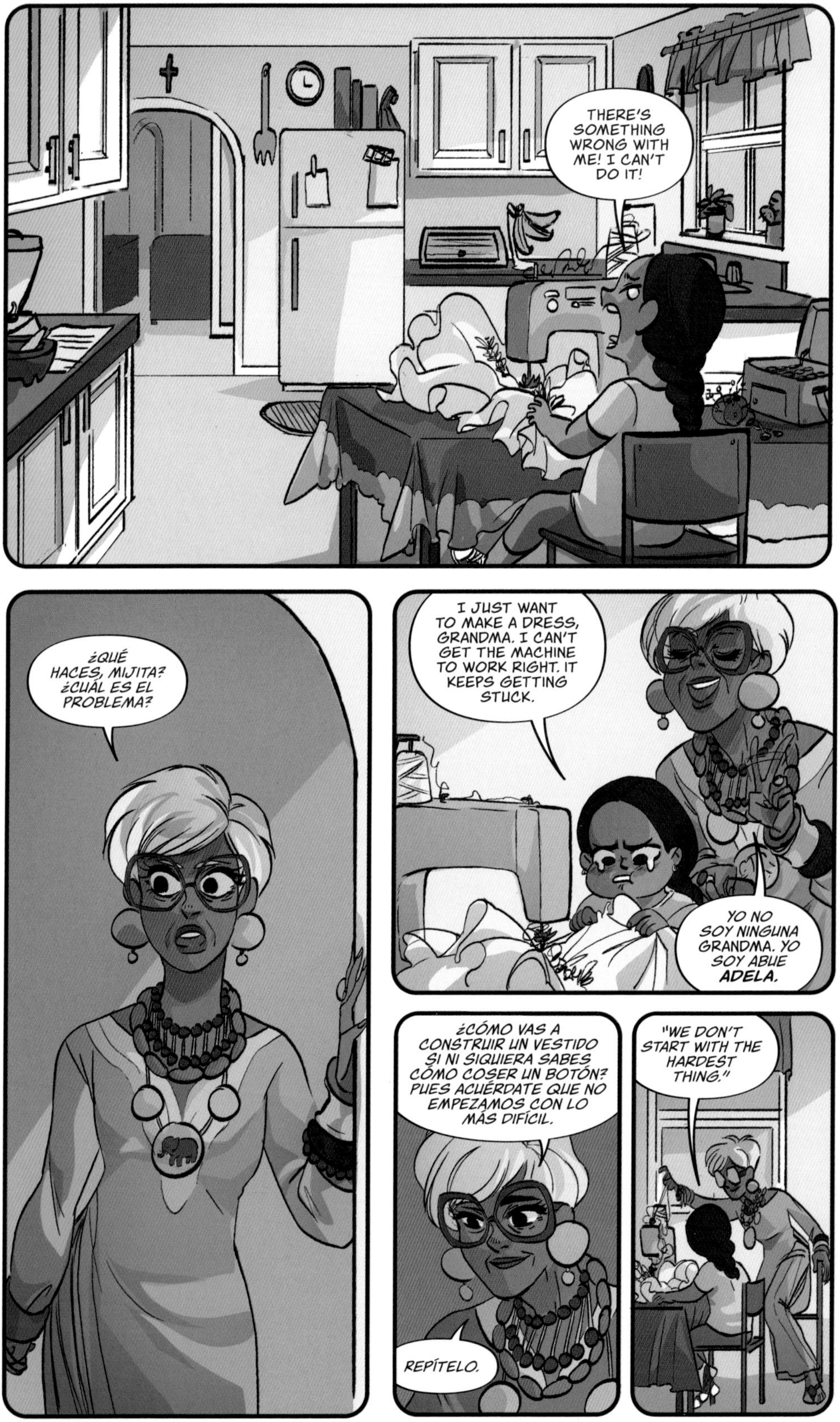
THERE'S SOMETHING WRONG WITH ME! I CAN'T DO IT!
¿QUÉ HACES, MIJITA? ¿CUÁL ES EL PROBLEMA?
I JUST WANT TO MAKE A DRESS, GRANDMA. I CAN'T GET THE MACHINE TO WORK RIGHT. IT KEEPS GETTING STUCK.
YO NO SOY NINGUNA GRANDMA. YO SOY ABUE **ADELA.**
¿CÓMO VAS A CONSTRUIR UN VESTIDO SI NI SIQUIERA SABES CÓMO COSER UN BOTÓN? PUES ACUÉRDATE QUE NO EMPEZAMOS CON LO MÁS DIFÍCIL.
REPÍTELO.
"WE DON'T START WITH THE HARDEST THING."

PÁSAME UNA AGUJA. CON CUIDADO.

GRACIAS. Y EL HILO TAMBIÉN.

ESCOJE UN BOTÓN ALLÍ DE MIS COSITAS.

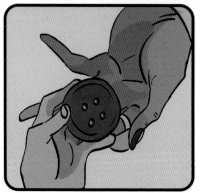

¡PERFECTO!

SI SABES CÓMO COSER UN BOTÓN, VAS A PODER PONERTE LA ROPA QUE HACES.

CUANDO NO SEPAS QUE HACER, REGRESA A LO BÁSICO.

REPÍTELO.

GOT IT. "WHEN YOU DON'T KNOW WHAT TO DO, **GO BACK TO THE BASICS.**"

GRACIAS, ABUE.

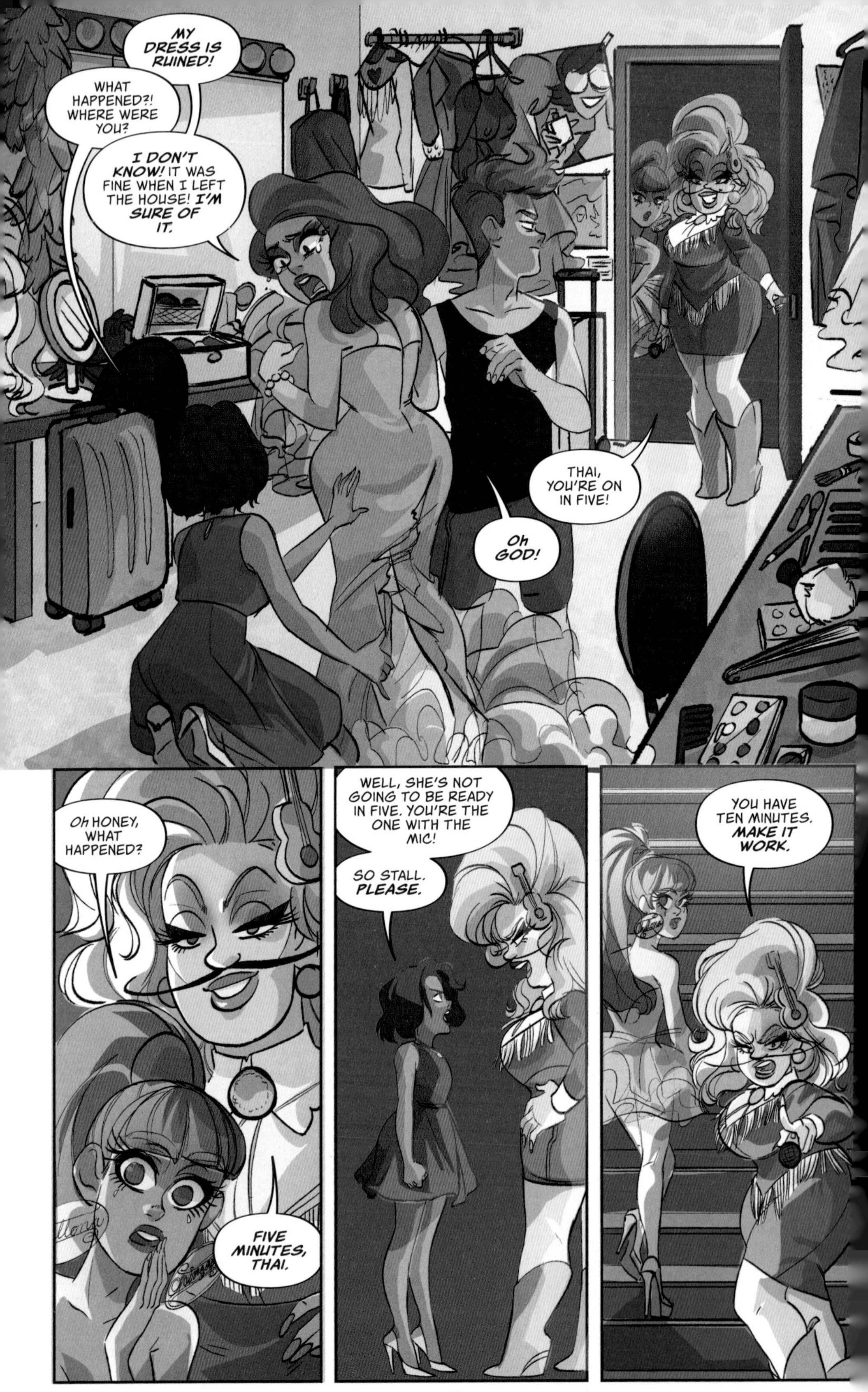

MY DRESS IS RUINED!
WHAT HAPPENED?! WHERE WERE YOU?
I DON'T KNOW! IT WAS FINE WHEN I LEFT THE HOUSE! I'M SURE OF IT.
THAI, YOU'RE ON IN FIVE!
Oh GOD!
Oh HONEY, WHAT HAPPENED?
FIVE MINUTES, THAI.
WELL, SHE'S NOT GOING TO BE READY IN FIVE. YOU'RE THE ONE WITH THE MIC!
SO STALL. PLEASE.
YOU HAVE TEN MINUTES. MAKE IT WORK.

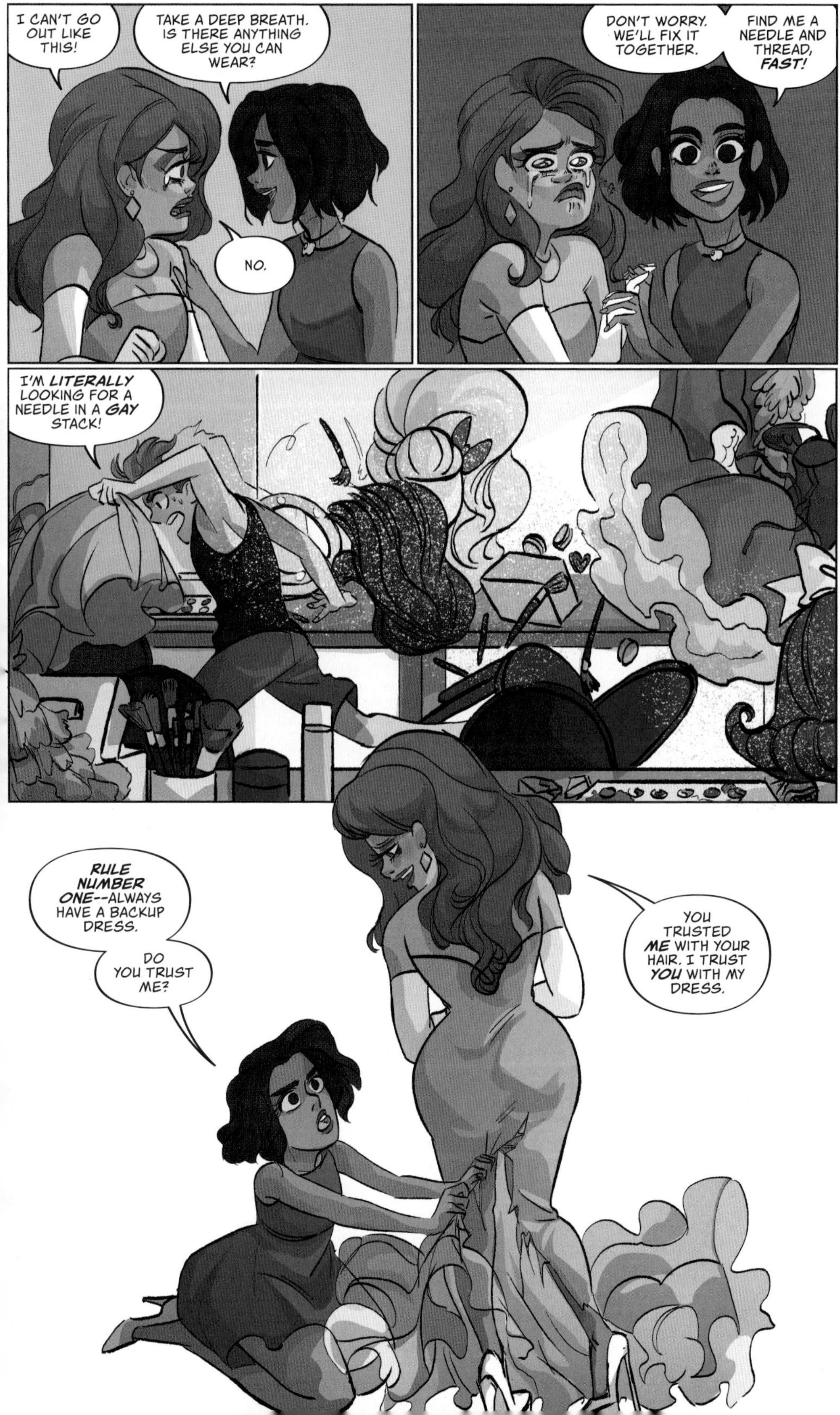
I CAN'T GO OUT LIKE THIS!
TAKE A DEEP BREATH. IS THERE ANYTHING ELSE YOU CAN WEAR?
NO.
DON'T WORRY. WE'LL FIX IT TOGETHER.
FIND ME A NEEDLE AND THREAD, FAST!
I'M LITERALLY LOOKING FOR A NEEDLE IN A GAY STACK!
RULE NUMBER ONE--ALWAYS HAVE A BACKUP DRESS.
DO YOU TRUST ME?
YOU TRUSTED ME WITH YOUR HAIR. I TRUST YOU WITH MY DRESS.

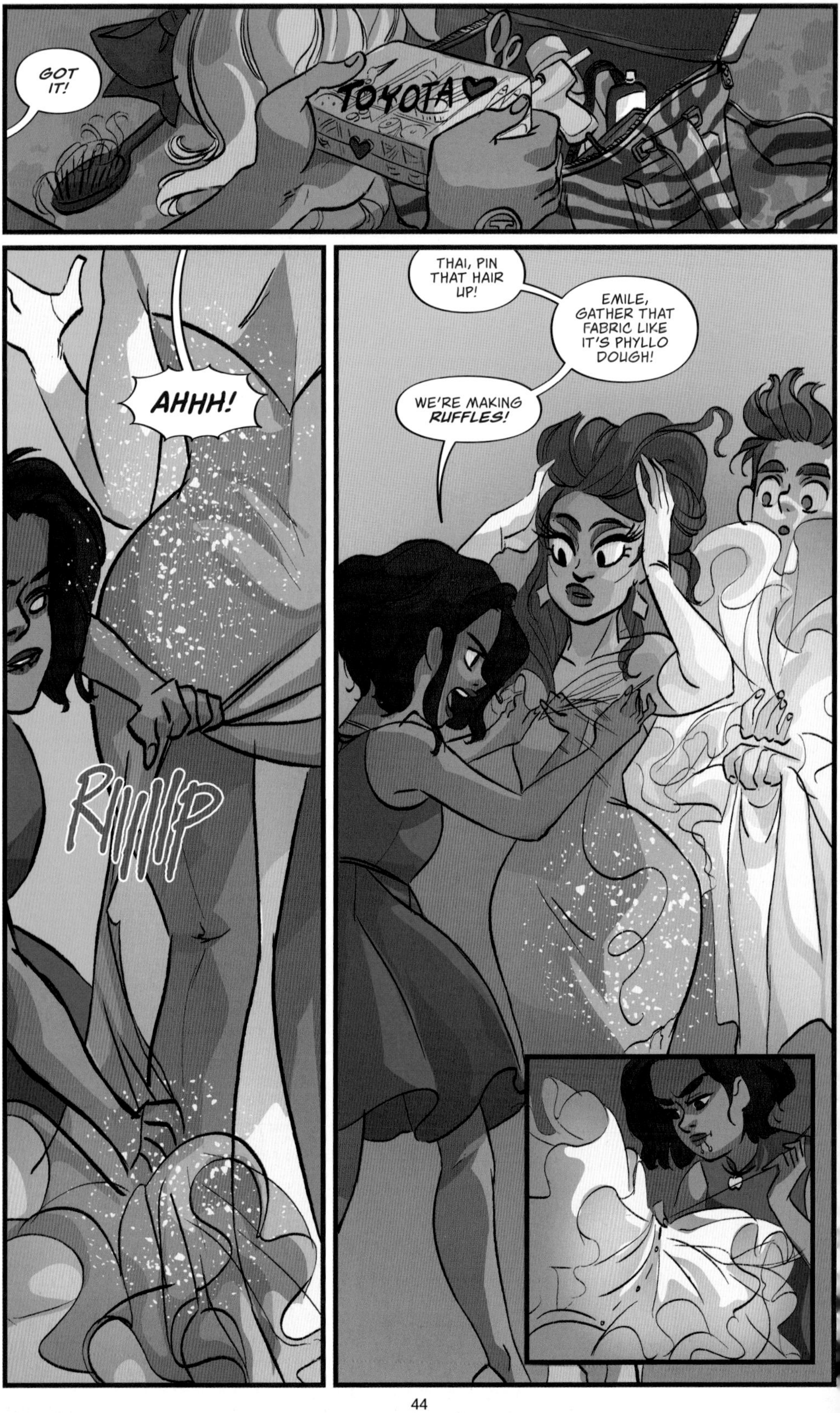
GOT IT!
TOYOTA
AHHH!
RIIIIP
THAI, PIN THAT HAIR UP!
EMILE, GATHER THAT FABRIC LIKE IT'S PHYLLO DOUGH!
WE'RE MAKING RUFFLES!

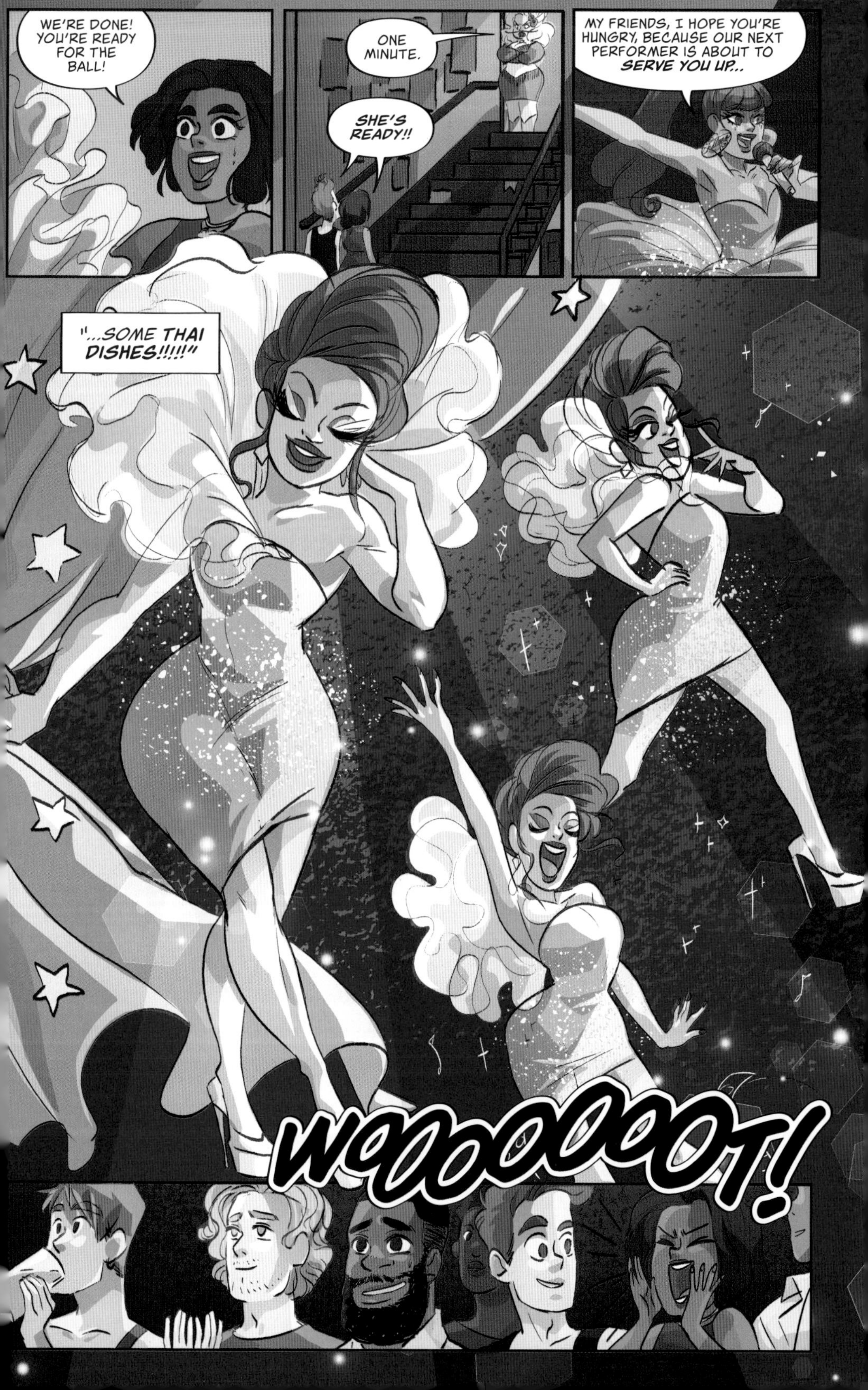
WE'RE DONE! YOU'RE READY FOR THE BALL!
ONE MINUTE.
SHE'S READY!!
MY FRIENDS, I HOPE YOU'RE HUNGRY, BECAUSE OUR NEXT PERFORMER IS ABOUT TO SERVE YOU UP...
"...SOME THAI DISHES!!!!!"
WOOOOOOOT!

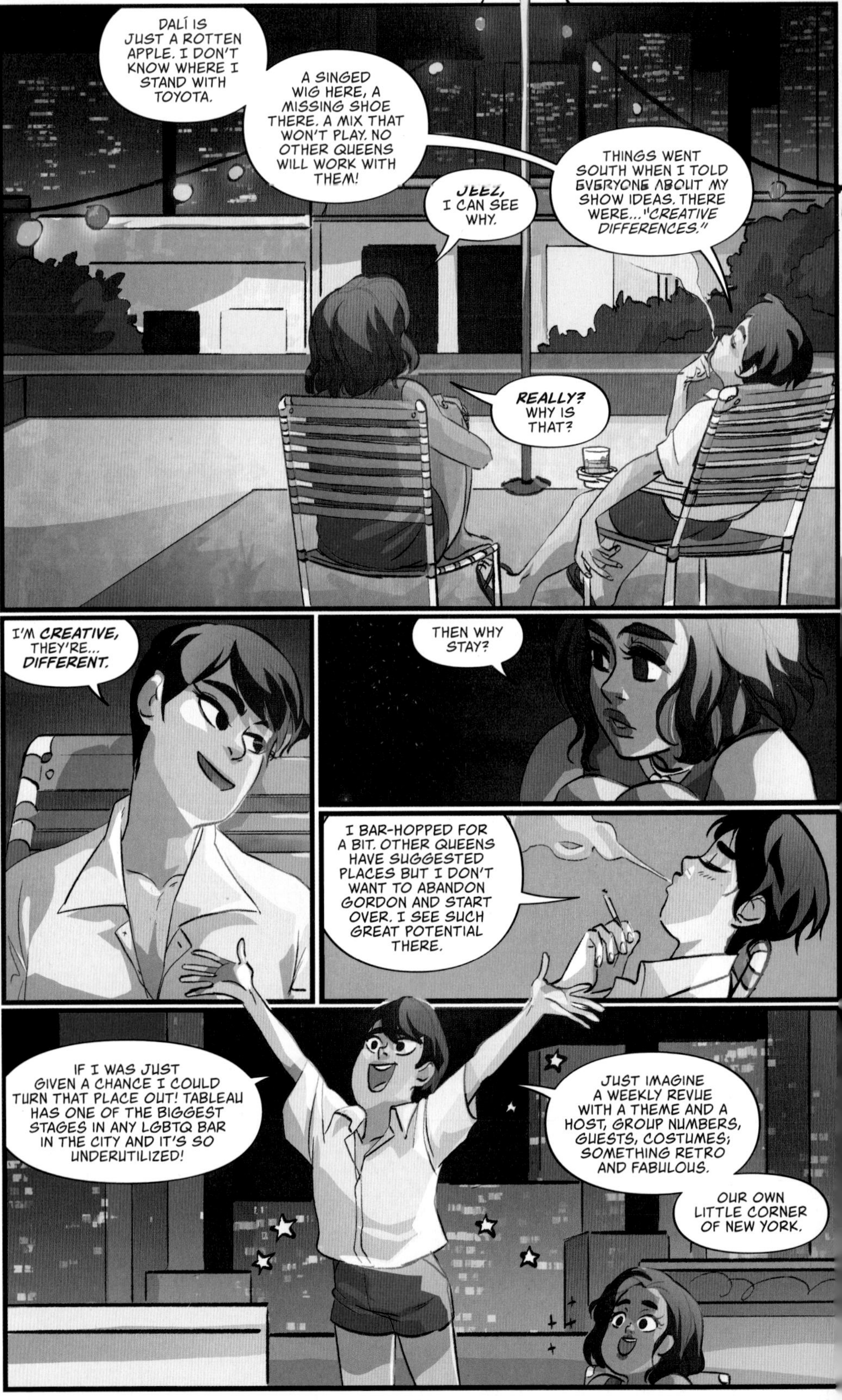
DALÍ IS JUST A ROTTEN APPLE. I DON'T KNOW WHERE I STAND WITH TOYOTA.
A SINGED WIG HERE, A MISSING SHOE THERE. A MIX THAT WON'T PLAY. NO OTHER QUEENS WILL WORK WITH THEM!
JEEZ, I CAN SEE WHY.
THINGS WENT SOUTH WHEN I TOLD EVERYONE ABOUT MY SHOW IDEAS. THERE WERE..."CREATIVE DIFFERENCES."
REALLY? WHY IS THAT?
I'M CREATIVE, THEY'RE... DIFFERENT.
THEN WHY STAY?
I BAR-HOPPED FOR A BIT. OTHER QUEENS HAVE SUGGESTED PLACES BUT I DON'T WANT TO ABANDON GORDON AND START OVER. I SEE SUCH GREAT POTENTIAL THERE.
IF I WAS JUST GIVEN A CHANCE I COULD TURN THAT PLACE OUT! TABLEAU HAS ONE OF THE BIGGEST STAGES IN ANY LGBTQ BAR IN THE CITY AND IT'S SO UNDERUTILIZED!
JUST IMAGINE A WEEKLY REVUE WITH A THEME AND A HOST, GROUP NUMBERS, GUESTS, COSTUMES; SOMETHING RETRO AND FABULOUS.
OUR OWN LITTLE CORNER OF NEW YORK.

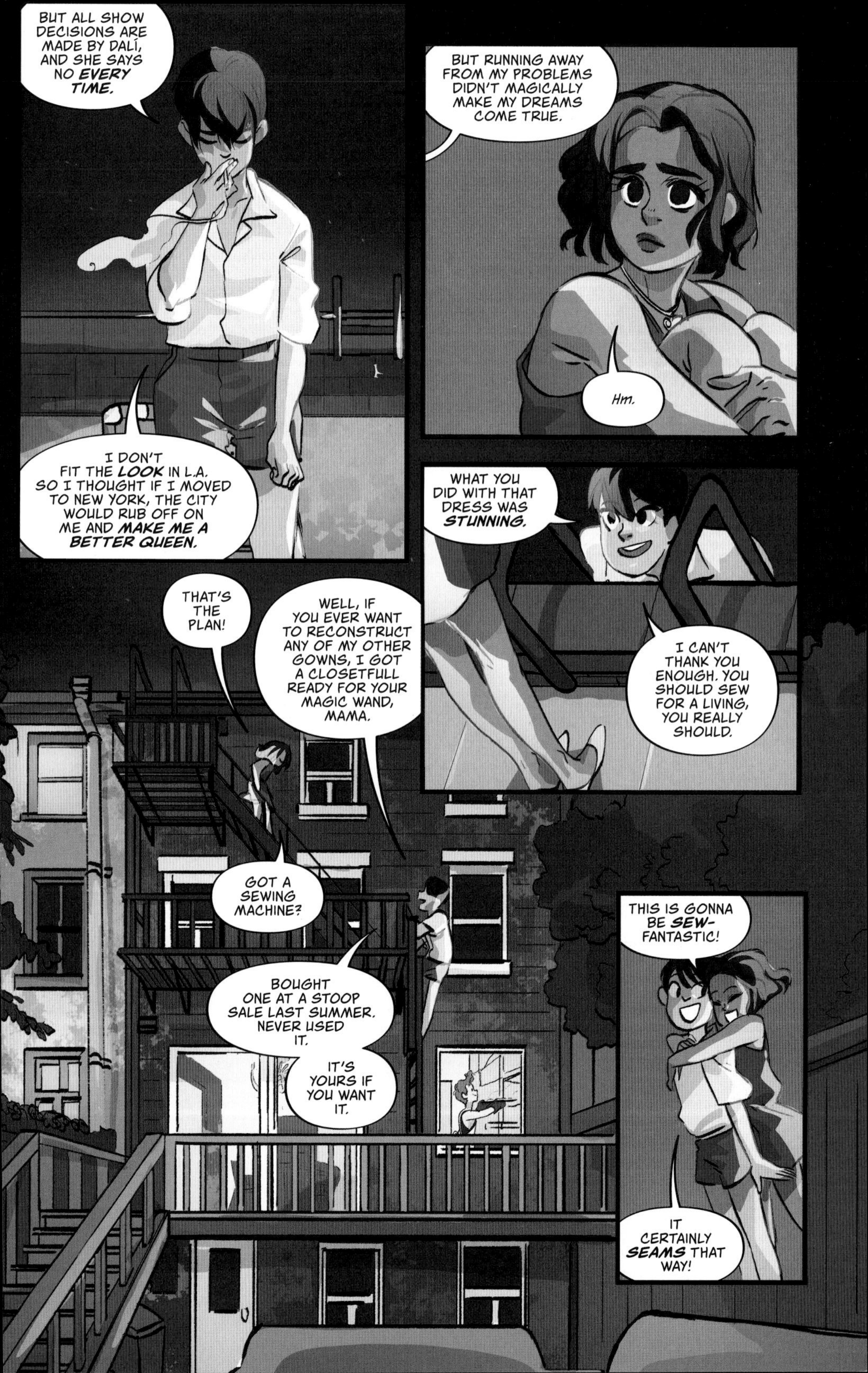
BUT ALL SHOW DECISIONS ARE MADE BY DALÍ, AND SHE SAYS NO *EVERY TIME.*
I DON'T FIT THE *LOOK* IN L.A. SO I THOUGHT IF I MOVED TO NEW YORK, THE CITY WOULD RUB OFF ON ME AND *MAKE ME A BETTER QUEEN.*
BUT RUNNING AWAY FROM MY PROBLEMS DIDN'T MAGICALLY MAKE MY DREAMS COME TRUE.
Hm.
WHAT YOU DID WITH THAT DRESS WAS *STUNNING.*
I CAN'T THANK YOU ENOUGH. YOU SHOULD SEW FOR A LIVING, YOU REALLY SHOULD.
THAT'S THE PLAN!
WELL, IF YOU EVER WANT TO RECONSTRUCT ANY OF MY OTHER GOWNS, I GOT A CLOSETFULL READY FOR YOUR MAGIC WAND, MAMA.
GOT A SEWING MACHINE?
BOUGHT ONE AT A STOOP SALE LAST SUMMER. NEVER USED IT.
IT'S YOURS IF YOU WANT IT.
THIS IS GONNA BE *SEW-*FANTASTIC!
IT CERTAINLY *SEAMS* THAT WAY!

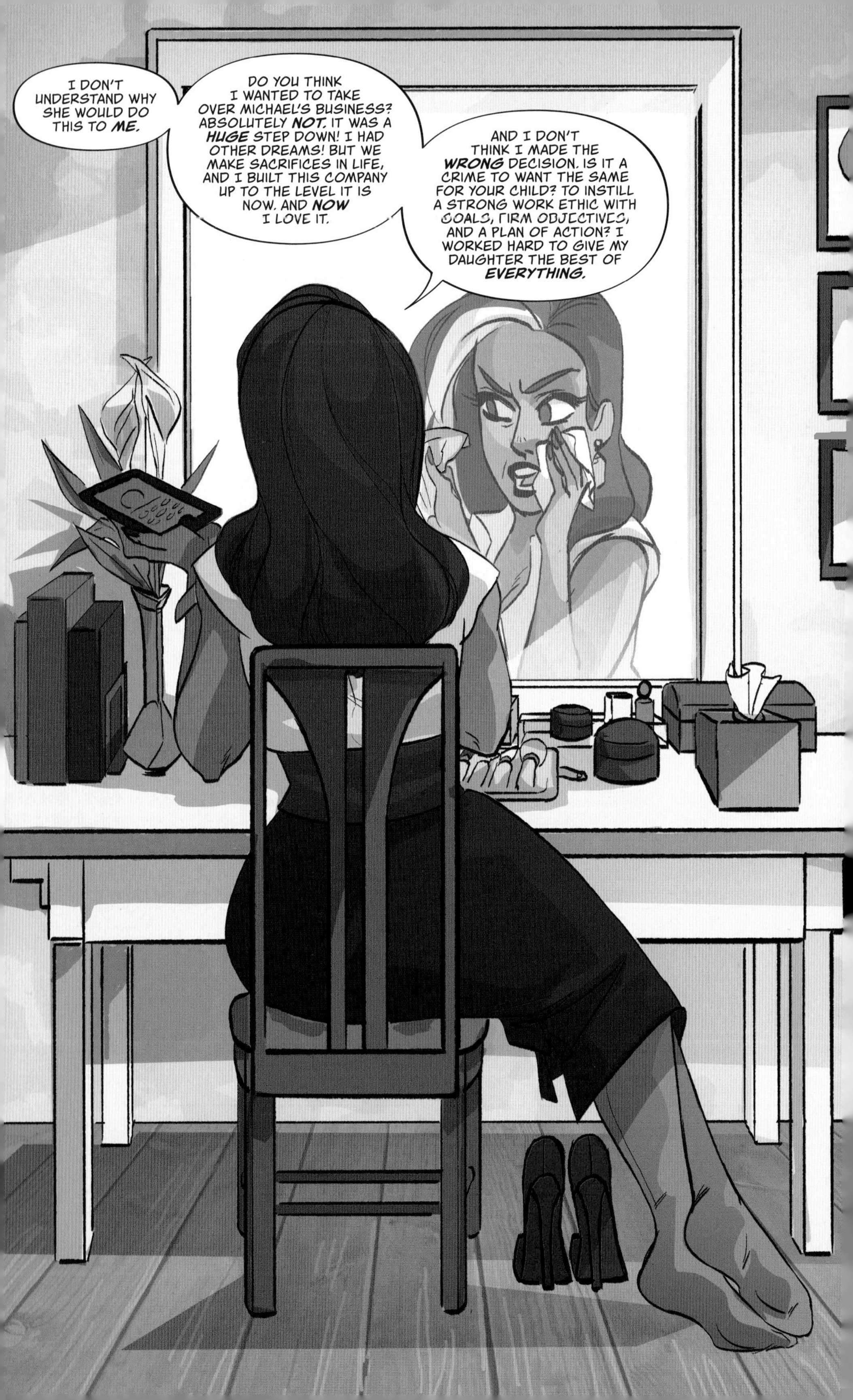
I DON'T UNDERSTAND WHY SHE WOULD DO THIS TO ME.
DO YOU THINK I WANTED TO TAKE OVER MICHAEL'S BUSINESS? ABSOLUTELY NOT. IT WAS A HUGE STEP DOWN! I HAD OTHER DREAMS! BUT WE MAKE SACRIFICES IN LIFE, AND I BUILT THIS COMPANY UP TO THE LEVEL IT IS NOW. AND NOW I LOVE IT.
AND I DON'T THINK I MADE THE WRONG DECISION. IS IT A CRIME TO WANT THE SAME FOR YOUR CHILD? TO INSTILL A STRONG WORK ETHIC WITH GOALS, FIRM OBJECTIVES, AND A PLAN OF ACTION? I WORKED HARD TO GIVE MY DAUGHTER THE BEST OF EVERYTHING.

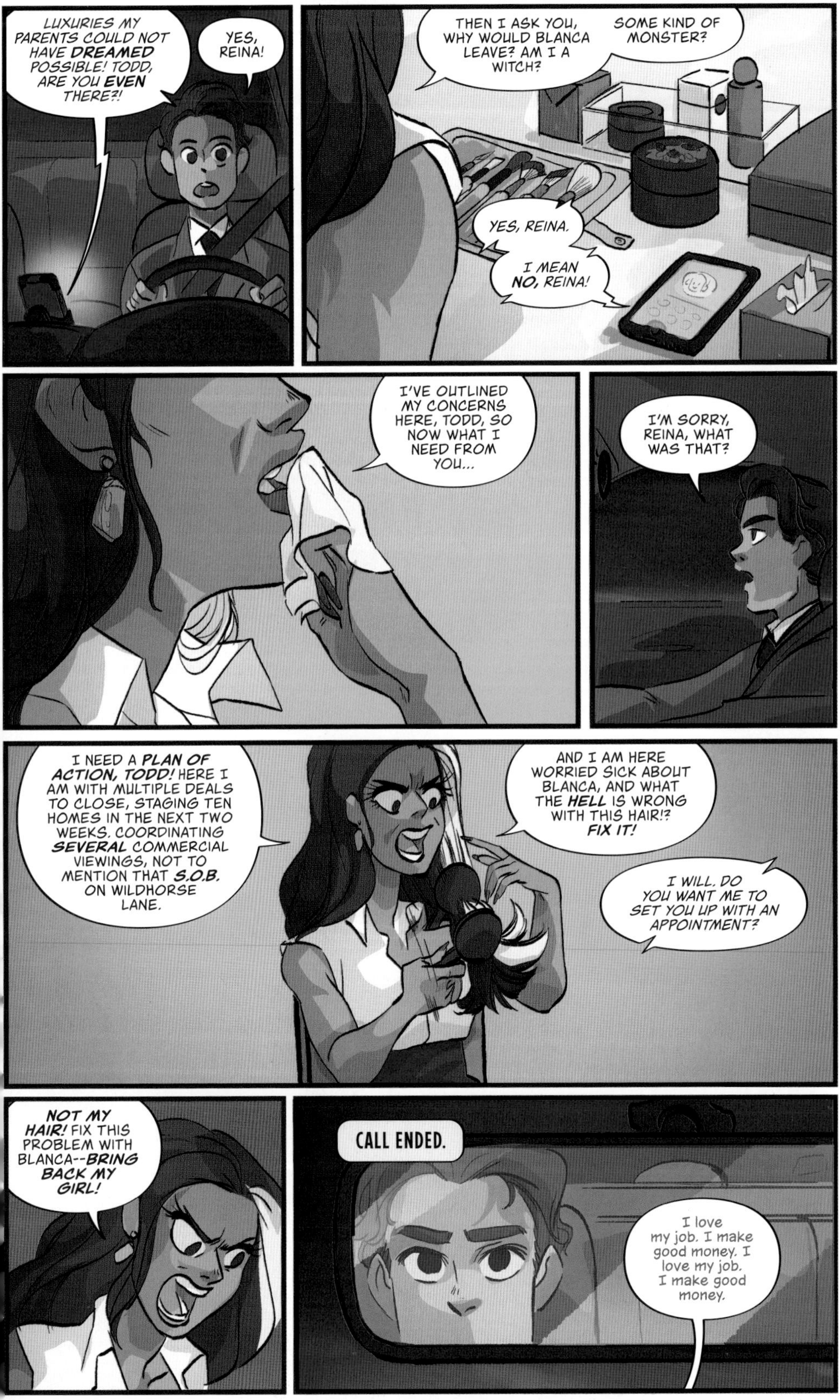
LUXURIES MY PARENTS COULD NOT HAVE DREAMED POSSIBLE! TODD, ARE YOU EVEN THERE?!
YES, REINA!
THEN I ASK YOU, WHY WOULD BLANCA LEAVE? AM I A WITCH?
SOME KIND OF MONSTER?
YES, REINA.
I MEAN NO, REINA!
I'VE OUTLINED MY CONCERNS HERE, TODD, SO NOW WHAT I NEED FROM YOU...
I'M SORRY, REINA, WHAT WAS THAT?
I NEED A PLAN OF ACTION, TODD! HERE I AM WITH MULTIPLE DEALS TO CLOSE, STAGING TEN HOMES IN THE NEXT TWO WEEKS. COORDINATING SEVERAL COMMERCIAL VIEWINGS, NOT TO MENTION THAT S.O.B. ON WILDHORSE LANE.
AND I AM HERE WORRIED SICK ABOUT BLANCA, AND WHAT THE HELL IS WRONG WITH THIS HAIR!? FIX IT!
I WILL. DO YOU WANT ME TO SET YOU UP WITH AN APPOINTMENT?
NOT MY HAIR! FIX THIS PROBLEM WITH BLANCA--BRING BACK MY GIRL!
CALL ENDED.
I love my job. I make good money. I love my job. I make good money.

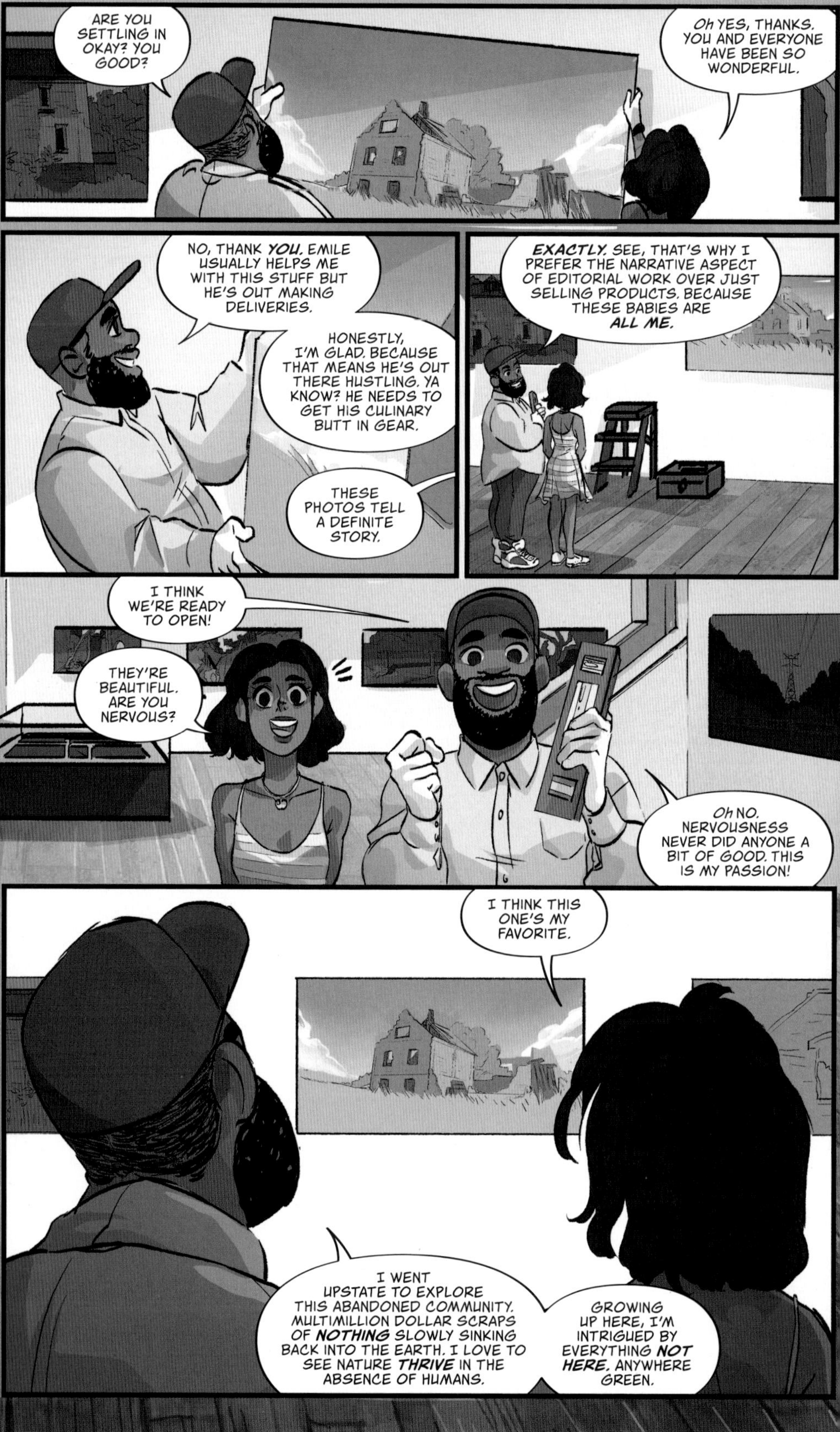
ARE YOU SETTLING IN OKAY? YOU GOOD?
Oh YES, THANKS. YOU AND EVERYONE HAVE BEEN SO WONDERFUL.
NO, THANK YOU. EMILE USUALLY HELPS ME WITH THIS STUFF BUT HE'S OUT MAKING DELIVERIES.
HONESTLY, I'M GLAD. BECAUSE THAT MEANS HE'S OUT THERE HUSTLING, YA KNOW? HE NEEDS TO GET HIS CULINARY BUTT IN GEAR.
THESE PHOTOS TELL A DEFINITE STORY.
EXACTLY. SEE, THAT'S WHY I PREFER THE NARRATIVE ASPECT OF EDITORIAL WORK OVER JUST SELLING PRODUCTS. BECAUSE THESE BABIES ARE ALL ME.
I THINK WE'RE READY TO OPEN!
THEY'RE BEAUTIFUL. ARE YOU NERVOUS?
Oh NO. NERVOUSNESS NEVER DID ANYONE A BIT OF GOOD. THIS IS MY PASSION!
I THINK THIS ONE'S MY FAVORITE.
I WENT UPSTATE TO EXPLORE THIS ABANDONED COMMUNITY. MULTIMILLION DOLLAR SCRAPS OF NOTHING SLOWLY SINKING BACK INTO THE EARTH. I LOVE TO SEE NATURE THRIVE IN THE ABSENCE OF HUMANS.
GROWING UP HERE, I'M INTRIGUED BY EVERYTHING NOT HERE. ANYWHERE GREEN.

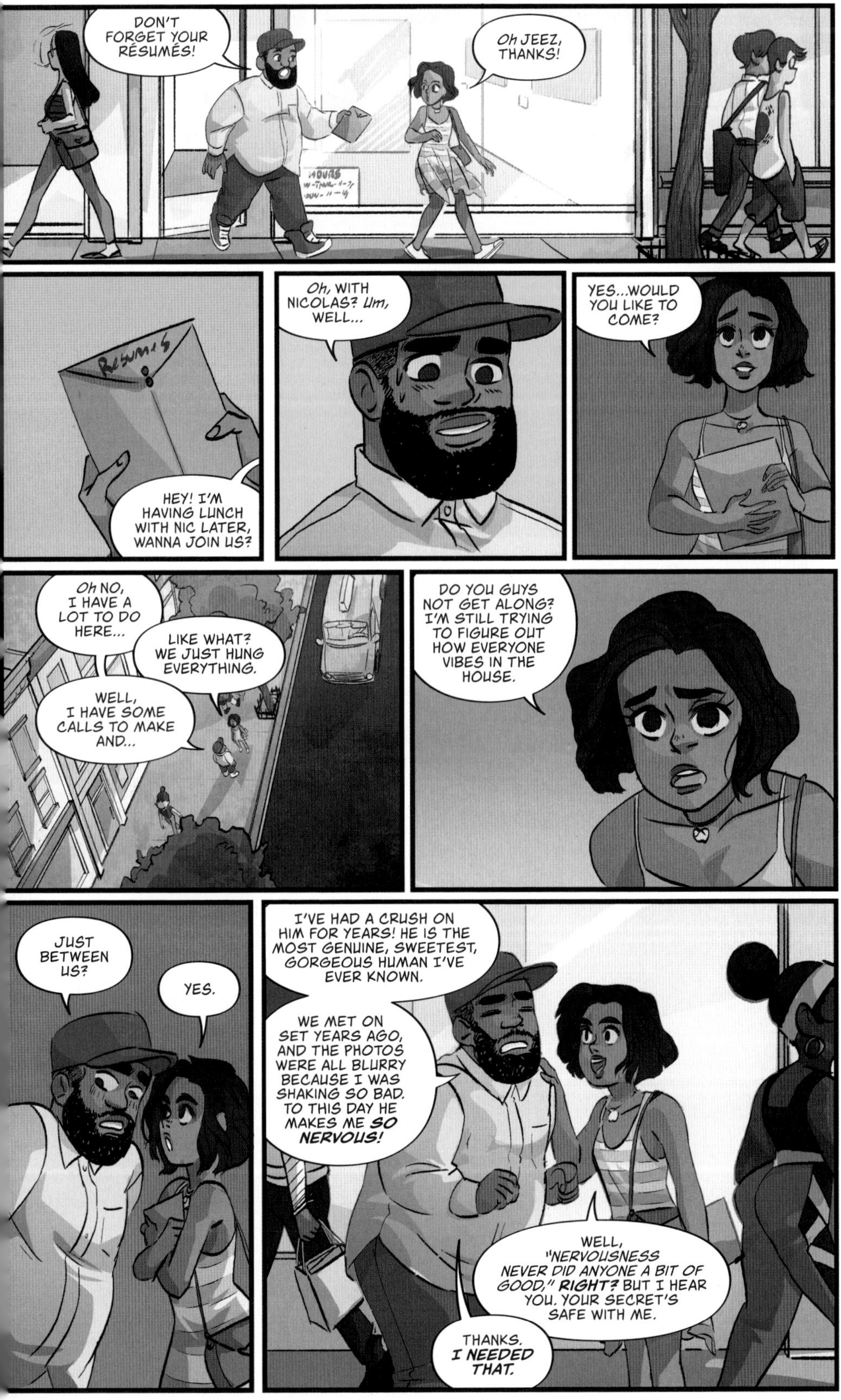
DON'T FORGET YOUR RÉSUMÉS!
Oh JEEZ, THANKS!
HEY! I'M HAVING LUNCH WITH NIC LATER, WANNA JOIN US?
Oh, WITH NICOLAS? Um, WELL...
YES...WOULD YOU LIKE TO COME?
Oh NO, I HAVE A LOT TO DO HERE...
LIKE WHAT? WE JUST HUNG EVERYTHING.
WELL, I HAVE SOME CALLS TO MAKE AND...
DO YOU GUYS NOT GET ALONG? I'M STILL TRYING TO FIGURE OUT HOW EVERYONE VIBES IN THE HOUSE.
JUST BETWEEN US?
YES.
I'VE HAD A CRUSH ON HIM FOR YEARS! HE IS THE MOST GENUINE, SWEETEST, GORGEOUS HUMAN I'VE EVER KNOWN.
WE MET ON SET YEARS AGO, AND THE PHOTOS WERE ALL BLURRY BECAUSE I WAS SHAKING SO BAD. TO THIS DAY HE MAKES ME **SO NERVOUS!**
WELL, "NERVOUSNESS NEVER DID ANYONE A BIT OF GOOD," **RIGHT?** BUT I HEAR YOU. YOUR SECRET'S SAFE WITH ME.
THANKS. **I NEEDED THAT.**

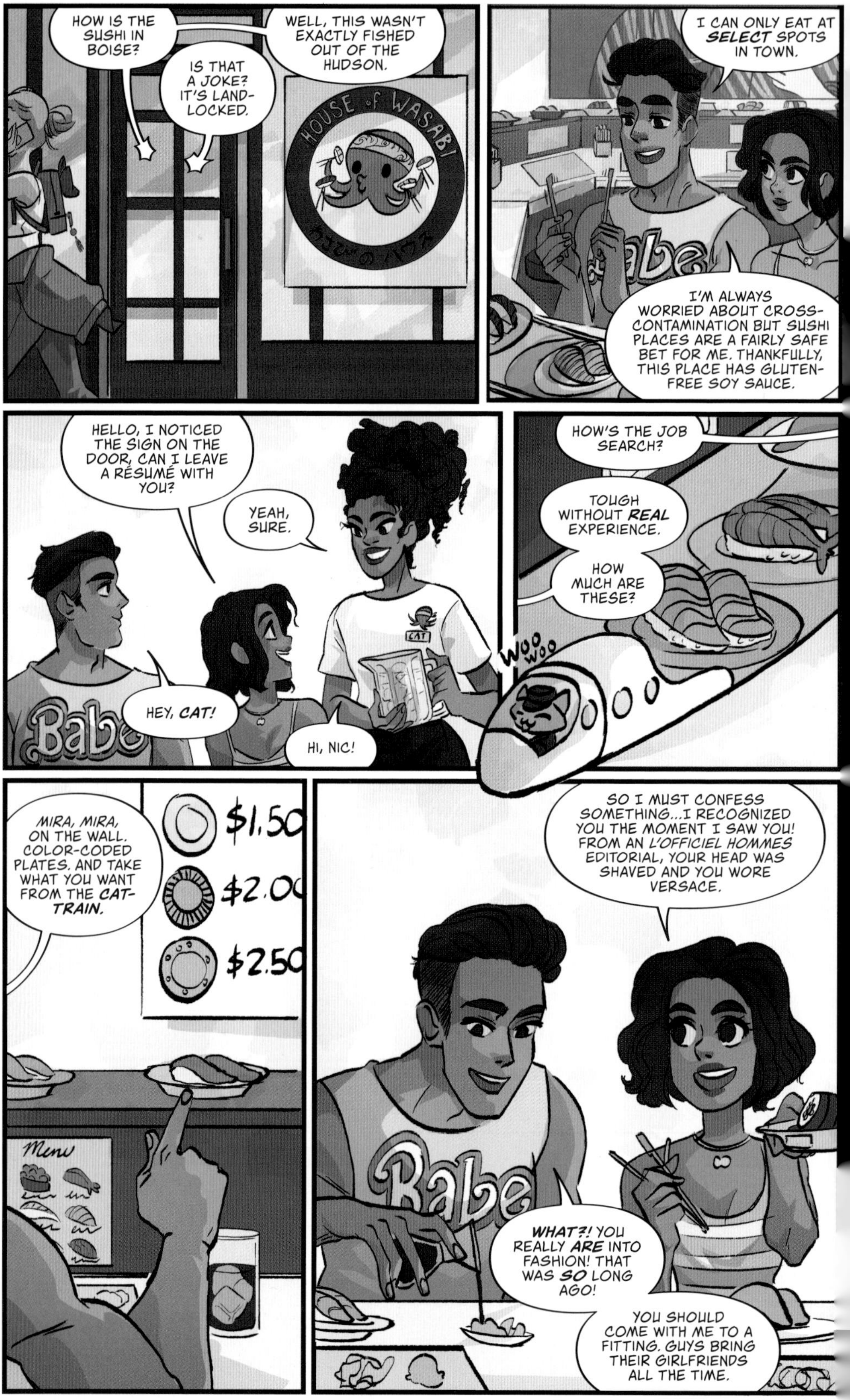
HOW IS THE SUSHI IN BOISE?
WELL, THIS WASN'T EXACTLY FISHED OUT OF THE HUDSON.
IS THAT A JOKE? IT'S LAND-LOCKED.
HOUSE of WASABI
I CAN ONLY EAT AT SELECT SPOTS IN TOWN.
I'M ALWAYS WORRIED ABOUT CROSS-CONTAMINATION BUT SUSHI PLACES ARE A FAIRLY SAFE BET FOR ME. THANKFULLY, THIS PLACE HAS GLUTEN-FREE SOY SAUCE.
HELLO, I NOTICED THE SIGN ON THE DOOR, CAN I LEAVE A RÉSUMÉ WITH YOU?
YEAH, SURE.
HEY, CAT!
HI, NIC!
CAT
HOW'S THE JOB SEARCH?
TOUGH WITHOUT REAL EXPERIENCE.
HOW MUCH ARE THESE?
WOO WOO
MIRA, MIRA, ON THE WALL. COLOR-CODED PLATES. AND TAKE WHAT YOU WANT FROM THE CAT-TRAIN.
$1.50
$2.00
$2.50
Menu
SO I MUST CONFESS SOMETHING...I RECOGNIZED YOU THE MOMENT I SAW YOU! FROM AN L'OFFICIEL HOMMES EDITORIAL, YOUR HEAD WAS SHAVED AND YOU WORE VERSACE.
WHAT?! YOU REALLY ARE INTO FASHION! THAT WAS SO LONG AGO!
YOU SHOULD COME WITH ME TO A FITTING. GUYS BRING THEIR GIRLFRIENDS ALL THE TIME.

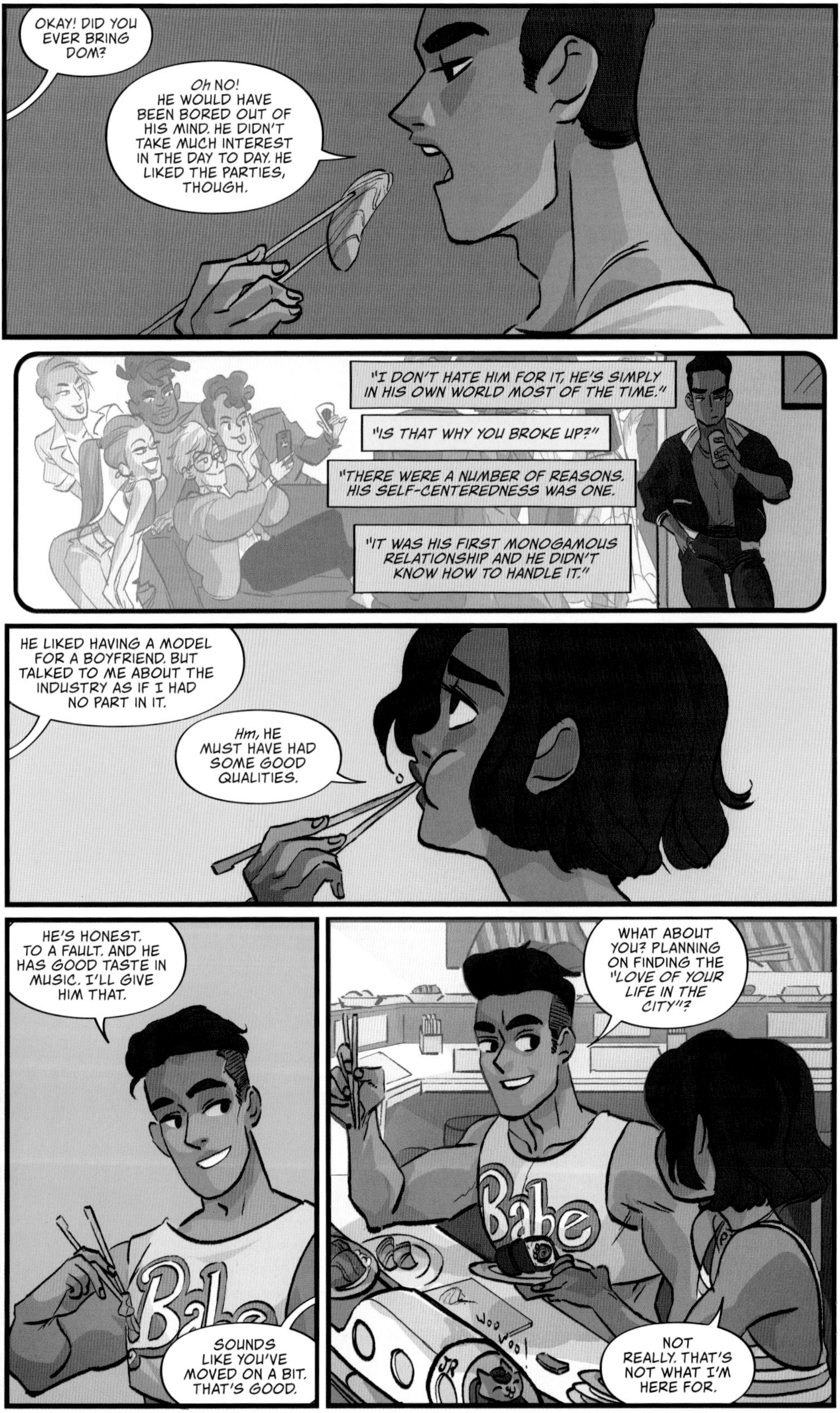
OKAY! DID YOU EVER BRING DOM?
Oh NO! HE WOULD HAVE BEEN BORED OUT OF HIS MIND. HE DIDN'T TAKE MUCH INTEREST IN THE DAY TO DAY. HE LIKED THE PARTIES, THOUGH.
"I DON'T HATE HIM FOR IT, HE'S SIMPLY IN HIS OWN WORLD MOST OF THE TIME."
"IS THAT WHY YOU BROKE UP?"
"THERE WERE A NUMBER OF REASONS. HIS SELF-CENTEREDNESS WAS ONE.
"IT WAS HIS FIRST MONOGAMOUS RELATIONSHIP AND HE DIDN'T KNOW HOW TO HANDLE IT."
HE LIKED HAVING A MODEL FOR A BOYFRIEND, BUT TALKED TO ME ABOUT THE INDUSTRY AS IF I HAD NO PART IN IT.
Hm, HE MUST HAVE HAD SOME GOOD QUALITIES.
HE'S HONEST. TO A FAULT. AND HE HAS GOOD TASTE IN MUSIC. I'LL GIVE HIM THAT.
Babe
SOUNDS LIKE YOU'VE MOVED ON A BIT. THAT'S GOOD.
WHAT ABOUT YOU? PLANNING ON FINDING THE "LOVE OF YOUR LIFE IN THE CITY"?
Babe
WOO WOO!
JR
NOT REALLY. THAT'S NOT WHAT I'M HERE FOR.

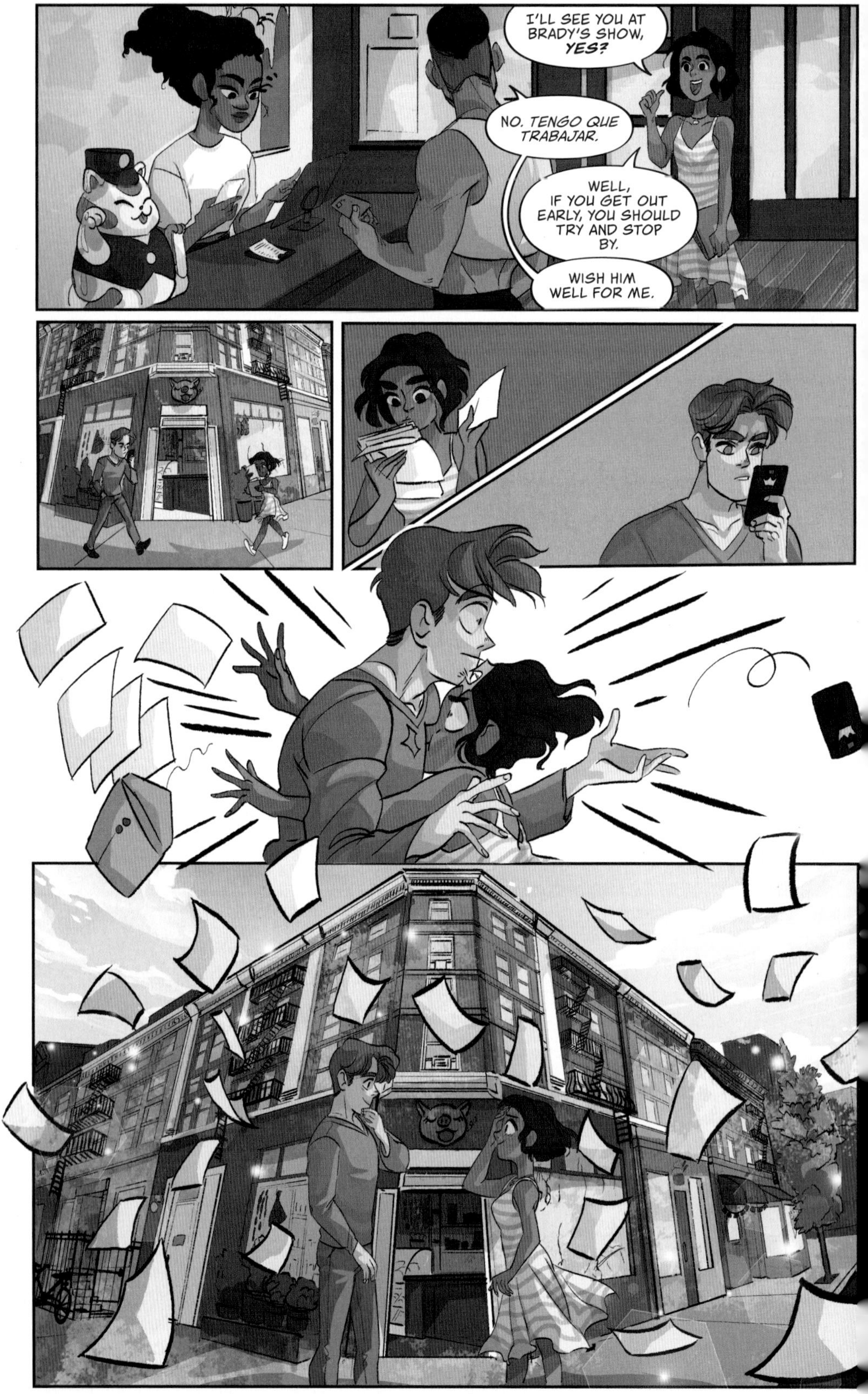
I'LL SEE YOU AT BRADY'S SHOW, YES?
NO. TENGO QUE TRABAJAR.
WELL, IF YOU GET OUT EARLY, YOU SHOULD TRY AND STOP BY.
WISH HIM WELL FOR ME.

Chapter Three

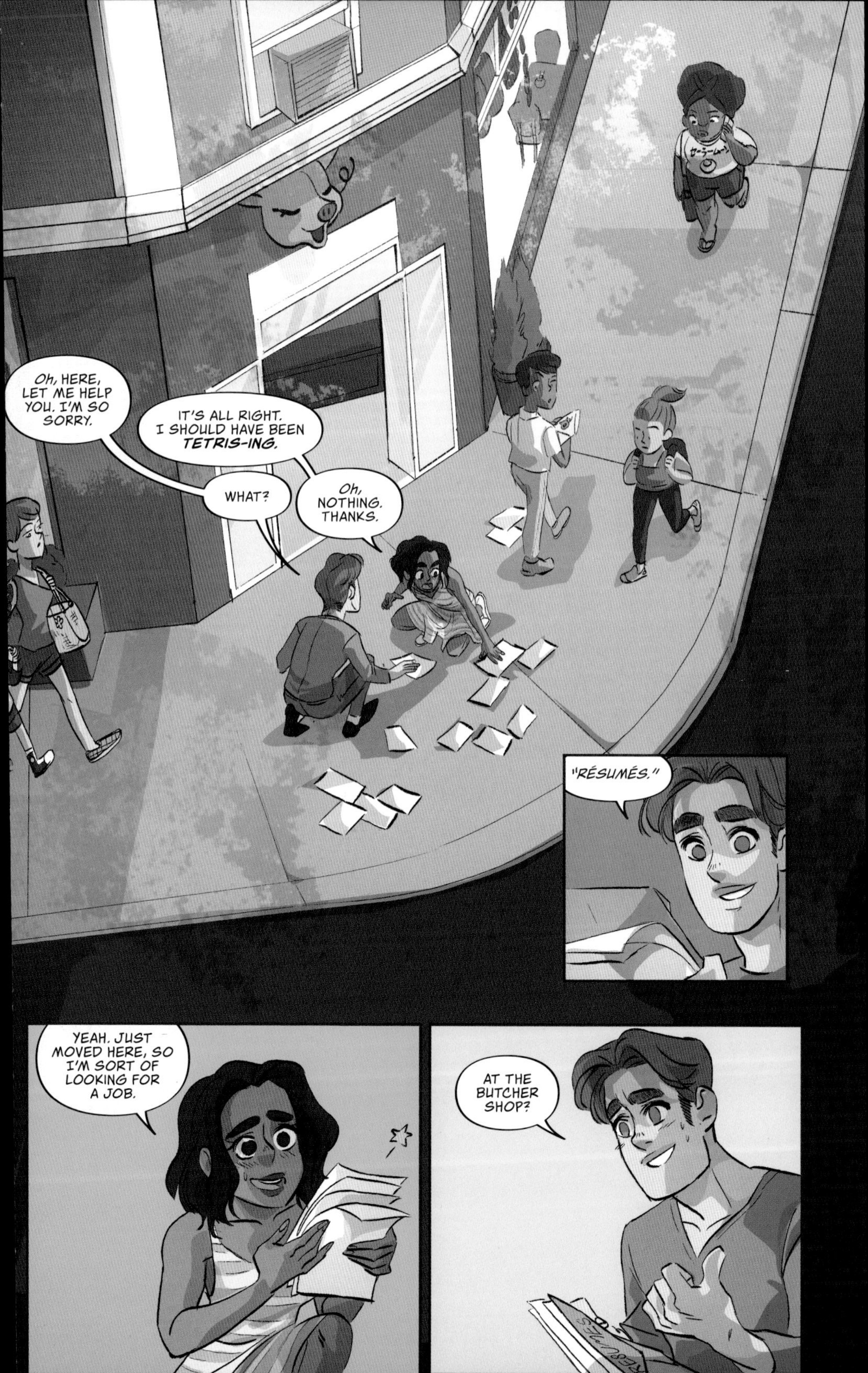
Oh, HERE, LET ME HELP YOU. I'M SO SORRY.
IT'S ALL RIGHT. I SHOULD HAVE BEEN **TETRIS-ING.**
WHAT?
Oh, NOTHING. THANKS.
"RÉSUMÉS."
YEAH. JUST MOVED HERE, SO I'M SORT OF LOOKING FOR A JOB.
AT THE BUTCHER SHOP?

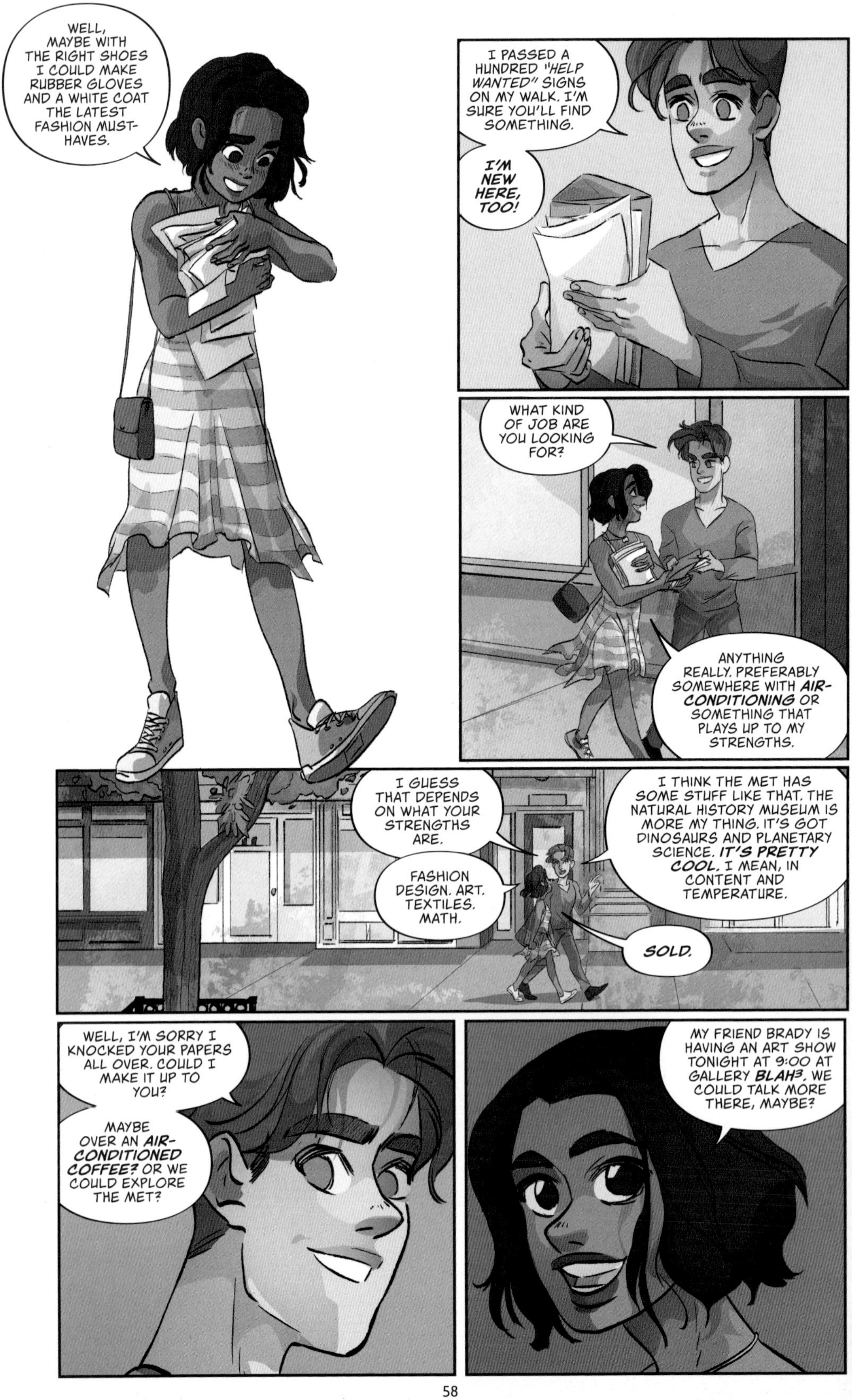

WELL, MAYBE WITH THE RIGHT SHOES I COULD MAKE RUBBER GLOVES AND A WHITE COAT THE LATEST FASHION MUST-HAVES.
I PASSED A HUNDRED "HELP WANTED" SIGNS ON MY WALK. I'M SURE YOU'LL FIND SOMETHING.
I'M NEW HERE, TOO!
WHAT KIND OF JOB ARE YOU LOOKING FOR?
ANYTHING REALLY. PREFERABLY SOMEWHERE WITH AIR-CONDITIONING OR SOMETHING THAT PLAYS UP TO MY STRENGTHS.
I GUESS THAT DEPENDS ON WHAT YOUR STRENGTHS ARE.
FASHION DESIGN. ART. TEXTILES. MATH.
I THINK THE MET HAS SOME STUFF LIKE THAT. THE NATURAL HISTORY MUSEUM IS MORE MY THING. IT'S GOT DINOSAURS AND PLANETARY SCIENCE. IT'S PRETTY COOL. I MEAN, IN CONTENT AND TEMPERATURE.
SOLD.
WELL, I'M SORRY I KNOCKED YOUR PAPERS ALL OVER. COULD I MAKE IT UP TO YOU?
MAYBE OVER AN AIR-CONDITIONED COFFEE? OR WE COULD EXPLORE THE MET?
MY FRIEND BRADY IS HAVING AN ART SHOW TONIGHT AT 9:00 AT GALLERY BLAH³. WE COULD TALK MORE THERE, MAYBE?

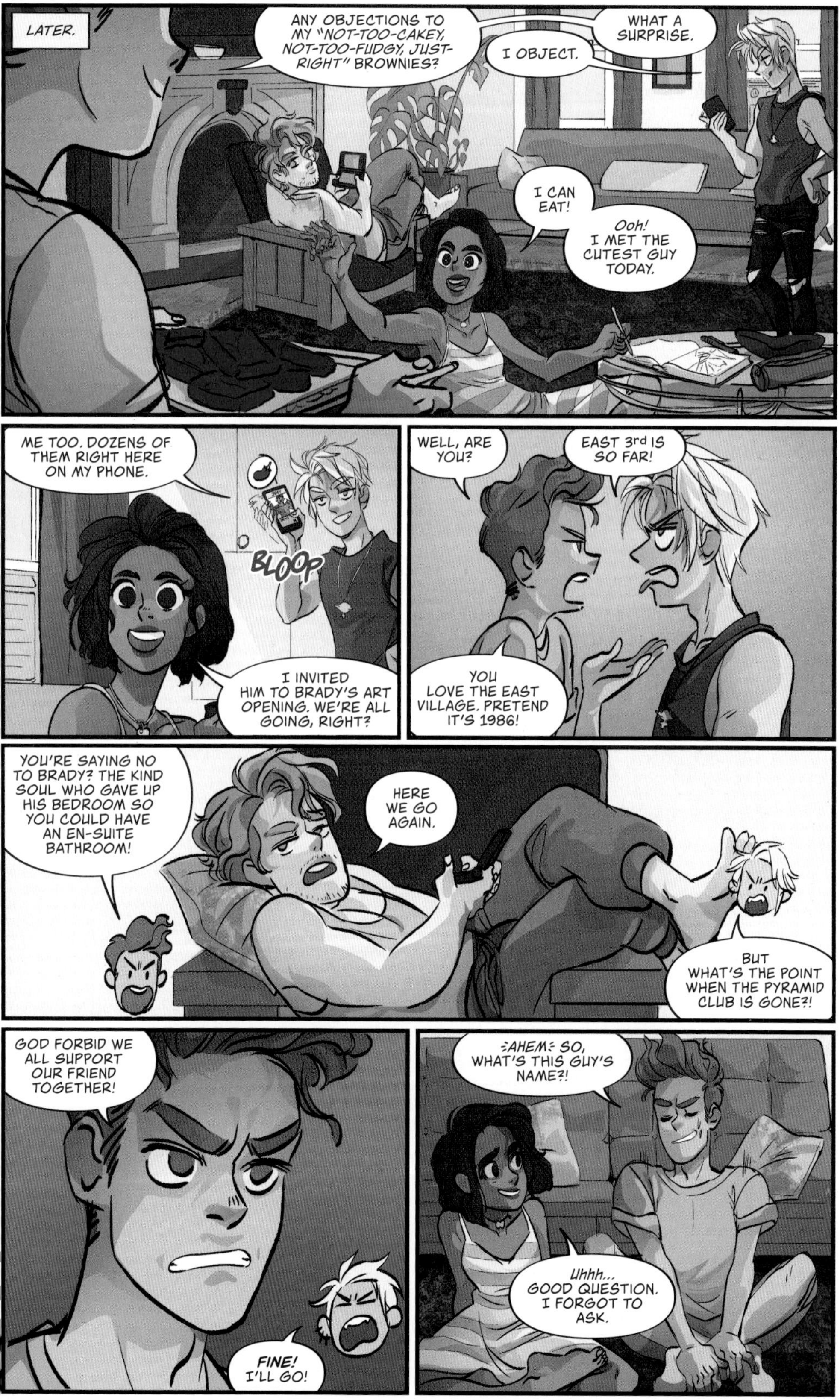
LATER.
ANY OBJECTIONS TO MY "NOT-TOO-CAKEY, NOT-TOO-FUDGY, JUST-RIGHT" BROWNIES?
I OBJECT.
WHAT A SURPRISE.
I CAN EAT!
Ooh! I MET THE CUTEST GUY TODAY.
ME TOO. DOZENS OF THEM RIGHT HERE ON MY PHONE.
BLOOP
I INVITED HIM TO BRADY'S ART OPENING. WE'RE ALL GOING, RIGHT?
WELL, ARE YOU?
EAST 3rd IS SO FAR!
YOU LOVE THE EAST VILLAGE. PRETEND IT'S 1986!
YOU'RE SAYING NO TO BRADY? THE KIND SOUL WHO GAVE UP HIS BEDROOM SO YOU COULD HAVE AN EN-SUITE BATHROOM!
HERE WE GO AGAIN.
BUT WHAT'S THE POINT WHEN THE PYRAMID CLUB IS GONE?!
GOD FORBID WE ALL SUPPORT OUR FRIEND TOGETHER!
FINE! I'LL GO!
AHEM SO, WHAT'S THIS GUY'S NAME?!
Uhhh... GOOD QUESTION. I FORGOT TO ASK.

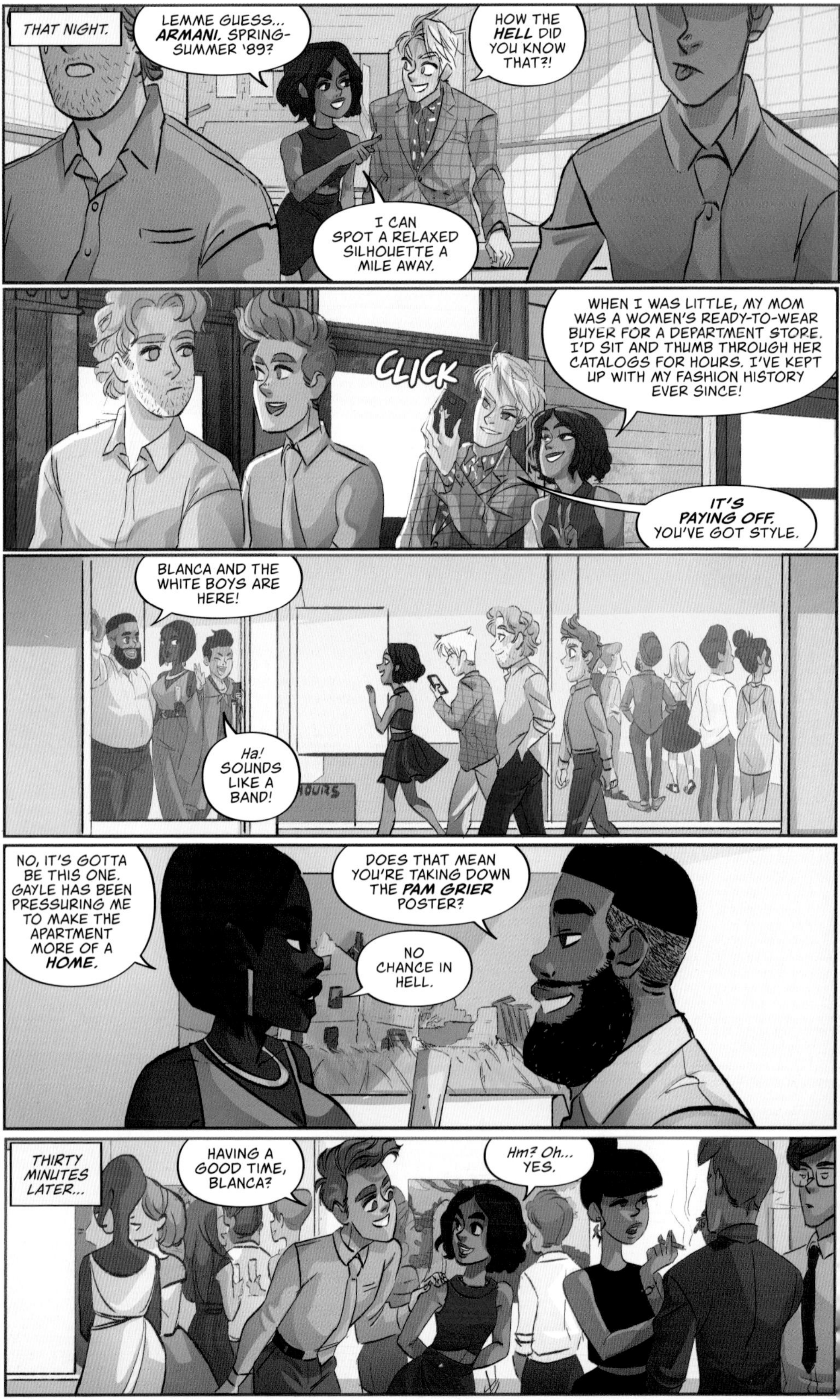
THAT NIGHT.
LEMME GUESS... ARMANI. SPRING-SUMMER '89?
HOW THE HELL DID YOU KNOW THAT?!
I CAN SPOT A RELAXED SILHOUETTE A MILE AWAY.
CLICK
WHEN I WAS LITTLE, MY MOM WAS A WOMEN'S READY-TO-WEAR BUYER FOR A DEPARTMENT STORE. I'D SIT AND THUMB THROUGH HER CATALOGS FOR HOURS. I'VE KEPT UP WITH MY FASHION HISTORY EVER SINCE!
IT'S PAYING OFF. YOU'VE GOT STYLE.
BLANCA AND THE WHITE BOYS ARE HERE!
Ha! SOUNDS LIKE A BAND!
HOURS
NO, IT'S GOTTA BE THIS ONE. GAYLE HAS BEEN PRESSURING ME TO MAKE THE APARTMENT MORE OF A HOME.
DOES THAT MEAN YOU'RE TAKING DOWN THE PAM GRIER POSTER?
NO CHANCE IN HELL.
THIRTY MINUTES LATER...
HAVING A GOOD TIME, BLANCA?
Hm? Oh... YES.

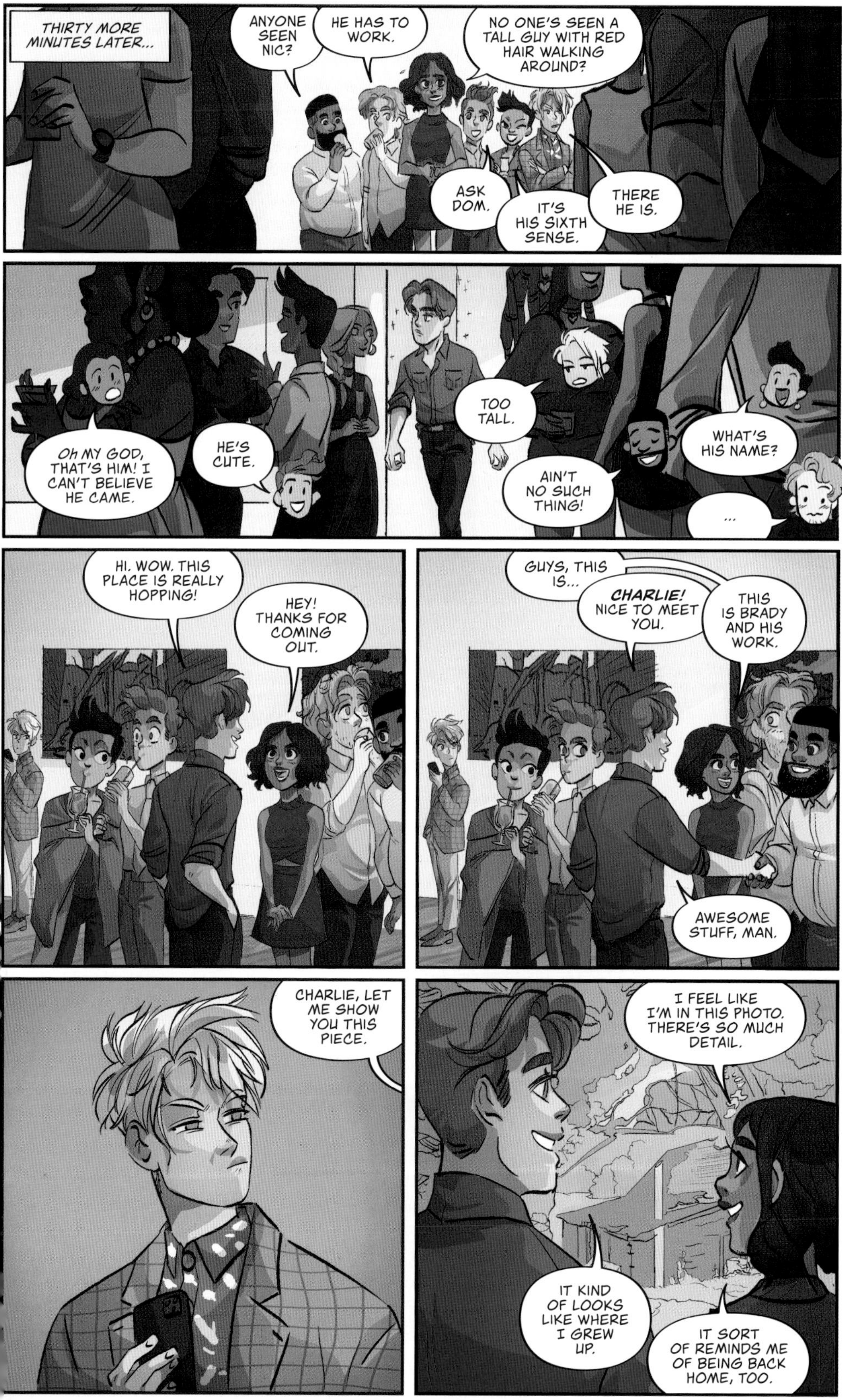
THIRTY MORE MINUTES LATER...
ANYONE SEEN NIC?
HE HAS TO WORK.
NO ONE'S SEEN A TALL GUY WITH RED HAIR WALKING AROUND?
ASK DOM.
IT'S HIS SIXTH SENSE.
THERE HE IS.
Oh MY GOD, THAT'S HIM! I CAN'T BELIEVE HE CAME.
HE'S CUTE.
TOO TALL.
AIN'T NO SUCH THING!
WHAT'S HIS NAME?
...
HI. WOW. THIS PLACE IS REALLY HOPPING!
HEY! THANKS FOR COMING OUT.
GUYS, THIS IS...
CHARLIE! NICE TO MEET YOU.
THIS IS BRADY AND HIS WORK.
AWESOME STUFF, MAN.
CHARLIE, LET ME SHOW YOU THIS PIECE.
I FEEL LIKE I'M IN THIS PHOTO. THERE'S SO MUCH DETAIL.
IT KIND OF LOOKS LIKE WHERE I GREW UP.
IT SORT OF REMINDS ME OF BEING BACK HOME, TOO.

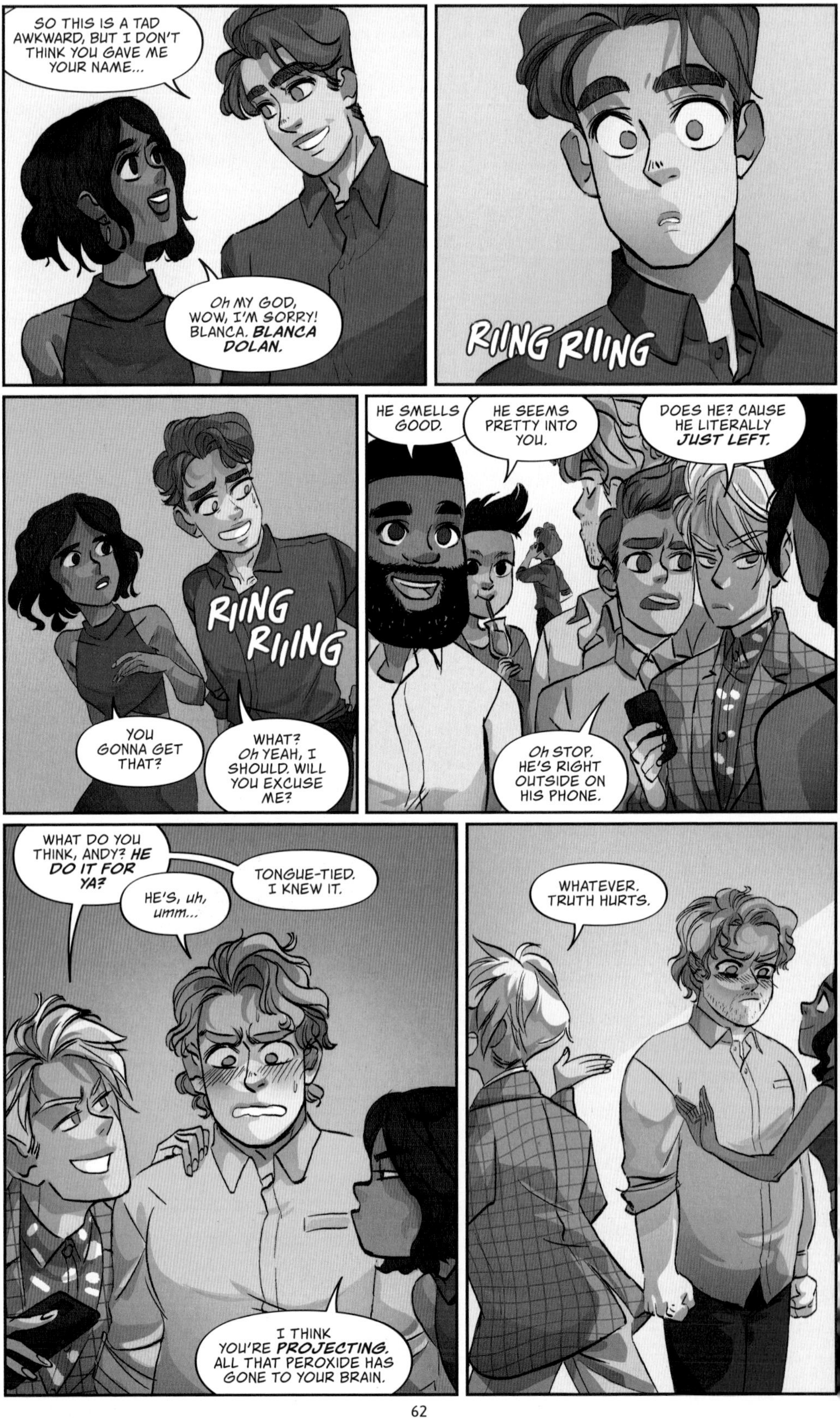
SO THIS IS A TAD AWKWARD, BUT I DON'T THINK YOU GAVE ME YOUR NAME...
Oh MY GOD, WOW, I'M SORRY! BLANCA. BLANCA DOLAN.
RIING RIIING
RIING RIIING
YOU GONNA GET THAT?
WHAT? Oh YEAH, I SHOULD. WILL YOU EXCUSE ME?
HE SMELLS GOOD.
HE SEEMS PRETTY INTO YOU.
DOES HE? CAUSE HE LITERALLY JUST LEFT.
Oh STOP. HE'S RIGHT OUTSIDE ON HIS PHONE.
WHAT DO YOU THINK, ANDY? HE DO IT FOR YA?
HE'S, uh, umm...
TONGUE-TIED. I KNEW IT.
I THINK YOU'RE PROJECTING. ALL THAT PEROXIDE HAS GONE TO YOUR BRAIN.
WHATEVER. TRUTH HURTS.

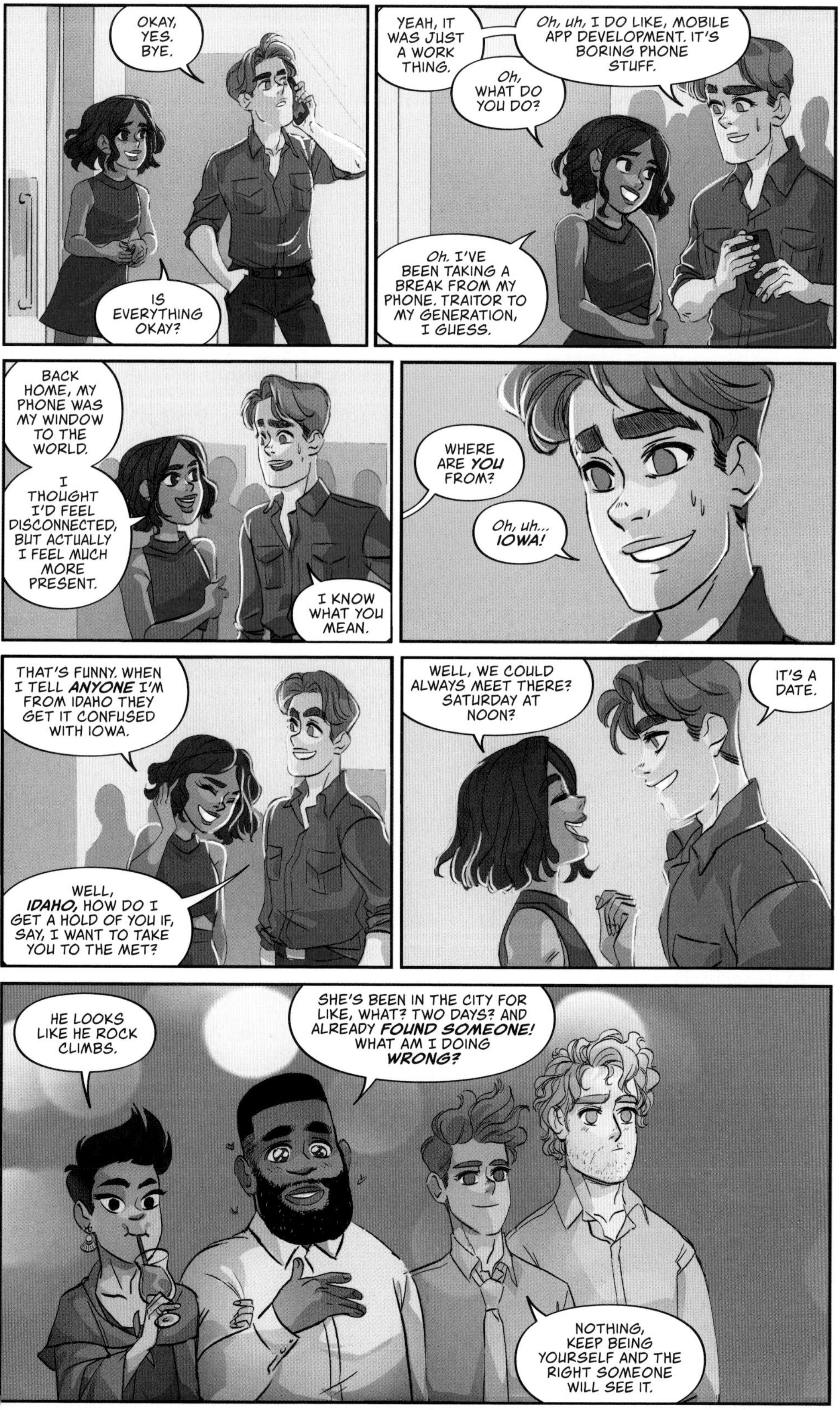
OKAY, YES. BYE.
IS EVERYTHING OKAY?
YEAH, IT WAS JUST A WORK THING.
Oh, WHAT DO YOU DO?
Oh, uh, I DO LIKE, MOBILE APP DEVELOPMENT. IT'S BORING PHONE STUFF.
Oh. I'VE BEEN TAKING A BREAK FROM MY PHONE. TRAITOR TO MY GENERATION, I GUESS.
BACK HOME, MY PHONE WAS MY WINDOW TO THE WORLD.
I THOUGHT I'D FEEL DISCONNECTED, BUT ACTUALLY I FEEL MUCH MORE PRESENT.
I KNOW WHAT YOU MEAN.
WHERE ARE YOU FROM?
Oh, uh... IOWA!
THAT'S FUNNY. WHEN I TELL ANYONE I'M FROM IDAHO THEY GET IT CONFUSED WITH IOWA.
WELL, IDAHO, HOW DO I GET A HOLD OF YOU IF, SAY, I WANT TO TAKE YOU TO THE MET?
WELL, WE COULD ALWAYS MEET THERE? SATURDAY AT NOON?
IT'S A DATE.
HE LOOKS LIKE HE ROCK CLIMBS.
SHE'S BEEN IN THE CITY FOR LIKE, WHAT? TWO DAYS? AND ALREADY FOUND SOMEONE! WHAT AM I DOING WRONG?
NOTHING, KEEP BEING YOURSELF AND THE RIGHT SOMEONE WILL SEE IT.

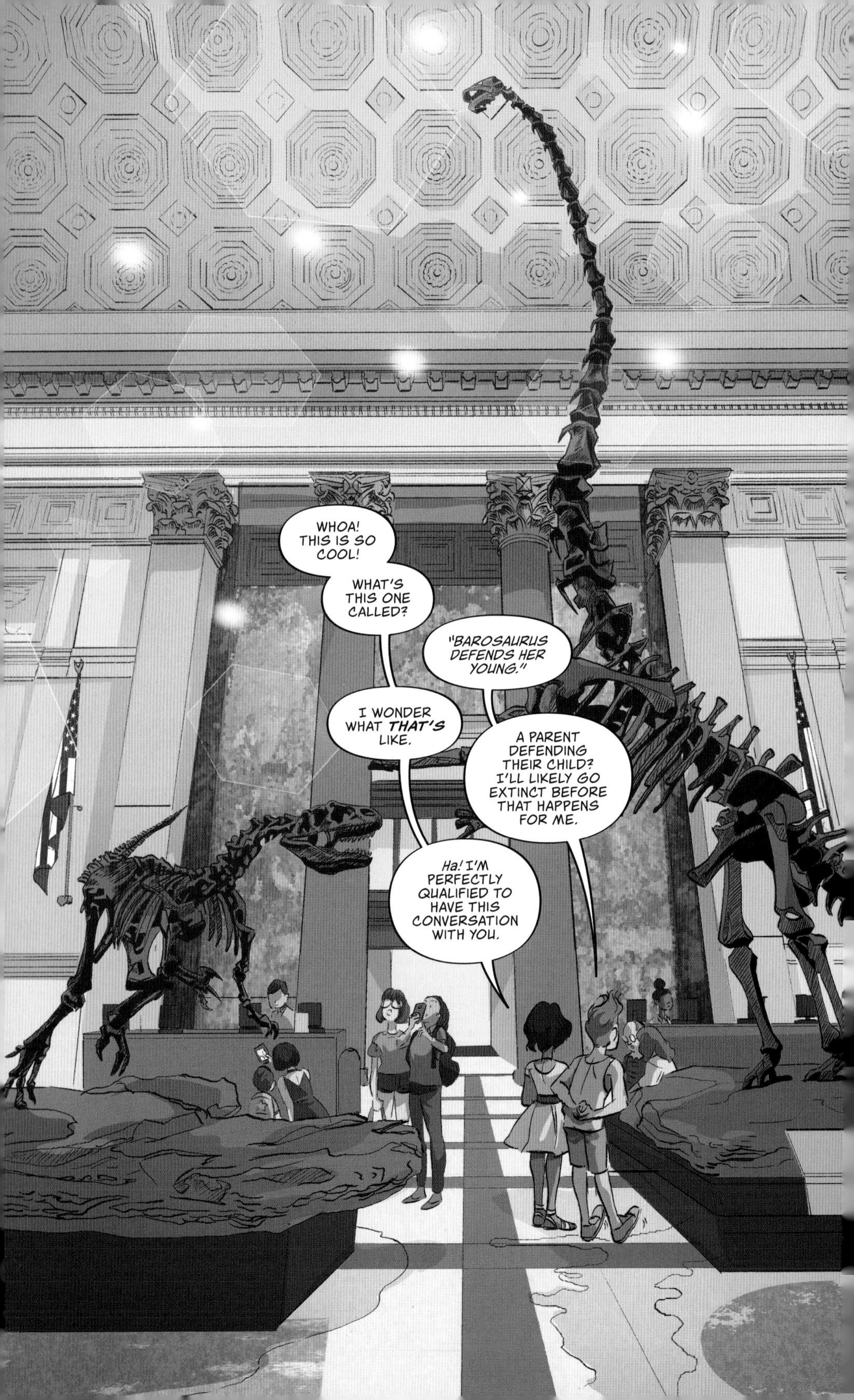
WHOA! THIS IS SO COOL!
WHAT'S THIS ONE CALLED?
"BAROSAURUS DEFENDS HER YOUNG."
I WONDER WHAT ***THAT'S*** LIKE.
A PARENT DEFENDING THEIR CHILD? I'LL LIKELY GO EXTINCT BEFORE THAT HAPPENS FOR ME.
Ha! I'M PERFECTLY QUALIFIED TO HAVE THIS CONVERSATION WITH YOU.

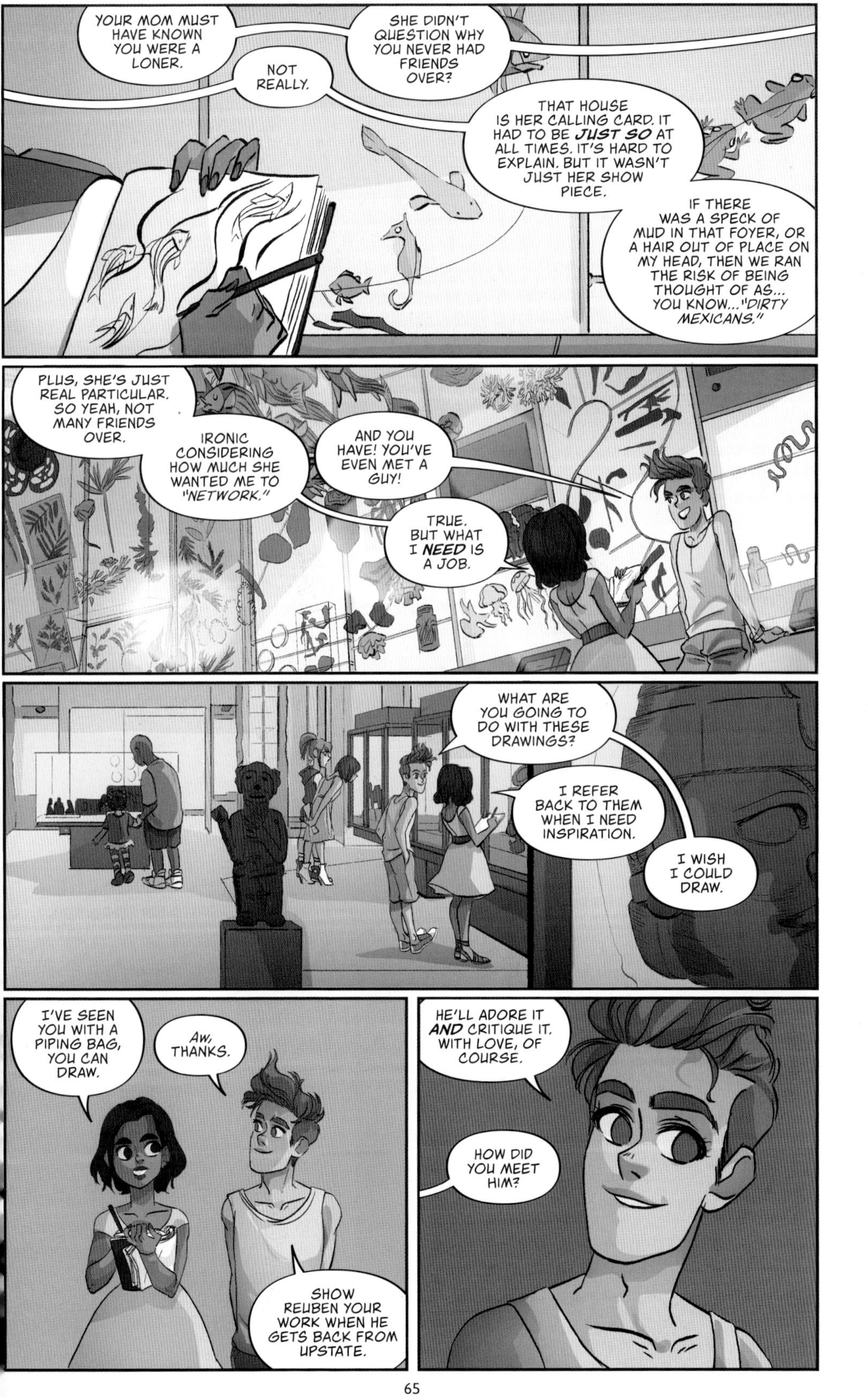
YOUR MOM MUST HAVE KNOWN YOU WERE A LONER.
NOT REALLY.
SHE DIDN'T QUESTION WHY YOU NEVER HAD FRIENDS OVER?
THAT HOUSE IS HER CALLING CARD. IT HAD TO BE JUST SO AT ALL TIMES. IT'S HARD TO EXPLAIN. BUT IT WASN'T JUST HER SHOW PIECE.
IF THERE WAS A SPECK OF MUD IN THAT FOYER, OR A HAIR OUT OF PLACE ON MY HEAD, THEN WE RAN THE RISK OF BEING THOUGHT OF AS... YOU KNOW..."DIRTY MEXICANS."
PLUS, SHE'S JUST REAL PARTICULAR. SO YEAH, NOT MANY FRIENDS OVER.
IRONIC CONSIDERING HOW MUCH SHE WANTED ME TO "NETWORK."
AND YOU HAVE! YOU'VE EVEN MET A GUY!
TRUE. BUT WHAT I NEED IS A JOB.
WHAT ARE YOU GOING TO DO WITH THESE DRAWINGS?
I REFER BACK TO THEM WHEN I NEED INSPIRATION.
I WISH I COULD DRAW.
I'VE SEEN YOU WITH A PIPING BAG, YOU CAN DRAW.
AW, THANKS.
SHOW REUBEN YOUR WORK WHEN HE GETS BACK FROM UPSTATE.
HE'LL ADORE IT AND CRITIQUE IT. WITH LOVE, OF COURSE.
HOW DID YOU MEET HIM?

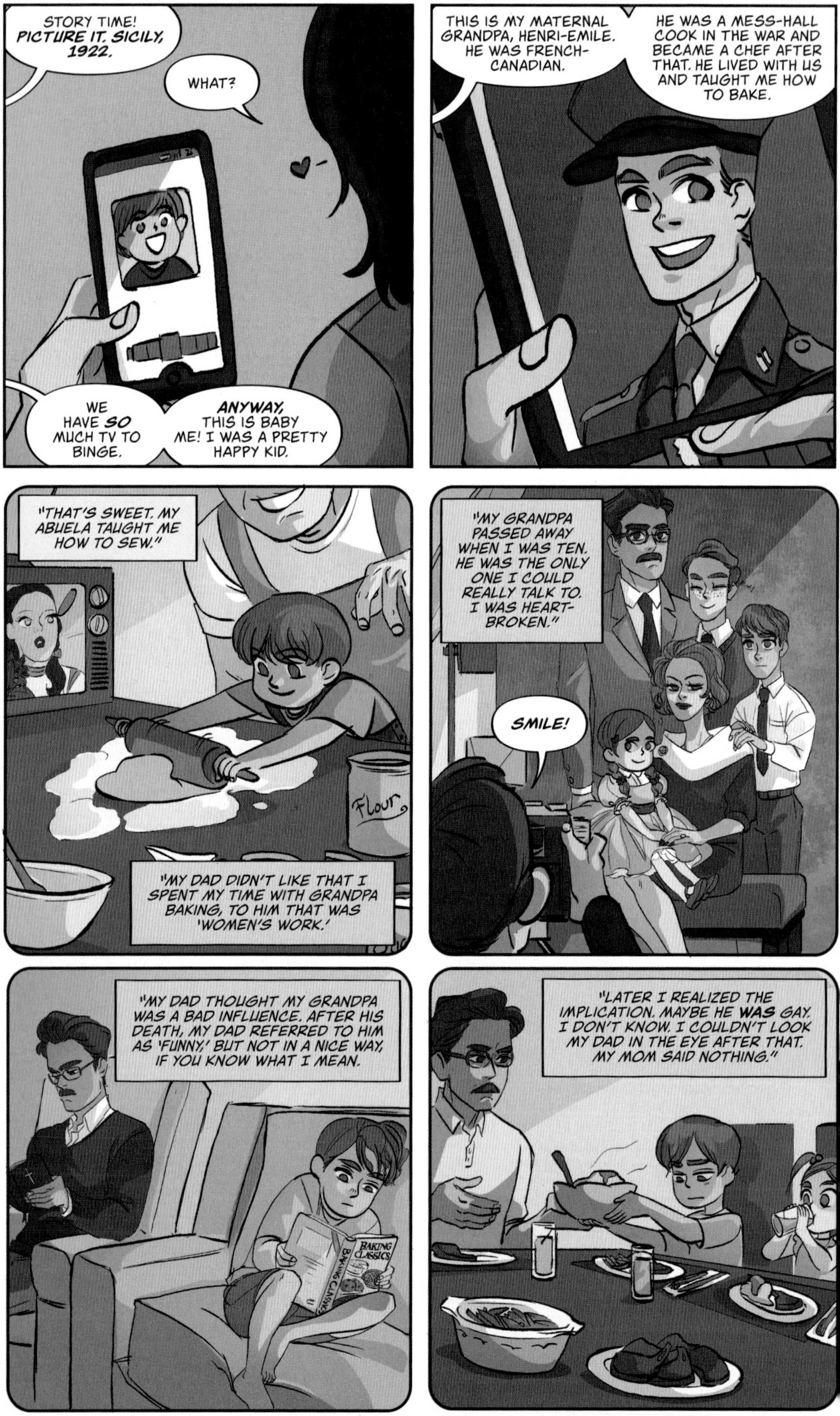

STORY TIME! PICTURE IT. SICILY, 1922.
WHAT?
WE HAVE SO MUCH TV TO BINGE.
ANYWAY, THIS IS BABY ME! I WAS A PRETTY HAPPY KID.
THIS IS MY MATERNAL GRANDPA, HENRI-EMILE. HE WAS FRENCH-CANADIAN.
HE WAS A MESS-HALL COOK IN THE WAR AND BECAME A CHEF AFTER THAT. HE LIVED WITH US AND TAUGHT ME HOW TO BAKE.
"THAT'S SWEET. MY ABUELA TAUGHT ME HOW TO SEW."
Flour
"MY DAD DIDN'T LIKE THAT I SPENT MY TIME WITH GRANDPA BAKING, TO HIM THAT WAS 'WOMEN'S WORK.'
"MY GRANDPA PASSED AWAY WHEN I WAS TEN. HE WAS THE ONLY ONE I COULD REALLY TALK TO. I WAS HEART-BROKEN."
SMILE!
"MY DAD THOUGHT MY GRANDPA WAS A BAD INFLUENCE. AFTER HIS DEATH, MY DAD REFERRED TO HIM AS 'FUNNY,' BUT NOT IN A NICE WAY, IF YOU KNOW WHAT I MEAN.
BAKING CLASSICS
"LATER I REALIZED THE IMPLICATION. MAYBE HE WAS GAY. I DON'T KNOW. I COULDN'T LOOK MY DAD IN THE EYE AFTER THAT. MY MOM SAID NOTHING."

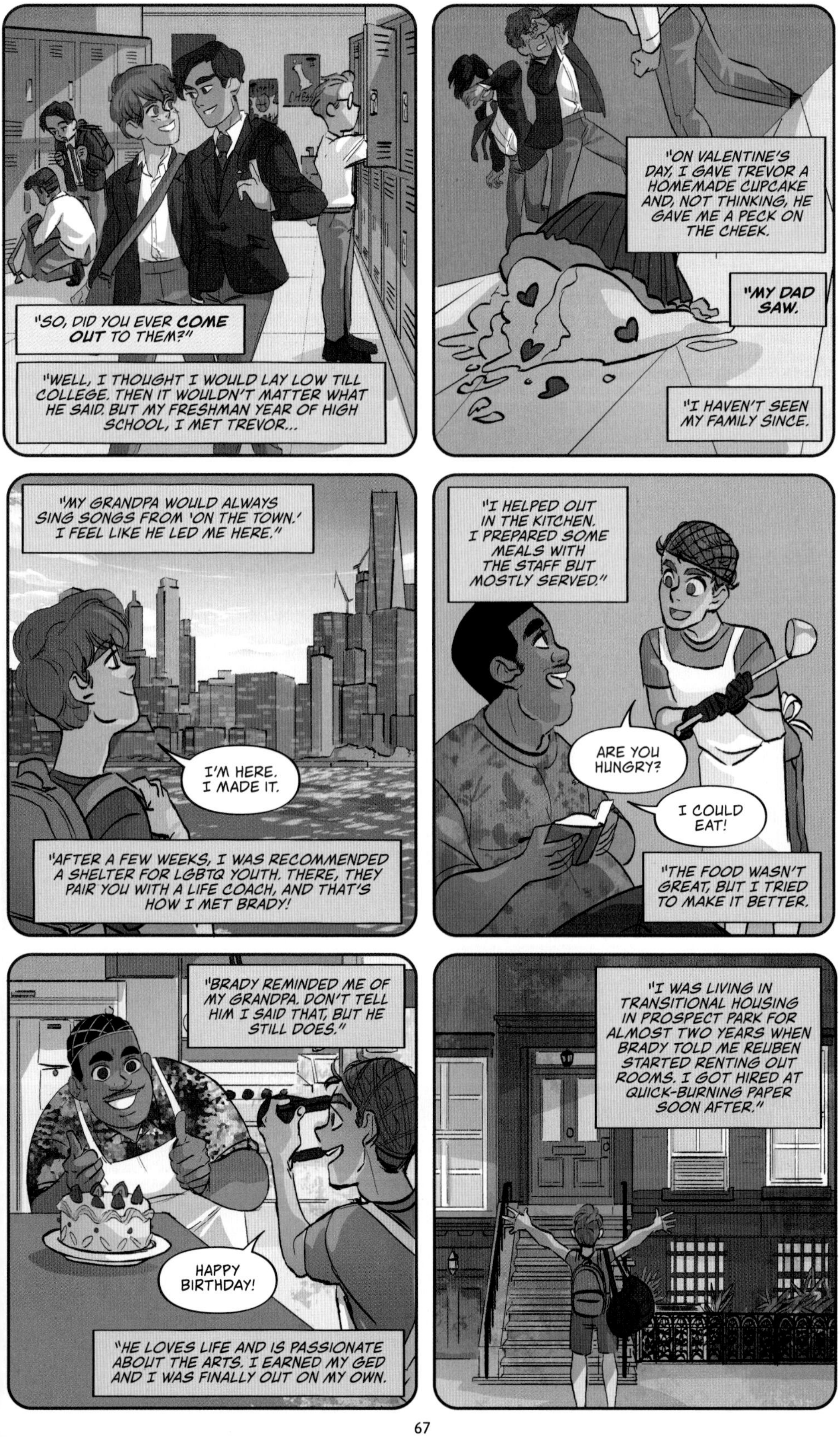
"SO, DID YOU EVER **COME OUT** TO THEM?"
"WELL, I THOUGHT I WOULD LAY LOW TILL COLLEGE. THEN IT WOULDN'T MATTER WHAT HE SAID. BUT MY FRESHMAN YEAR OF HIGH SCHOOL, I MET TREVOR...
"ON VALENTINE'S DAY, I GAVE TREVOR A HOMEMADE CUPCAKE AND, NOT THINKING, HE GAVE ME A PECK ON THE CHEEK.
"MY DAD SAW.
"I HAVEN'T SEEN MY FAMILY SINCE.
"MY GRANDPA WOULD ALWAYS SING SONGS FROM 'ON THE TOWN.' I FEEL LIKE HE LED ME HERE."
I'M HERE. I MADE IT.
"AFTER A FEW WEEKS, I WAS RECOMMENDED A SHELTER FOR LGBTQ YOUTH. THERE, THEY PAIR YOU WITH A LIFE COACH, AND THAT'S HOW I MET BRADY!
"I HELPED OUT IN THE KITCHEN. I PREPARED SOME MEALS WITH THE STAFF BUT MOSTLY SERVED."
ARE YOU HUNGRY?
I COULD EAT!
"THE FOOD WASN'T GREAT, BUT I TRIED TO MAKE IT BETTER.
"BRADY REMINDED ME OF MY GRANDPA. DON'T TELL HIM I SAID THAT, BUT HE STILL DOES."
HAPPY BIRTHDAY!
"HE LOVES LIFE AND IS PASSIONATE ABOUT THE ARTS. I EARNED MY GED AND I WAS FINALLY OUT ON MY OWN.
"I WAS LIVING IN TRANSITIONAL HOUSING IN PROSPECT PARK FOR ALMOST TWO YEARS WHEN BRADY TOLD ME REUBEN STARTED RENTING OUT ROOMS. I GOT HIRED AT QUICK-BURNING PAPER SOON AFTER."

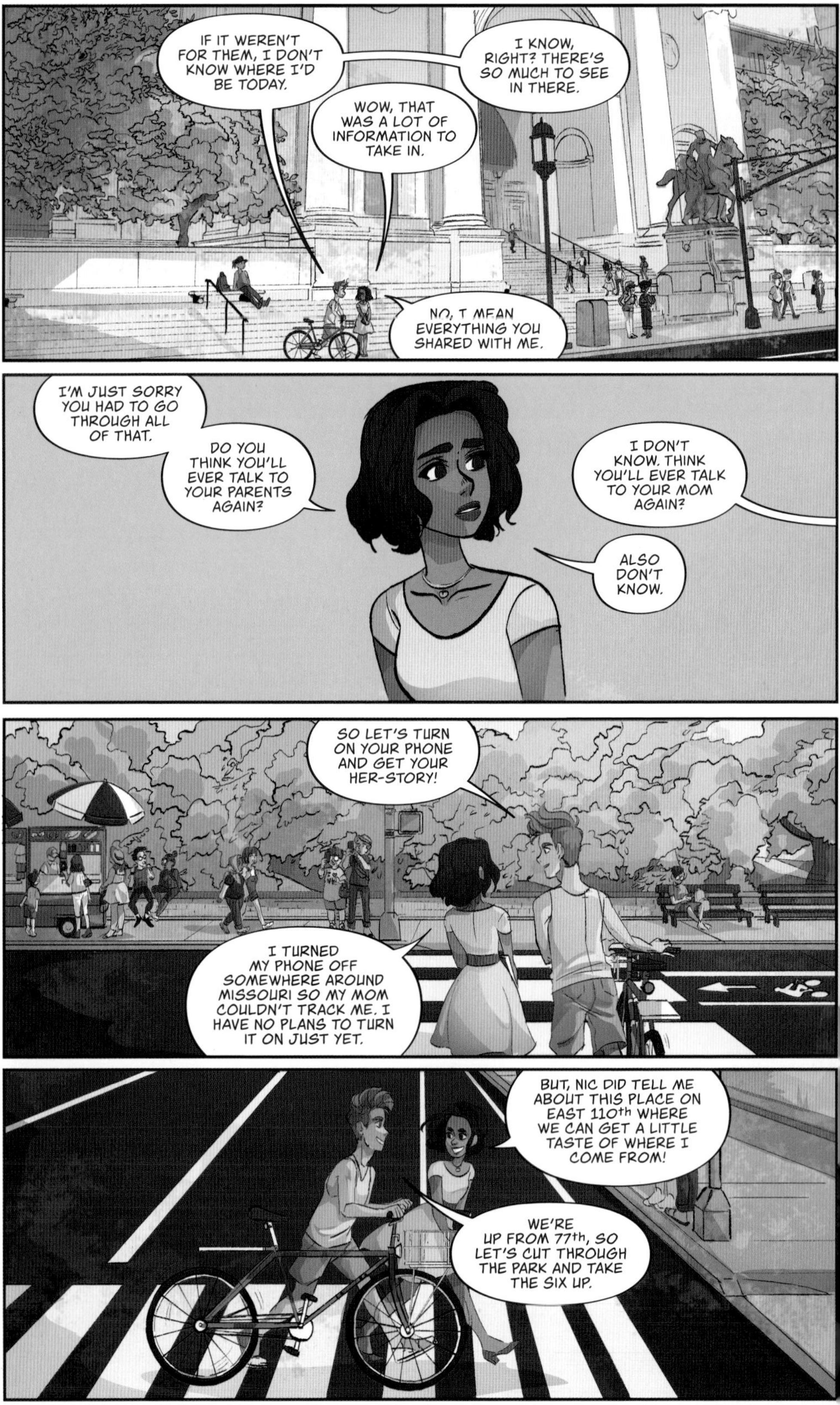
IF IT WEREN'T FOR THEM, I DON'T KNOW WHERE I'D BE TODAY.
I KNOW, RIGHT? THERE'S SO MUCH TO SEE IN THERE.
WOW, THAT WAS A LOT OF INFORMATION TO TAKE IN.
NO, I MEAN EVERYTHING YOU SHARED WITH ME.
I'M JUST SORRY YOU HAD TO GO THROUGH ALL OF THAT.
DO YOU THINK YOU'LL EVER TALK TO YOUR PARENTS AGAIN?
I DON'T KNOW. THINK YOU'LL EVER TALK TO YOUR MOM AGAIN?
ALSO DON'T KNOW.
SO LET'S TURN ON YOUR PHONE AND GET YOUR HER-STORY!
I TURNED MY PHONE OFF SOMEWHERE AROUND MISSOURI SO MY MOM COULDN'T TRACK ME. I HAVE NO PLANS TO TURN IT ON JUST YET.
BUT, NIC DID TELL ME ABOUT THIS PLACE ON EAST 110th WHERE WE CAN GET A LITTLE TASTE OF WHERE I COME FROM!
WE'RE UP FROM 77th, SO LET'S CUT THROUGH THE PARK AND TAKE THE SIX UP.

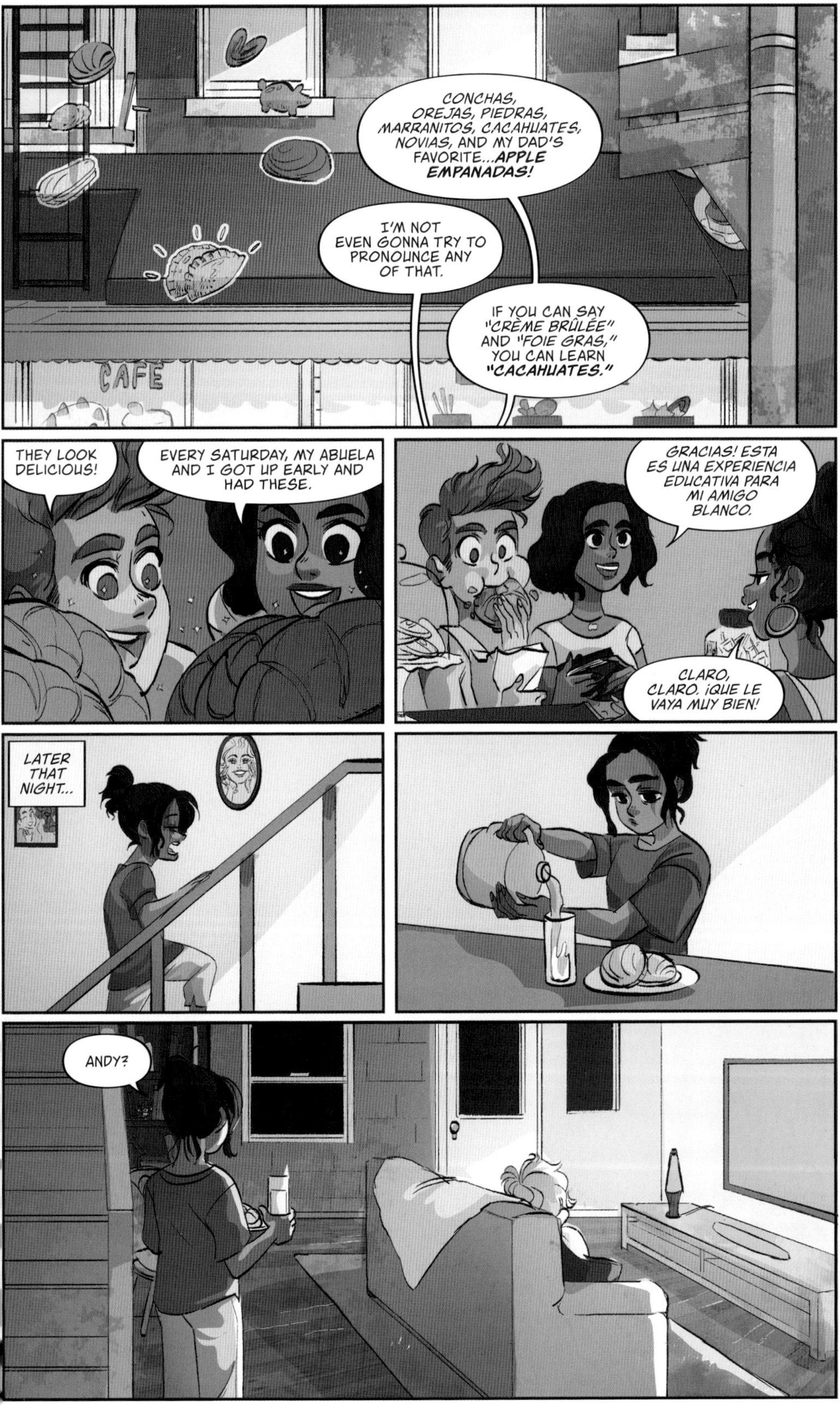
CONCHAS, OREJAS, PIEDRAS, MARRANITOS, CACAHUATES, NOVIAS, AND MY DAD'S FAVORITE...APPLE EMPANADAS!
I'M NOT EVEN GONNA TRY TO PRONOUNCE ANY OF THAT.
IF YOU CAN SAY "CRÈME BRÛLÉE" AND "FOIE GRAS," YOU CAN LEARN "CACAHUATES."
CAFE
THEY LOOK DELICIOUS!
EVERY SATURDAY, MY ABUELA AND I GOT UP EARLY AND HAD THESE.
GRACIAS! ESTA ES UNA EXPERIENCIA EDUCATIVA PARA MI AMIGO BLANCO.
CLARO, CLARO. ¡QUE LE VAYA MUY BIEN!
LATER THAT NIGHT...
ANDY?

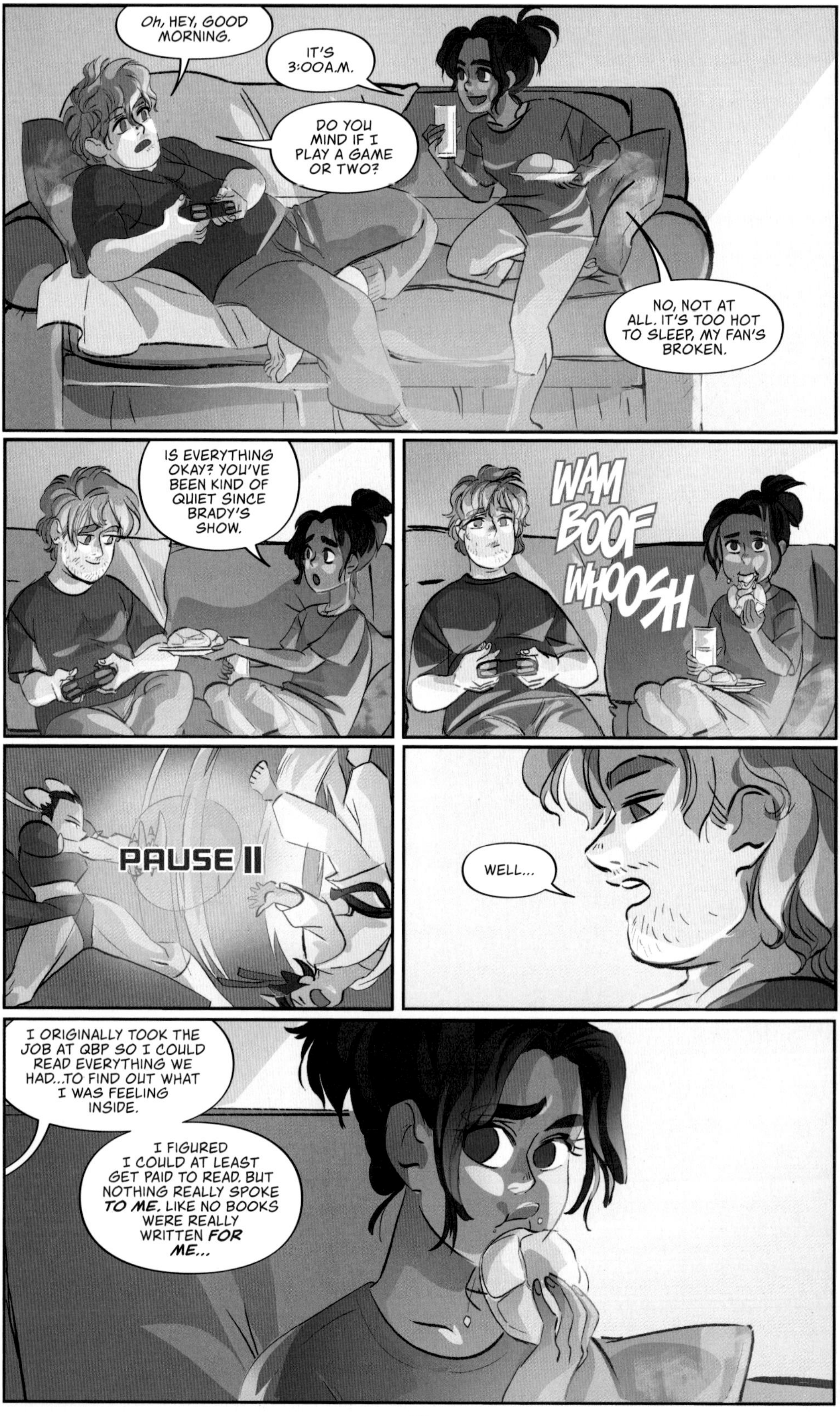
Oh, HEY, GOOD MORNING.
IT'S 3:00A.M.
DO YOU MIND IF I PLAY A GAME OR TWO?
NO, NOT AT ALL. IT'S TOO HOT TO SLEEP, MY FAN'S BROKEN.
IS EVERYTHING OKAY? YOU'VE BEEN KIND OF QUIET SINCE BRADY'S SHOW.
WAM
BOOF
WHOOSH
PAUSE II
WELL...
I ORIGINALLY TOOK THE JOB AT QBP SO I COULD READ EVERYTHING WE HAD...TO FIND OUT WHAT I WAS FEELING INSIDE.
I FIGURED I COULD AT LEAST GET PAID TO READ. BUT NOTHING REALLY SPOKE ***TO ME.*** LIKE NO BOOKS WERE REALLY WRITTEN ***FOR ME...***

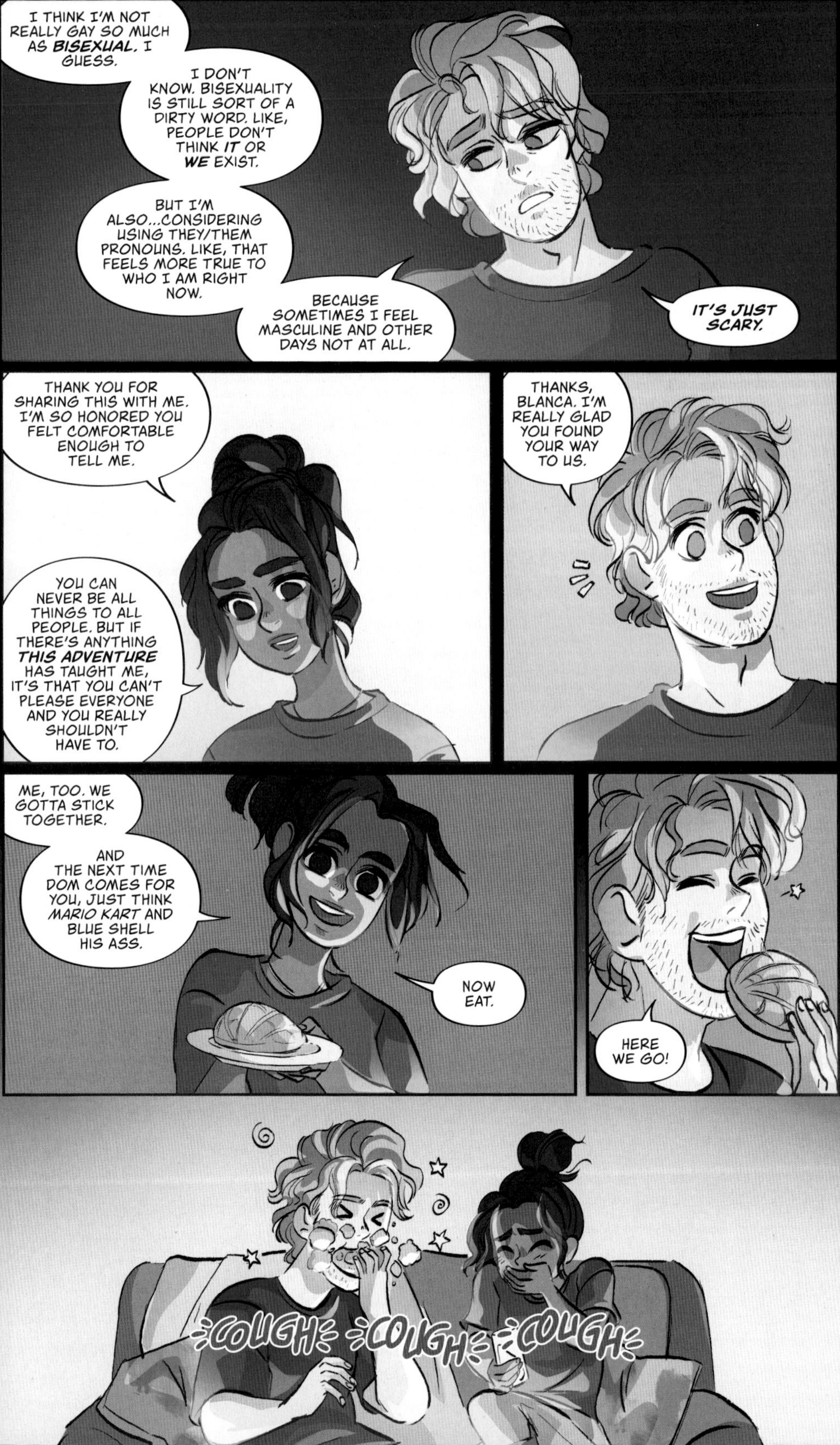
I THINK I'M NOT REALLY GAY SO MUCH AS **BISEXUAL**, I GUESS.
I DON'T KNOW. BISEXUALITY IS STILL SORT OF A DIRTY WORD. LIKE, PEOPLE DON'T THINK *IT* OR *WE* EXIST.
BUT I'M ALSO...CONSIDERING USING THEY/THEM PRONOUNS. LIKE, THAT FEELS MORE TRUE TO WHO I AM RIGHT NOW.
BECAUSE SOMETIMES I FEEL MASCULINE AND OTHER DAYS NOT AT ALL.
IT'S JUST SCARY.
THANK YOU FOR SHARING THIS WITH ME. I'M SO HONORED YOU FELT COMFORTABLE ENOUGH TO TELL ME.
YOU CAN NEVER BE ALL THINGS TO ALL PEOPLE. BUT IF THERE'S ANYTHING ***THIS ADVENTURE*** HAS TAUGHT ME, IT'S THAT YOU CAN'T PLEASE EVERYONE AND YOU REALLY SHOULDN'T HAVE TO.
THANKS, BLANCA. I'M REALLY GLAD YOU FOUND YOUR WAY TO US.
ME, TOO. WE GOTTA STICK TOGETHER.
AND THE NEXT TIME DOM COMES FOR YOU, JUST THINK *MARIO KART* AND BLUE SHELL HIS ASS.
NOW EAT.
HERE WE GO!
COUGH COUGH COUGH

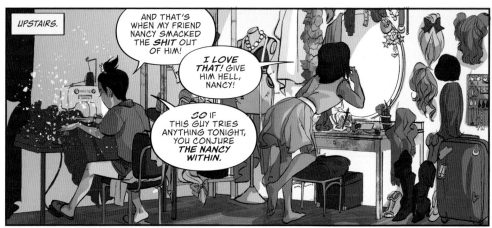

UPSTAIRS.

AND THAT'S WHEN MY FRIEND NANCY SMACKED THE *SHIT* OUT OF HIM!

I LOVE THAT! GIVE HIM HELL, NANCY!

SO IF THIS GUY TRIES ANYTHING TONIGHT, YOU CONJURE THE NANCY WITHIN.

DOWNSTAIRS.

HI, BRADY. HOW'D THE SHOW GO?

Oh, NICOLAS! HEY! IT WENT REALLY WELL.

I SOLD A FEW PIECES! AND GOT SOME SHOW OFFERS. THAT AND I WAS ASKED TO SPEAK AT SYRACUSE UNIVERSITY OVER THE NEXT COUPLE WEEKS.

WANT ME TO GO UNDERCOVER AND LURK FROM A DISTANCE? I HAVE A WIDE-BRIMMED HAT!

YOU'RE SWEET. THANKS. I'LL BE FINE, THOUGH.

THIS EXHIBIT THEY HAVE SOUNDS *SO ME!*

OF COURSE YOU SOLD WORK! *YOU'RE INCREDIBLE.*

THANKS, NICOLAS.

ANYTIME, BABY.

I'M OFF!

I'LL WALK YOU OUT. I'M GOING TO THE BODEGA.

HAVE A GREAT TIME IN SYRACUSE.

LET'S HOOK UP WHEN YOU GET BACK.

HOOK...UP?

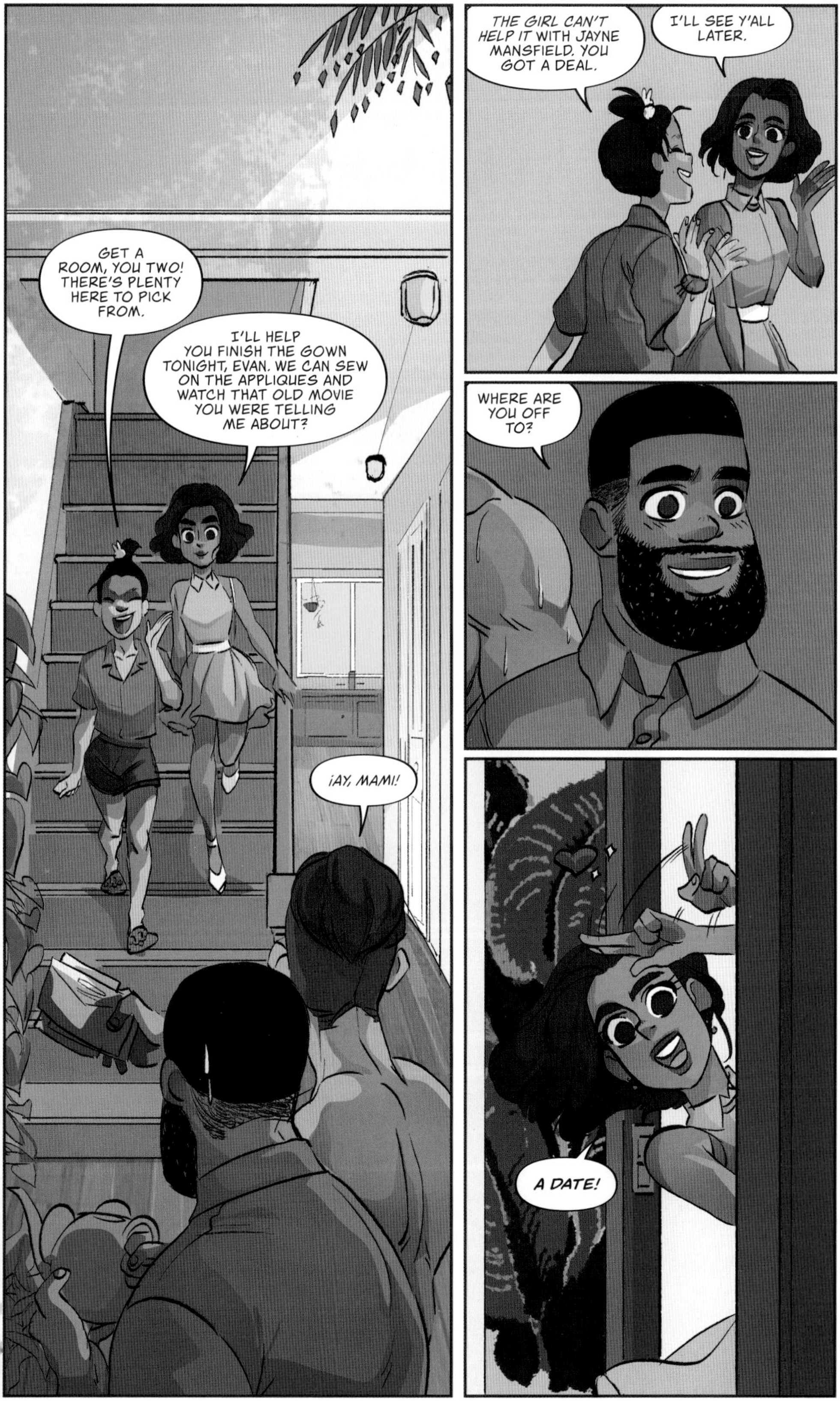
GET A ROOM, YOU TWO! THERE'S PLENTY HERE TO PICK FROM.
I'LL HELP YOU FINISH THE GOWN TONIGHT, EVAN. WE CAN SEW ON THE APPLIQUES AND WATCH THAT OLD MOVIE YOU WERE TELLING ME ABOUT?
¡AY, MAMI!
THE GIRL CAN'T HELP IT WITH JAYNE MANSFIELD. YOU GOT A DEAL.
I'LL SEE Y'ALL LATER.
WHERE ARE YOU OFF TO?
A DATE!

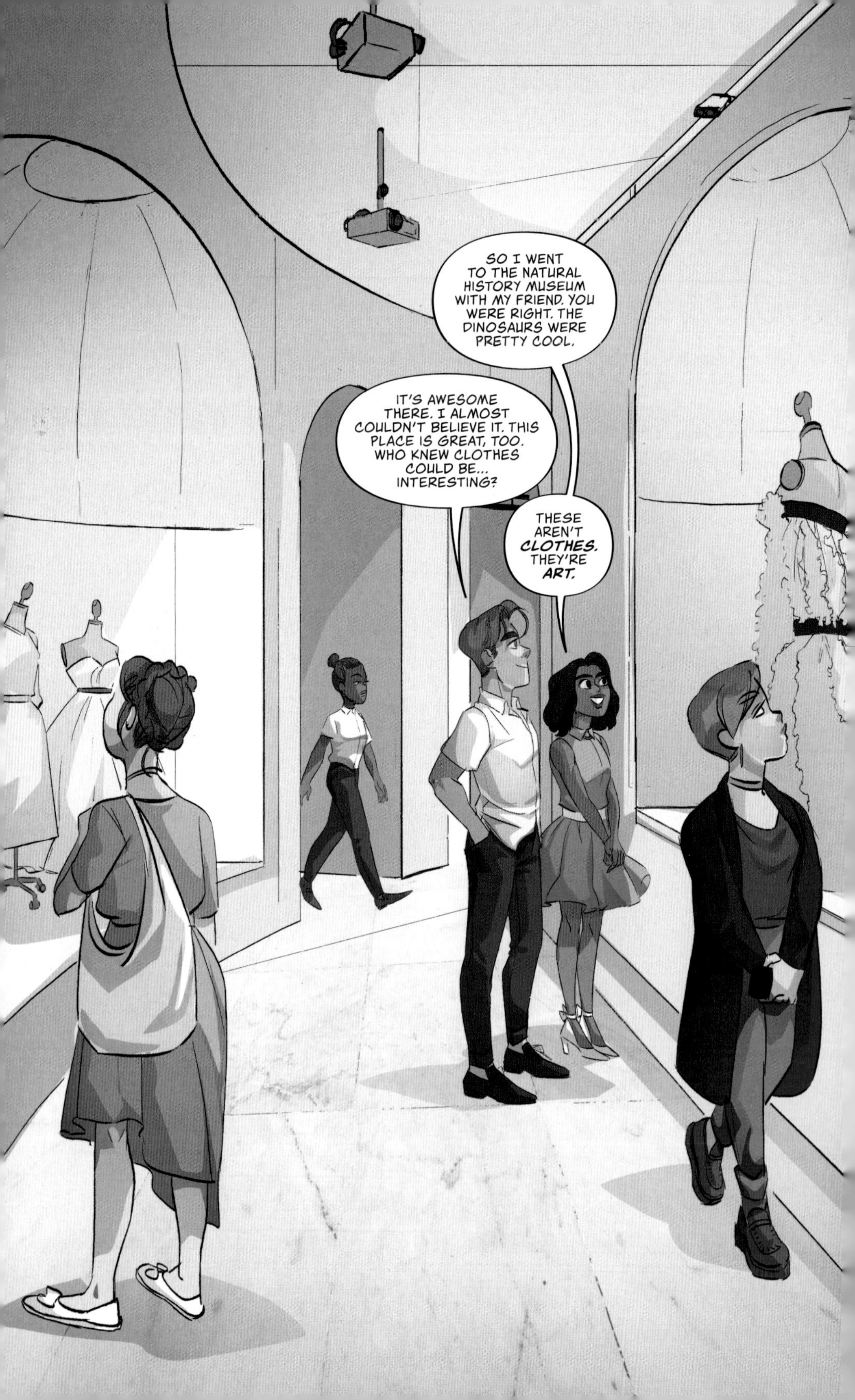
SO I WENT TO THE NATURAL HISTORY MUSEUM WITH MY FRIEND. YOU WERE RIGHT. THE DINOSAURS WERE PRETTY COOL.
IT'S AWESOME THERE. I ALMOST COULDN'T BELIEVE IT. THIS PLACE IS GREAT, TOO. WHO KNEW CLOTHES COULD BE... INTERESTING?
THESE AREN'T ***CLOTHES.*** THEY'RE ***ART.***

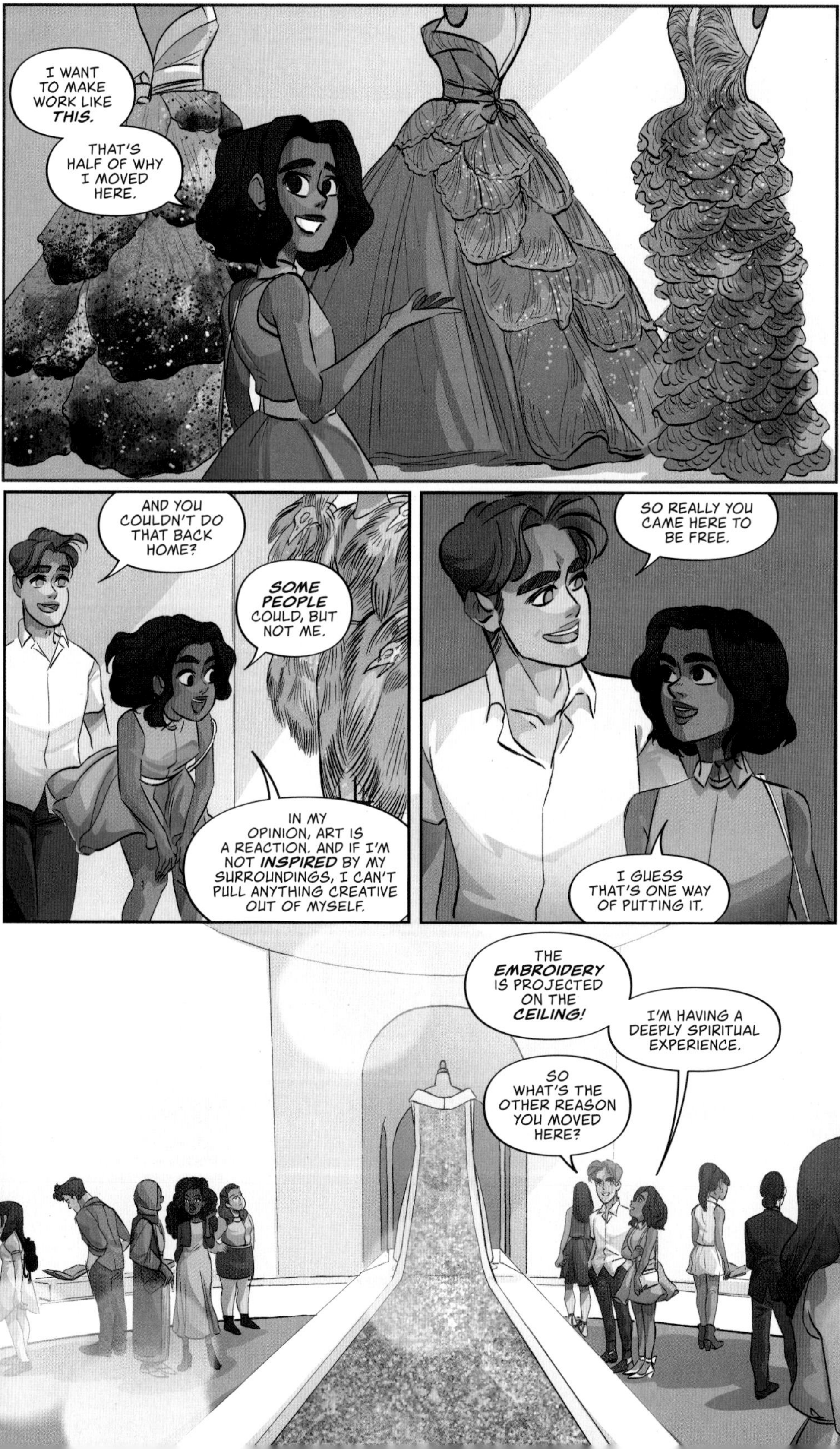
I WANT TO MAKE WORK LIKE ***THIS.***
THAT'S HALF OF WHY I MOVED HERE.
AND YOU COULDN'T DO THAT BACK HOME?
SOME PEOPLE COULD, BUT NOT ME.
IN MY OPINION, ART IS A REACTION. AND IF I'M NOT ***INSPIRED*** BY MY SURROUNDINGS, I CAN'T PULL ANYTHING CREATIVE OUT OF MYSELF.
SO REALLY YOU CAME HERE TO BE FREE.
I GUESS THAT'S ONE WAY OF PUTTING IT.
THE ***EMBROIDERY*** IS PROJECTED ON THE ***CEILING!***
I'M HAVING A DEEPLY SPIRITUAL EXPERIENCE.
SO WHAT'S THE OTHER REASON YOU MOVED HERE?

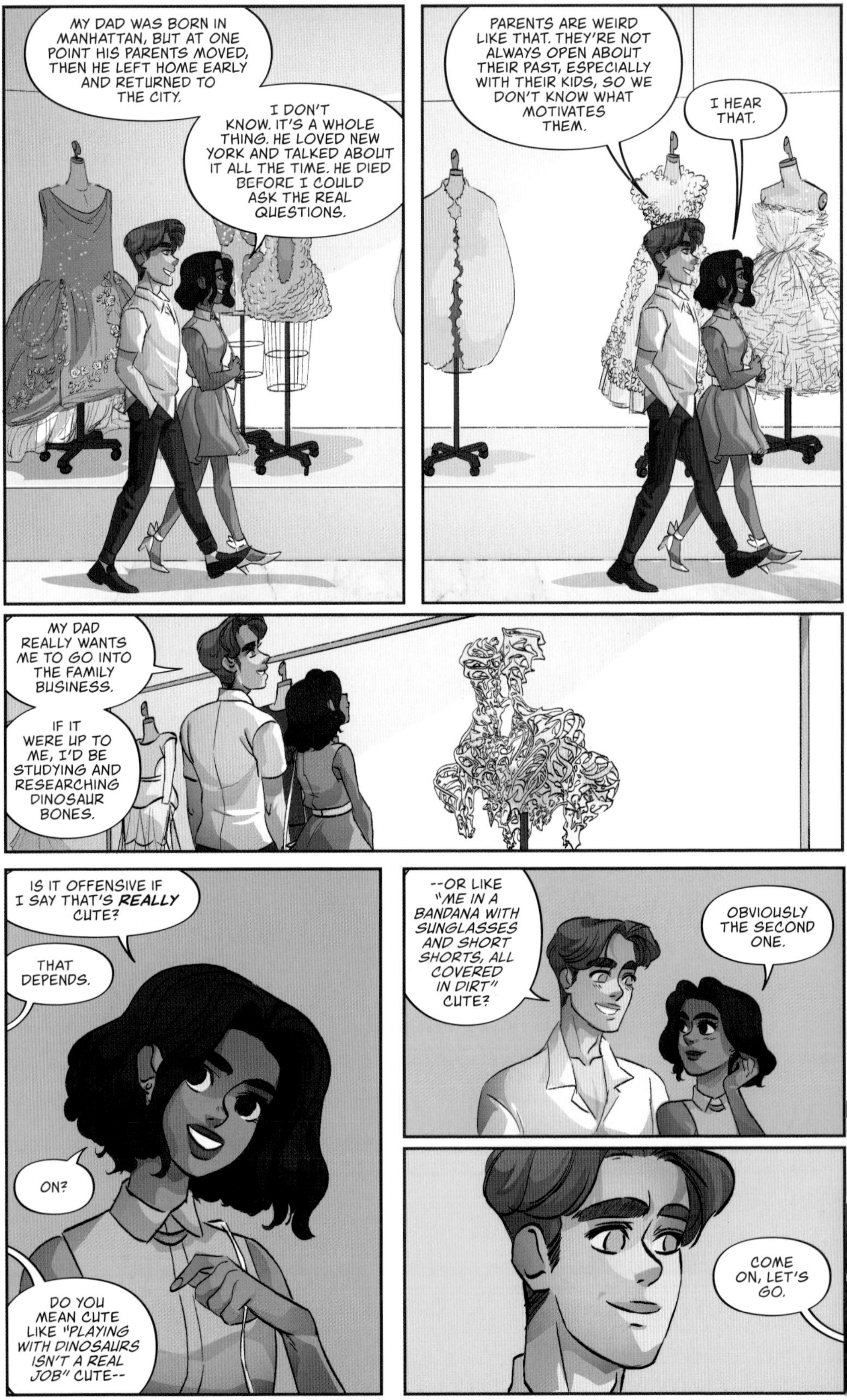

MY DAD WAS BORN IN MANHATTAN, BUT AT ONE POINT HIS PARENTS MOVED, THEN HE LEFT HOME EARLY AND RETURNED TO THE CITY.
I DON'T KNOW. IT'S A WHOLE THING. HE LOVED NEW YORK AND TALKED ABOUT IT ALL THE TIME. HE DIED BEFORE I COULD ASK THE REAL QUESTIONS.
PARENTS ARE WEIRD LIKE THAT. THEY'RE NOT ALWAYS OPEN ABOUT THEIR PAST, ESPECIALLY WITH THEIR KIDS, SO WE DON'T KNOW WHAT MOTIVATES THEM.
I HEAR THAT.
MY DAD REALLY WANTS ME TO GO INTO THE FAMILY BUSINESS.
IF IT WERE UP TO ME, I'D BE STUDYING AND RESEARCHING DINOSAUR BONES.
IS IT OFFENSIVE IF I SAY THAT'S ***REALLY*** CUTE?
THAT DEPENDS.
ON?
DO YOU MEAN CUTE LIKE "PLAYING WITH DINOSAURS ISN'T A REAL JOB" CUTE--
--OR LIKE "ME IN A BANDANA WITH SUNGLASSES AND SHORT SHORTS, ALL COVERED IN DIRT" CUTE?
OBVIOUSLY THE SECOND ONE.
COME ON, LET'S GO.

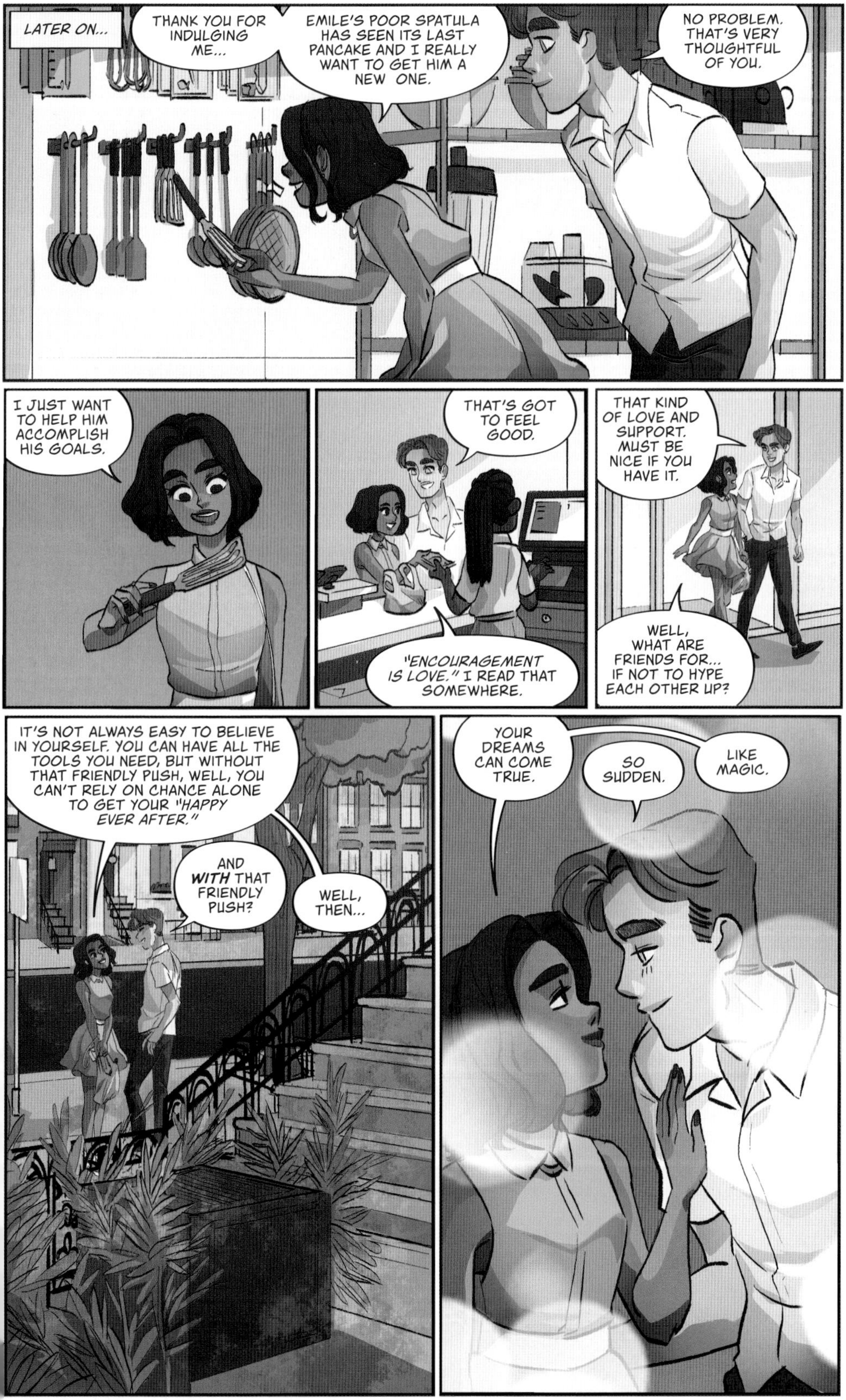
LATER ON...
THANK YOU FOR INDULGING ME...
EMILE'S POOR SPATULA HAS SEEN ITS LAST PANCAKE AND I REALLY WANT TO GET HIM A NEW ONE.
NO PROBLEM. THAT'S VERY THOUGHTFUL OF YOU.
I JUST WANT TO HELP HIM ACCOMPLISH HIS GOALS.
THAT'S GOT TO FEEL GOOD.
"ENCOURAGEMENT IS LOVE." I READ THAT SOMEWHERE.
THAT KIND OF LOVE AND SUPPORT. MUST BE NICE IF YOU HAVE IT.
WELL, WHAT ARE FRIENDS FOR... IF NOT TO HYPE EACH OTHER UP?
IT'S NOT ALWAYS EASY TO BELIEVE IN YOURSELF. YOU CAN HAVE ALL THE TOOLS YOU NEED, BUT WITHOUT THAT FRIENDLY PUSH, WELL, YOU CAN'T RELY ON CHANCE ALONE TO GET YOUR "HAPPY EVER AFTER."
AND WITH THAT FRIENDLY PUSH?
WELL, THEN...
YOUR DREAMS CAN COME TRUE.
SO SUDDEN.
LIKE MAGIC.

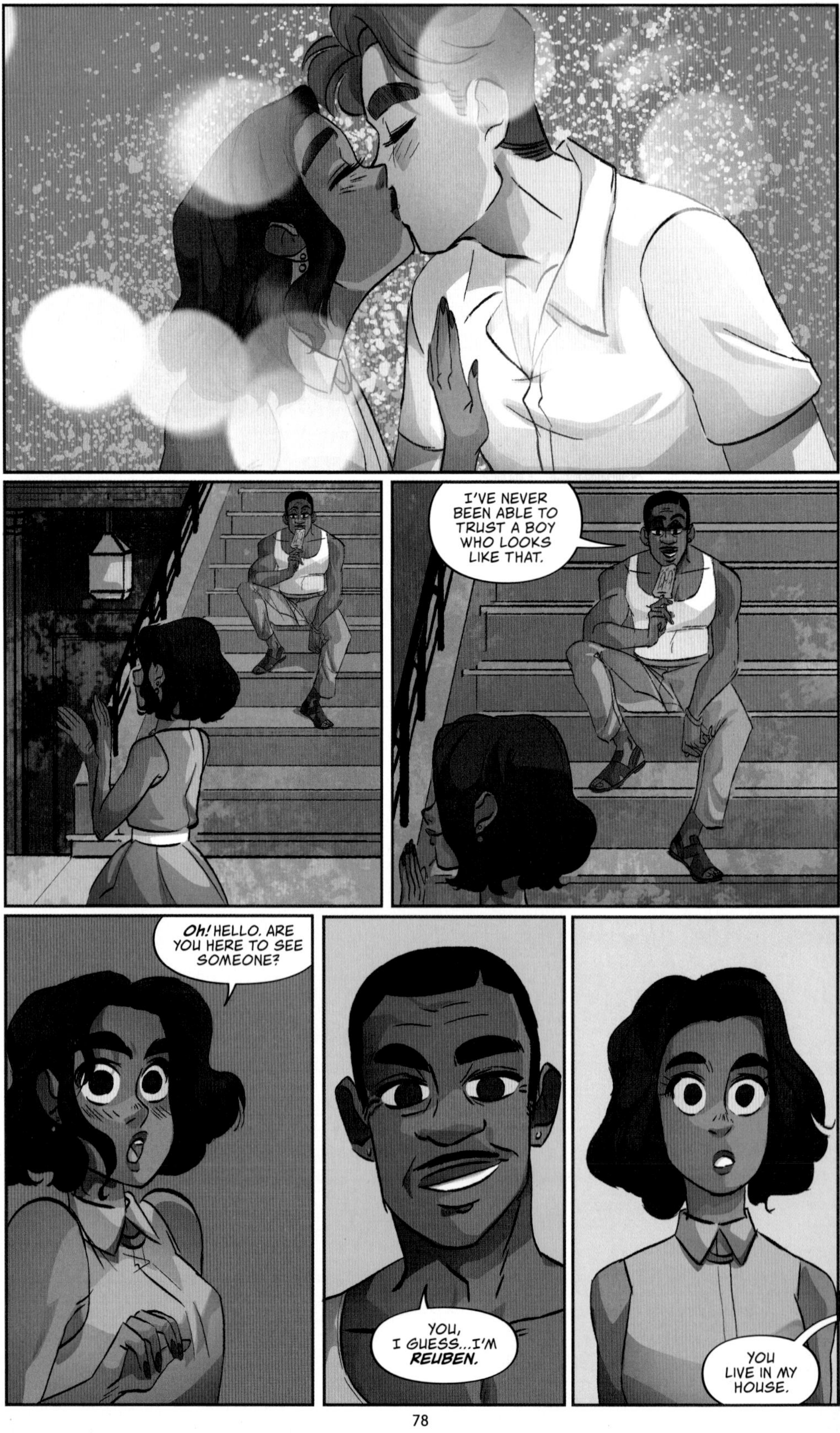
I'VE NEVER BEEN ABLE TO TRUST A BOY WHO LOOKS LIKE THAT.
Oh! HELLO. ARE YOU HERE TO SEE SOMEONE?
YOU, I GUESS...I'M ***REUBEN.***
YOU LIVE IN MY HOUSE.

Chapter Four

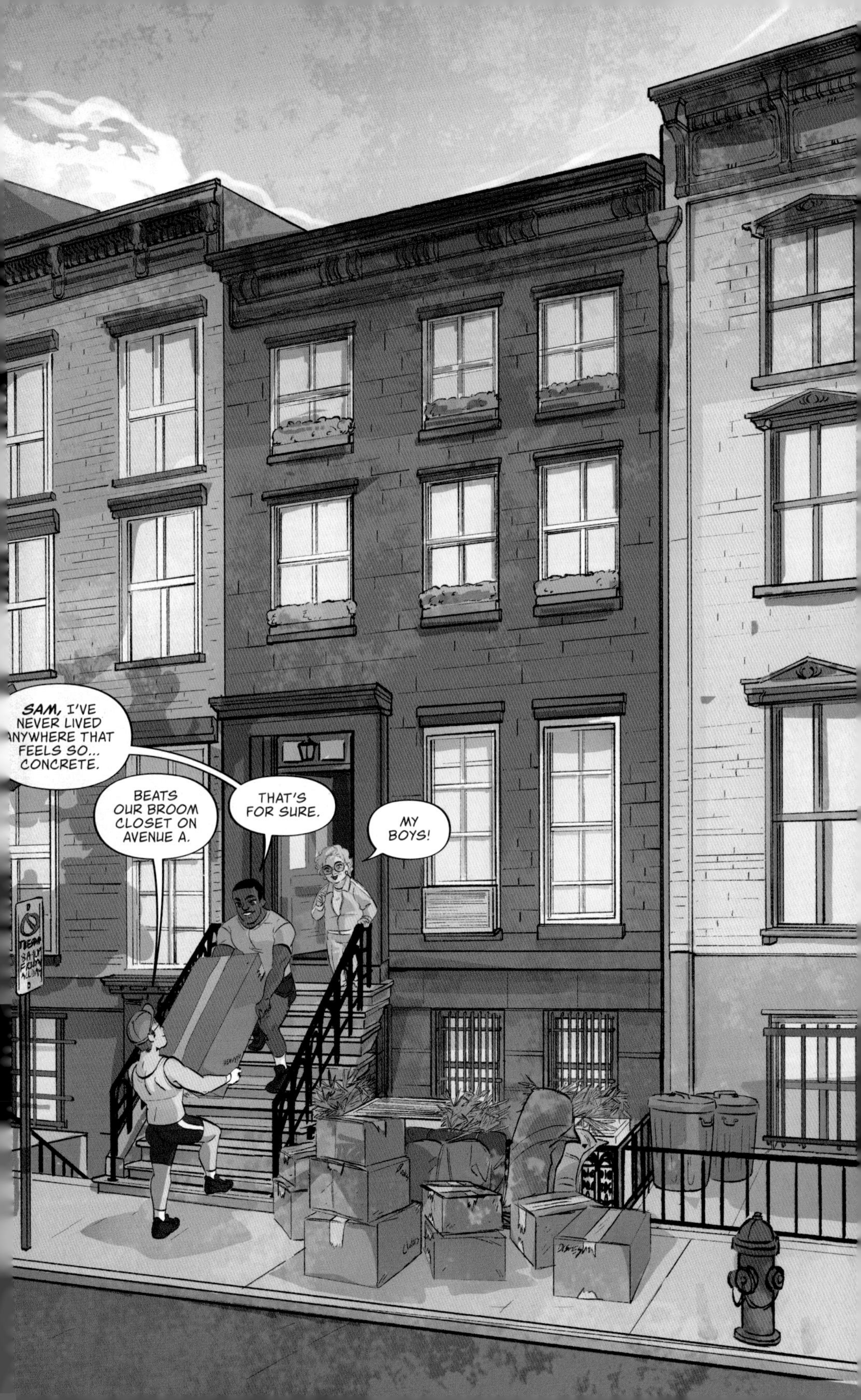
SAM, I'VE NEVER LIVED ANYWHERE THAT FEELS SO... CONCRETE.
BEATS OUR BROOM CLOSET ON AVENUE A.
THAT'S FOR SURE.
MY BOYS!

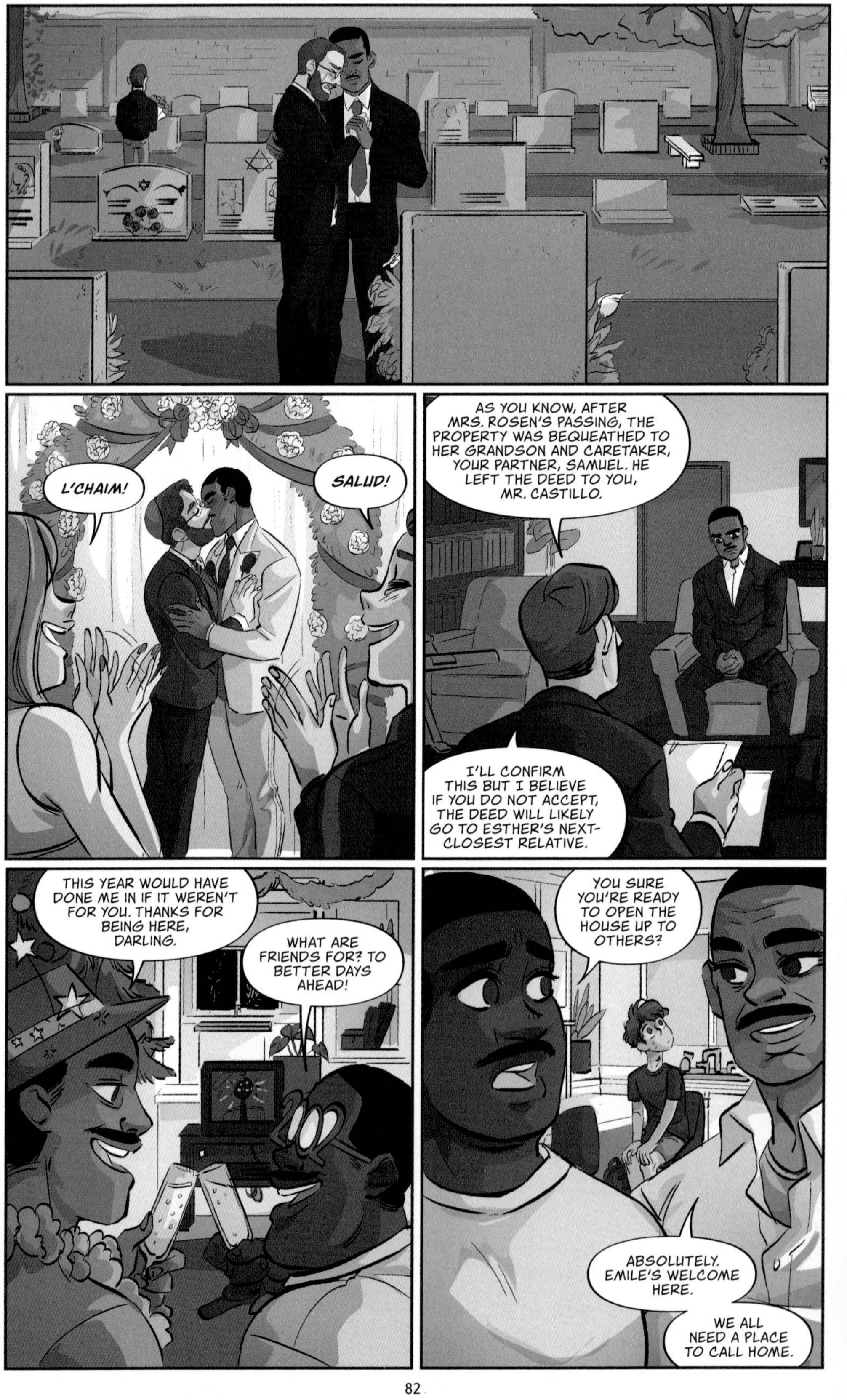
L'CHAIM!
SALUD!
AS YOU KNOW, AFTER MRS. ROSEN'S PASSING, THE PROPERTY WAS BEQUEATHED TO HER GRANDSON AND CARETAKER, YOUR PARTNER, SAMUEL. HE LEFT THE DEED TO YOU, MR. CASTILLO.
I'LL CONFIRM THIS BUT I BELIEVE IF YOU DO NOT ACCEPT, THE DEED WILL LIKELY GO TO ESTHER'S NEXT-CLOSEST RELATIVE.
THIS YEAR WOULD HAVE DONE ME IN IF IT WEREN'T FOR YOU. THANKS FOR BEING HERE, DARLING.
WHAT ARE FRIENDS FOR? TO BETTER DAYS AHEAD!
YOU SURE YOU'RE READY TO OPEN THE HOUSE UP TO OTHERS?
ABSOLUTELY. EMILE'S WELCOME HERE.
WE ALL NEED A PLACE TO CALL HOME.

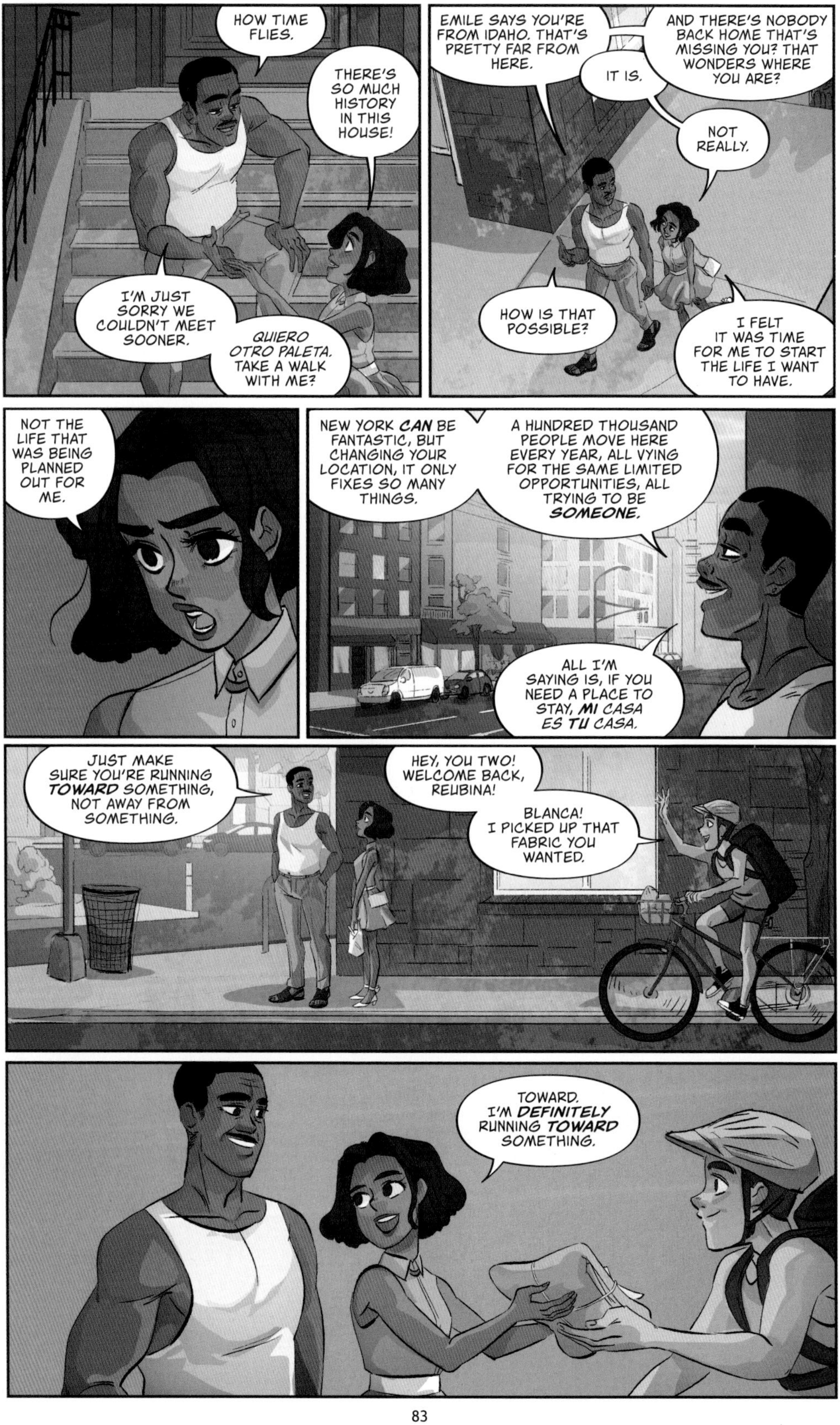

HOW TIME FLIES.
THERE'S SO MUCH HISTORY IN THIS HOUSE!
I'M JUST SORRY WE COULDN'T MEET SOONER.
QUIERO OTRO PALETA. TAKE A WALK WITH ME?
EMILE SAYS YOU'RE FROM IDAHO. THAT'S PRETTY FAR FROM HERE.
IT IS.
AND THERE'S NOBODY BACK HOME THAT'S MISSING YOU? THAT WONDERS WHERE YOU ARE?
NOT REALLY.
HOW IS THAT POSSIBLE?
I FELT IT WAS TIME FOR ME TO START THE LIFE I WANT TO HAVE.
NOT THE LIFE THAT WAS BEING PLANNED OUT FOR ME.
NEW YORK **CAN** BE FANTASTIC, BUT CHANGING YOUR LOCATION, IT ONLY FIXES SO MANY THINGS.
A HUNDRED THOUSAND PEOPLE MOVE HERE EVERY YEAR, ALL VYING FOR THE SAME LIMITED OPPORTUNITIES, ALL TRYING TO BE ***SOMEONE.***
ALL I'M SAYING IS, IF YOU NEED A PLACE TO STAY, ***MI*** CASA ES ***TU*** CASA.
JUST MAKE SURE YOU'RE RUNNING ***TOWARD*** SOMETHING, NOT AWAY FROM SOMETHING.
HEY, YOU TWO! WELCOME BACK, REUBINA!
BLANCA! I PICKED UP THAT FABRIC YOU WANTED.
TOWARD. I'M ***DEFINITELY*** RUNNING ***TOWARD*** SOMETHING.

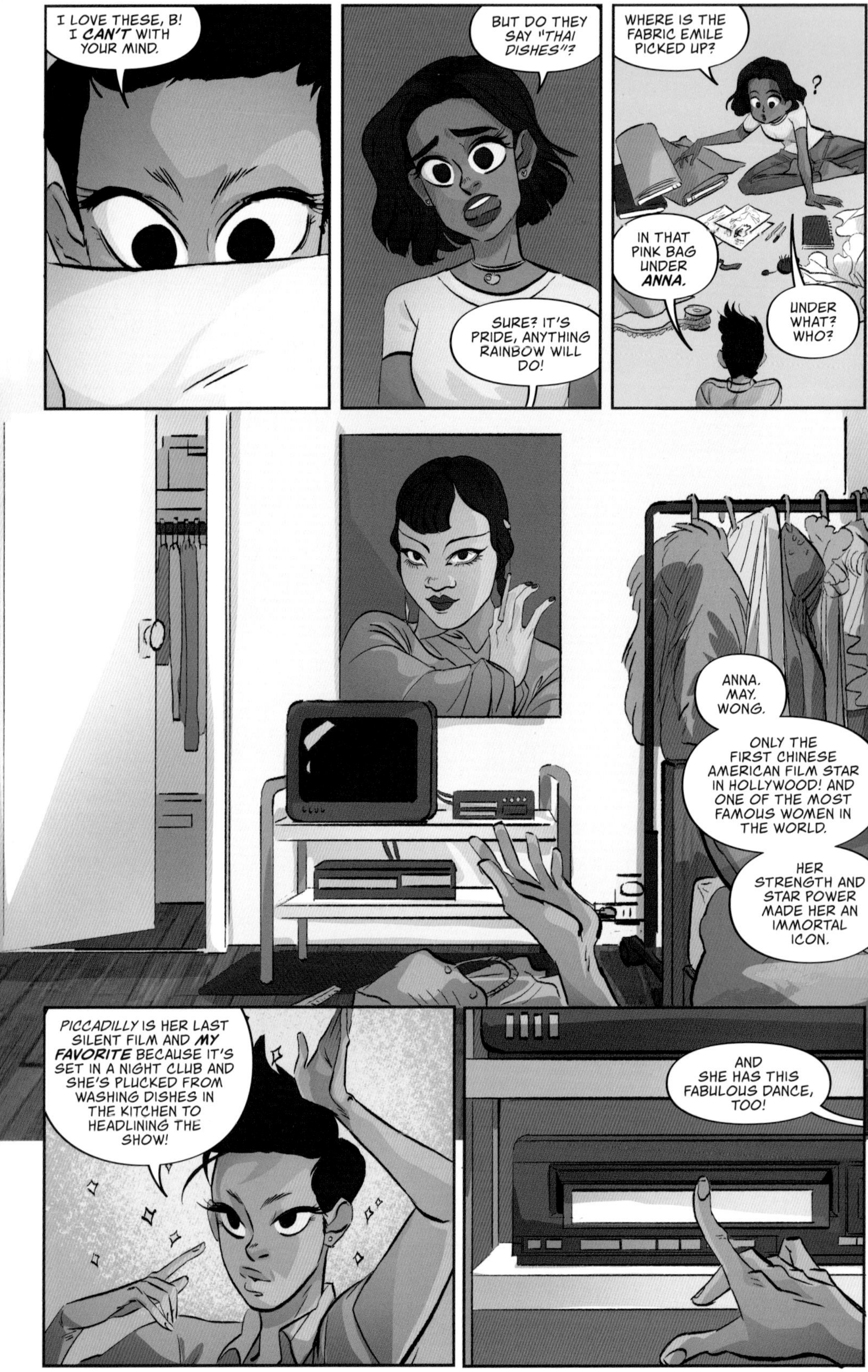
I LOVE THESE, B! I *CAN'T* WITH YOUR MIND.
BUT DO THEY SAY "*THAI DISHES*"?
SURE? IT'S PRIDE, ANYTHING RAINBOW WILL DO!
WHERE IS THE FABRIC EMILE PICKED UP?
?
IN THAT PINK BAG UNDER **ANNA.**
UNDER WHAT? WHO?
ANNA. MAY. WONG.
ONLY THE FIRST CHINESE AMERICAN FILM STAR IN HOLLYWOOD! AND ONE OF THE MOST FAMOUS WOMEN IN THE WORLD.
HER STRENGTH AND STAR POWER MADE HER AN IMMORTAL ICON.
PICCADILLY IS HER LAST SILENT FILM AND ***MY FAVORITE*** BECAUSE IT'S SET IN A NIGHT CLUB AND SHE'S PLUCKED FROM WASHING DISHES IN THE KITCHEN TO HEADLINING THE SHOW!
AND SHE HAS THIS FABULOUS DANCE, TOO!

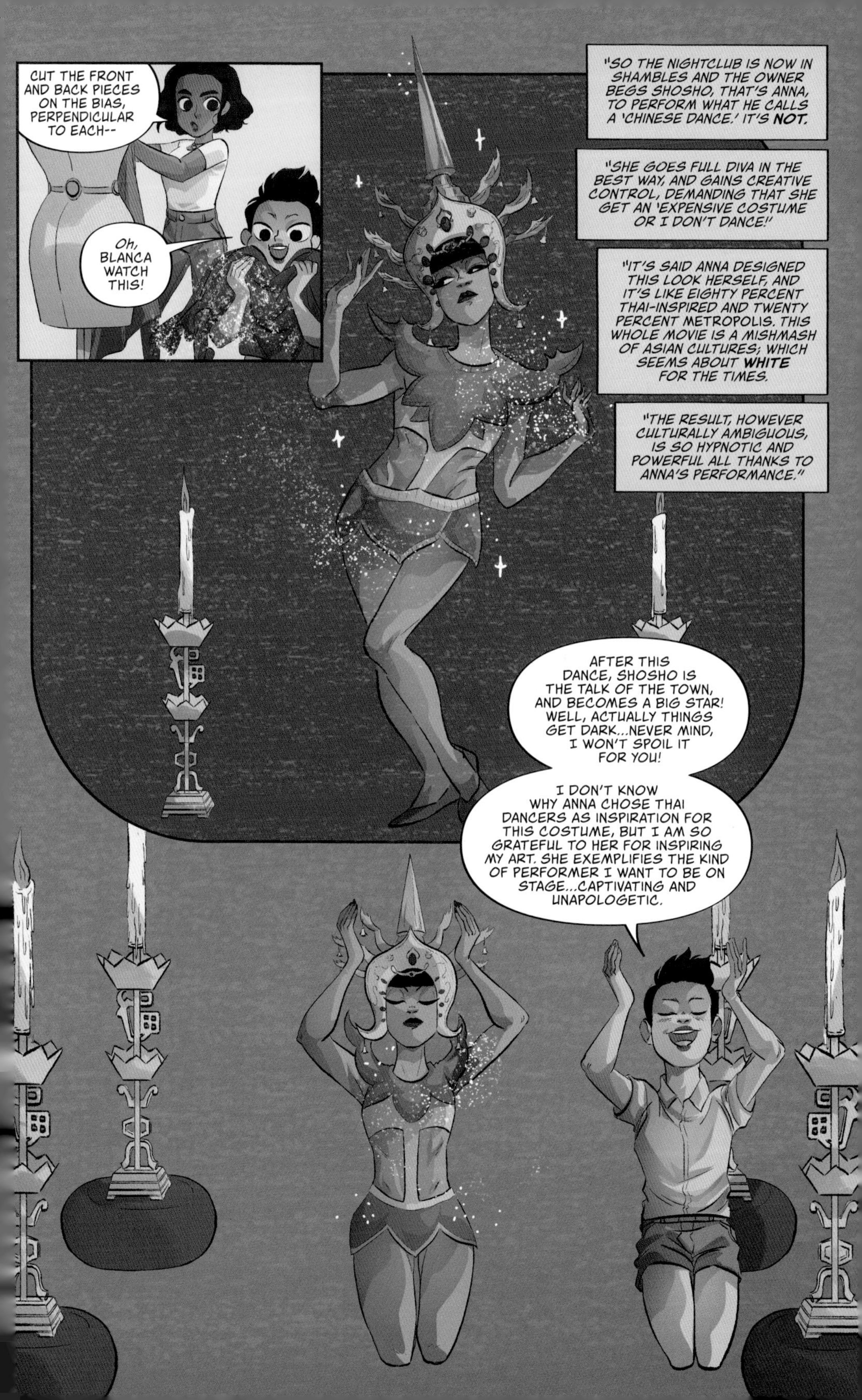
CUT THE FRONT AND BACK PIECES ON THE BIAS, PERPENDICULAR TO EACH--
Oh, BLANCA WATCH THIS!
"SO THE NIGHTCLUB IS NOW IN SHAMBLES AND THE OWNER BEGS SHOSHO, THAT'S ANNA, TO PERFORM WHAT HE CALLS A 'CHINESE DANCE.' IT'S **NOT.**
"SHE GOES FULL DIVA IN THE BEST WAY, AND GAINS CREATIVE CONTROL, DEMANDING THAT SHE GET AN 'EXPENSIVE COSTUME OR I DON'T DANCE!'
"IT'S SAID ANNA DESIGNED THIS LOOK HERSELF, AND IT'S LIKE EIGHTY PERCENT THAI-INSPIRED AND TWENTY PERCENT METROPOLIS. THIS WHOLE MOVIE IS A MISHMASH OF ASIAN CULTURES; WHICH SEEMS ABOUT **WHITE** FOR THE TIMES.
"THE RESULT, HOWEVER CULTURALLY AMBIGUOUS, IS SO HYPNOTIC AND POWERFUL ALL THANKS TO ANNA'S PERFORMANCE."
AFTER THIS DANCE, SHOSHO IS THE TALK OF THE TOWN, AND BECOMES A BIG STAR! WELL, ACTUALLY THINGS GET DARK...NEVER MIND, I WON'T SPOIL IT FOR YOU!
I DON'T KNOW WHY ANNA CHOSE THAI DANCERS AS INSPIRATION FOR THIS COSTUME, BUT I AM SO GRATEFUL TO HER FOR INSPIRING MY ART. SHE EXEMPLIFIES THE KIND OF PERFORMER I WANT TO BE ON STAGE...CAPTIVATING AND UNAPOLOGETIC.

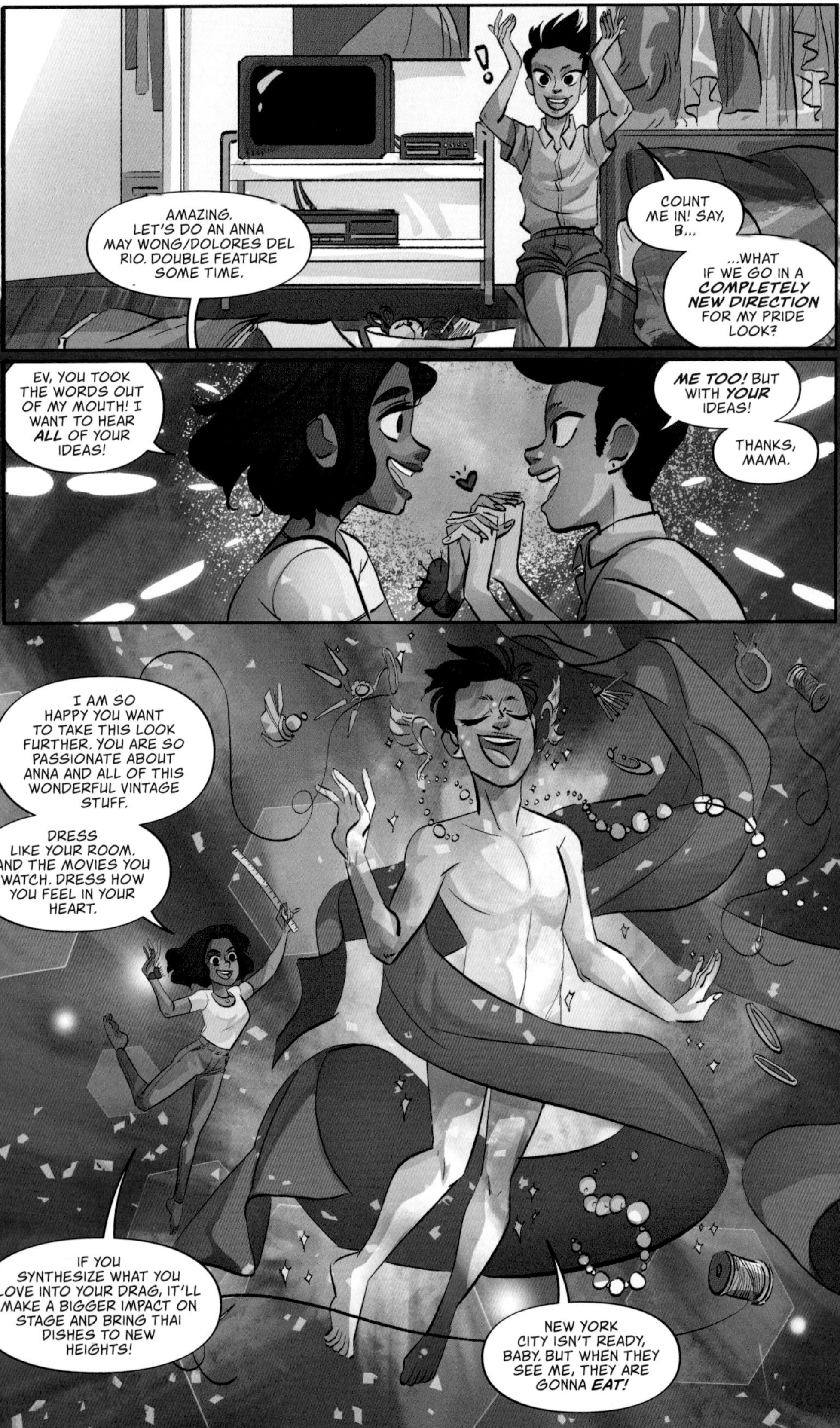

AMAZING. LET'S DO AN ANNA MAY WONG/DOLORES DEL RIO. DOUBLE FEATURE SOME TIME.
COUNT ME IN! SAY, B...
...WHAT IF WE GO IN A COMPLETELY NEW DIRECTION FOR MY PRIDE LOOK?
EV, YOU TOOK THE WORDS OUT OF MY MOUTH! I WANT TO HEAR ALL OF YOUR IDEAS!
ME TOO! BUT WITH YOUR IDEAS!
THANKS, MAMA.
I AM SO HAPPY YOU WANT TO TAKE THIS LOOK FURTHER. YOU ARE SO PASSIONATE ABOUT ANNA AND ALL OF THIS WONDERFUL VINTAGE STUFF.
DRESS LIKE YOUR ROOM. AND THE MOVIES YOU WATCH. DRESS HOW YOU FEEL IN YOUR HEART.
IF YOU SYNTHESIZE WHAT YOU LOVE INTO YOUR DRAG, IT'LL MAKE A BIGGER IMPACT ON STAGE AND BRING THAI DISHES TO NEW HEIGHTS!
NEW YORK CITY ISN'T READY, BABY. BUT WHEN THEY SEE ME, THEY ARE GONNA EAT!

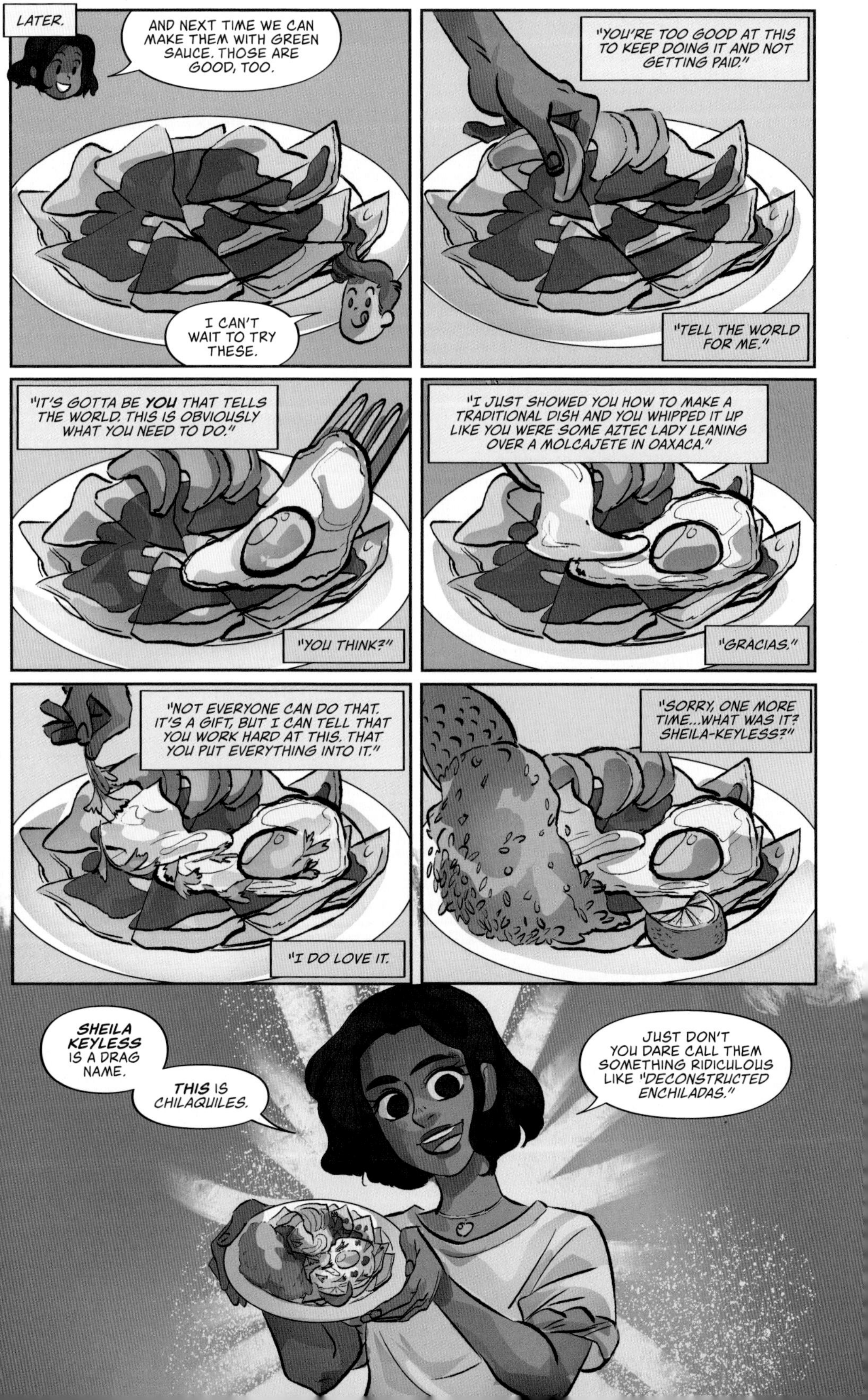
LATER.
AND NEXT TIME WE CAN MAKE THEM WITH GREEN SAUCE. THOSE ARE GOOD, TOO.
I CAN'T WAIT TO TRY THESE.
"YOU'RE TOO GOOD AT THIS TO KEEP DOING IT AND NOT GETTING PAID."
"TELL THE WORLD FOR ME."
"IT'S GOTTA BE YOU THAT TELLS THE WORLD. THIS IS OBVIOUSLY WHAT YOU NEED TO DO."
"YOU THINK?"
"I JUST SHOWED YOU HOW TO MAKE A TRADITIONAL DISH AND YOU WHIPPED IT UP LIKE YOU WERE SOME AZTEC LADY LEANING OVER A MOLCAJETE IN OAXACA."
"GRACIAS."
"NOT EVERYONE CAN DO THAT. IT'S A GIFT, BUT I CAN TELL THAT YOU WORK HARD AT THIS. THAT YOU PUT EVERYTHING INTO IT."
"I DO LOVE IT.
"SORRY, ONE MORE TIME...WHAT WAS IT? SHEILA-KEYLESS?"
SHEILA KEYLESS IS A DRAG NAME.
THIS IS CHILAQUILES.
JUST DON'T YOU DARE CALL THEM SOMETHING RIDICULOUS LIKE "DECONSTRUCTED ENCHILADAS."

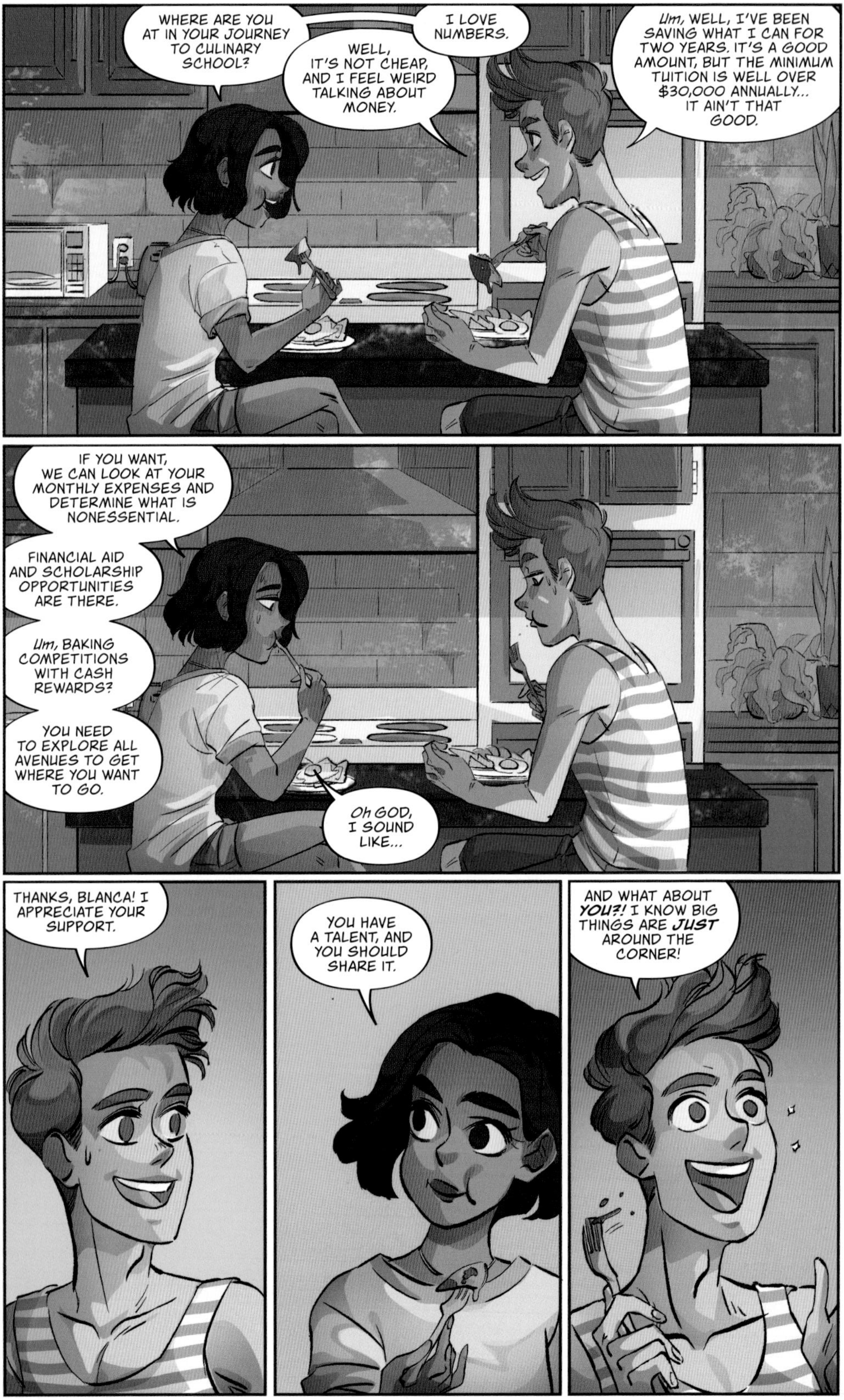
WHERE ARE YOU AT IN YOUR JOURNEY TO CULINARY SCHOOL?
I LOVE NUMBERS.
WELL, IT'S NOT CHEAP, AND I FEEL WEIRD TALKING ABOUT MONEY.
Um, WELL, I'VE BEEN SAVING WHAT I CAN FOR TWO YEARS. IT'S A GOOD AMOUNT, BUT THE MINIMUM TUITION IS WELL OVER $30,000 ANNUALLY... IT AIN'T THAT GOOD.
IF YOU WANT, WE CAN LOOK AT YOUR MONTHLY EXPENSES AND DETERMINE WHAT IS NONESSENTIAL.
FINANCIAL AID AND SCHOLARSHIP OPPORTUNITIES ARE THERE.
Um, BAKING COMPETITIONS WITH CASH REWARDS?
YOU NEED TO EXPLORE ALL AVENUES TO GET WHERE YOU WANT TO GO.
Oh GOD, I SOUND LIKE...
THANKS, BLANCA! I APPRECIATE YOUR SUPPORT.
YOU HAVE A TALENT, AND YOU SHOULD SHARE IT.
AND WHAT ABOUT ***YOU?!*** I KNOW BIG THINGS ARE ***JUST*** AROUND THE CORNER!

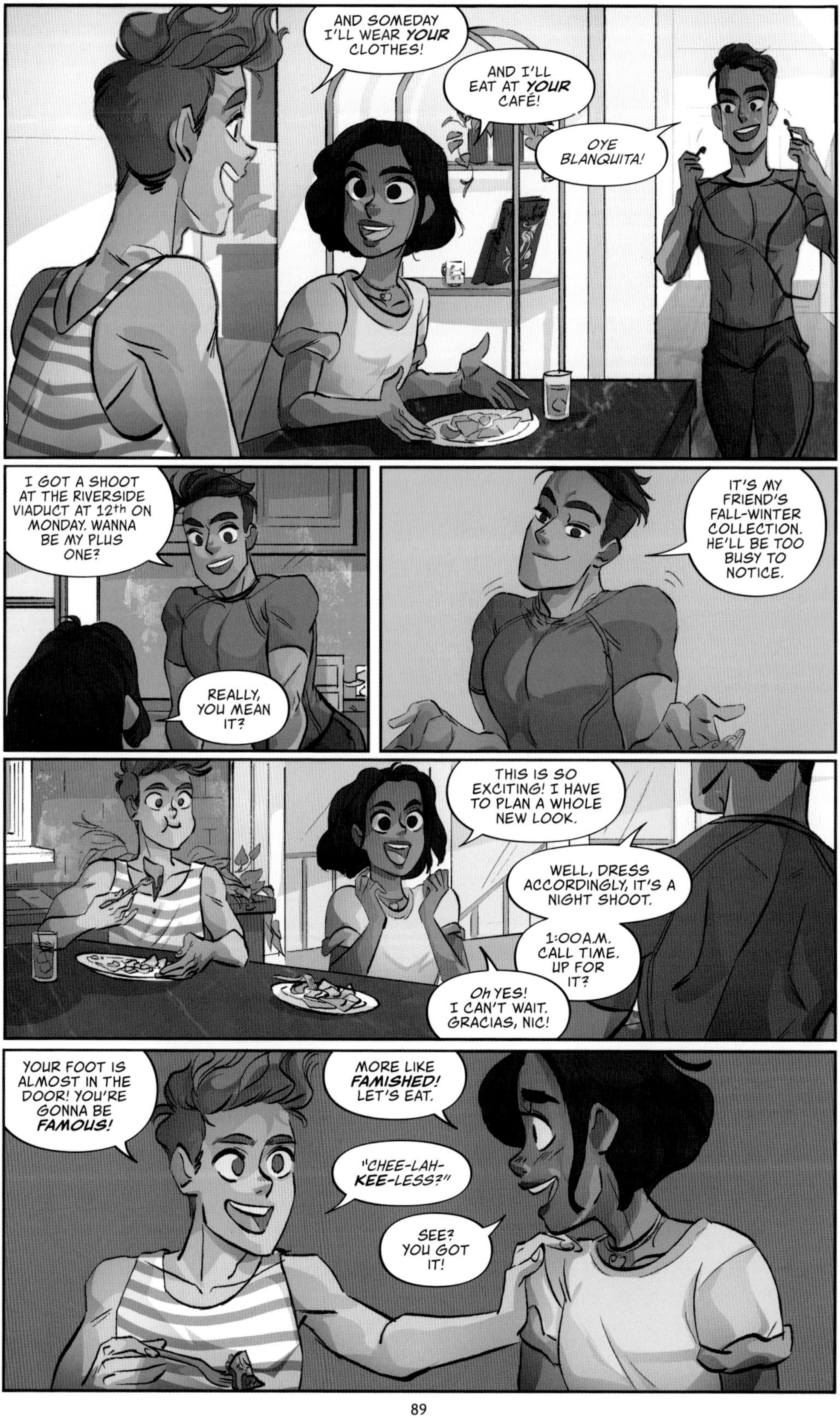
AND SOMEDAY I'LL WEAR YOUR CLOTHES!
AND I'LL EAT AT YOUR CAFÉ!
OYE BLANQUITA!
I GOT A SHOOT AT THE RIVERSIDE VIADUCT AT 12th ON MONDAY. WANNA BE MY PLUS ONE?
REALLY, YOU MEAN IT?
IT'S MY FRIEND'S FALL-WINTER COLLECTION. HE'LL BE TOO BUSY TO NOTICE.
THIS IS SO EXCITING! I HAVE TO PLAN A WHOLE NEW LOOK.
WELL, DRESS ACCORDINGLY, IT'S A NIGHT SHOOT.
1:00A.M. CALL TIME. UP FOR IT?
Oh YES! I CAN'T WAIT. GRACIAS, NIC!
YOUR FOOT IS ALMOST IN THE DOOR! YOU'RE GONNA BE FAMOUS!
MORE LIKE FAMISHED! LET'S EAT.
"CHEE-LAH-KEE-LESS?"
SEE? YOU GOT IT!

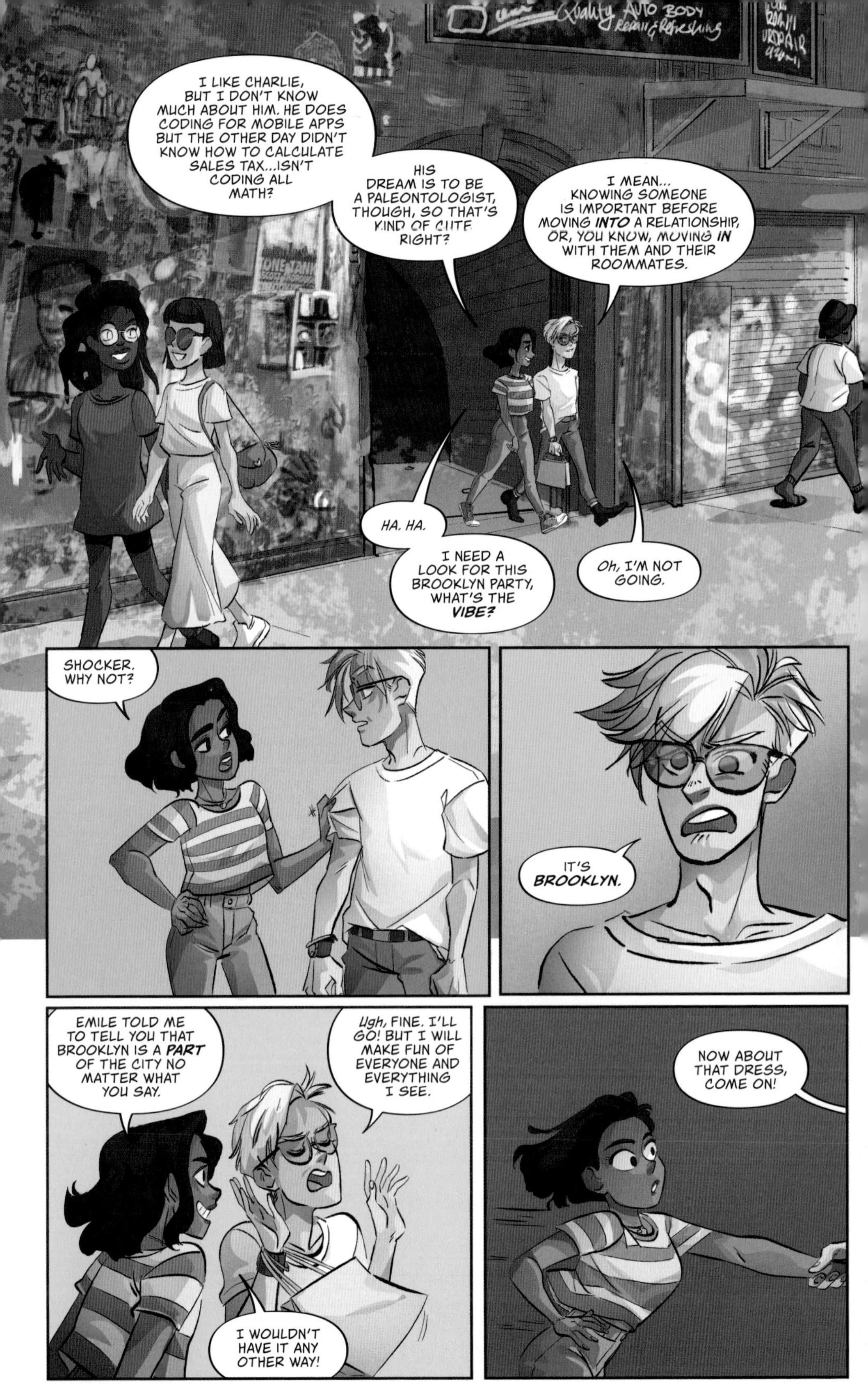
Quality AUTO BODY Repair & Refinishing
I LIKE CHARLIE, BUT I DON'T KNOW MUCH ABOUT HIM. HE DOES CODING FOR MOBILE APPS BUT THE OTHER DAY DIDN'T KNOW HOW TO CALCULATE SALES TAX...ISN'T CODING ALL MATH?
HIS DREAM IS TO BE A PALEONTOLOGIST, THOUGH, SO THAT'S KIND OF CUTE RIGHT?
I MEAN... KNOWING SOMEONE IS IMPORTANT BEFORE MOVING *INTO* A RELATIONSHIP, OR, YOU KNOW, MOVING *IN* WITH THEM AND THEIR ROOMMATES.
HA. HA.
I NEED A LOOK FOR THIS BROOKLYN PARTY, WHAT'S THE ***VIBE?***
Oh, I'M NOT GOING.
SHOCKER. WHY NOT?
IT'S ***BROOKLYN.***
EMILE TOLD ME TO TELL YOU THAT BROOKLYN IS A ***PART*** OF THE CITY NO MATTER WHAT YOU SAY.
Ugh, FINE. I'LL GO! BUT I WILL MAKE FUN OF EVERYONE AND EVERYTHING I SEE.
I WOULDN'T HAVE IT ANY OTHER WAY!
NOW ABOUT THAT DRESS, COME ON!

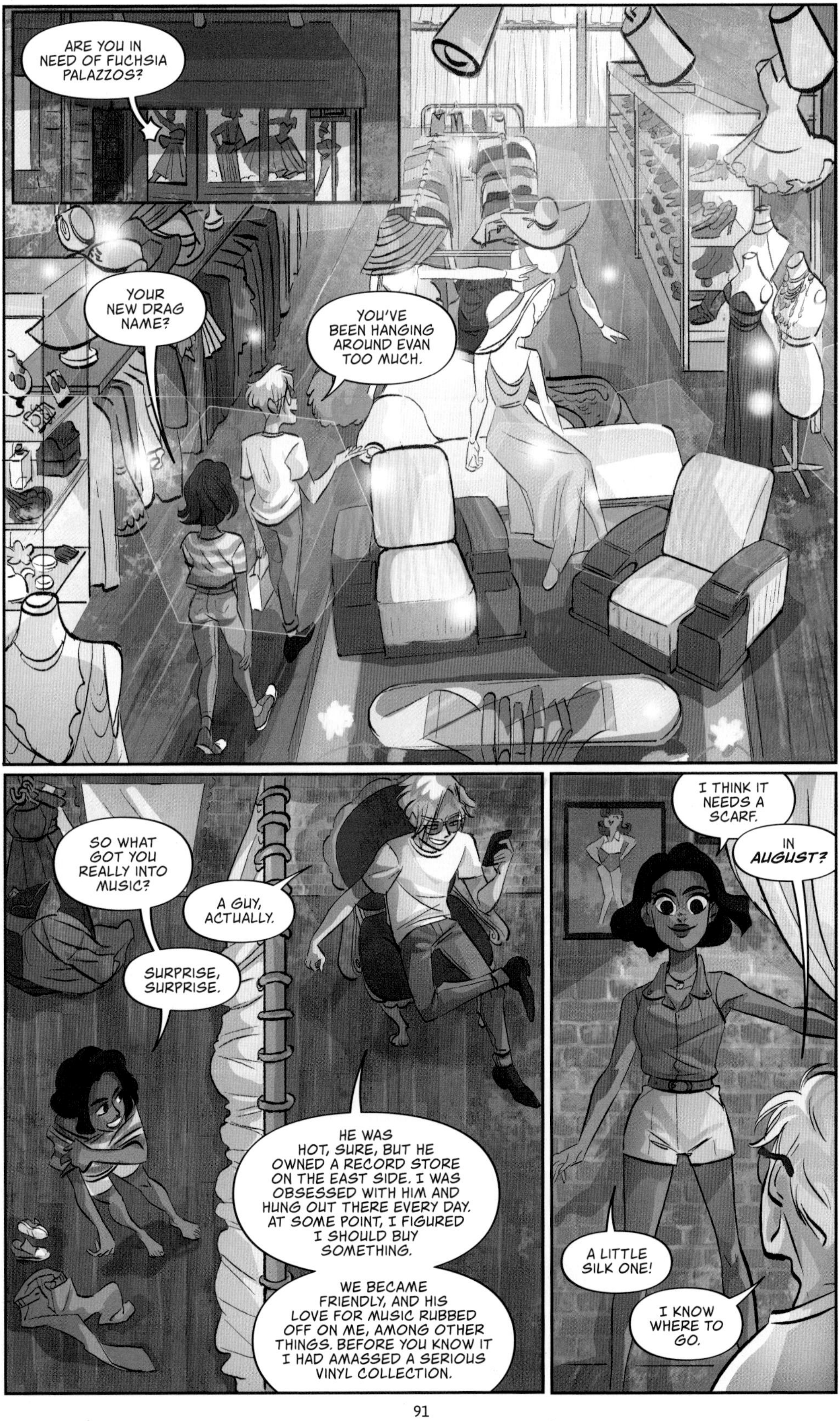
ARE YOU IN NEED OF FUCHSIA PALAZZOS?
YOUR NEW DRAG NAME?
YOU'VE BEEN HANGING AROUND EVAN TOO MUCH.
SO WHAT GOT YOU REALLY INTO MUSIC?
A GUY, ACTUALLY.
SURPRISE, SURPRISE.
HE WAS HOT, SURE, BUT HE OWNED A RECORD STORE ON THE EAST SIDE. I WAS OBSESSED WITH HIM AND HUNG OUT THERE EVERY DAY. AT SOME POINT, I FIGURED I SHOULD BUY SOMETHING.
WE BECAME FRIENDLY, AND HIS LOVE FOR MUSIC RUBBED OFF ON ME, AMONG OTHER THINGS. BEFORE YOU KNOW IT I HAD AMASSED A SERIOUS VINYL COLLECTION.
I THINK IT NEEDS A SCARF.
IN AUGUST?
A LITTLE SILK ONE!
I KNOW WHERE TO GO.

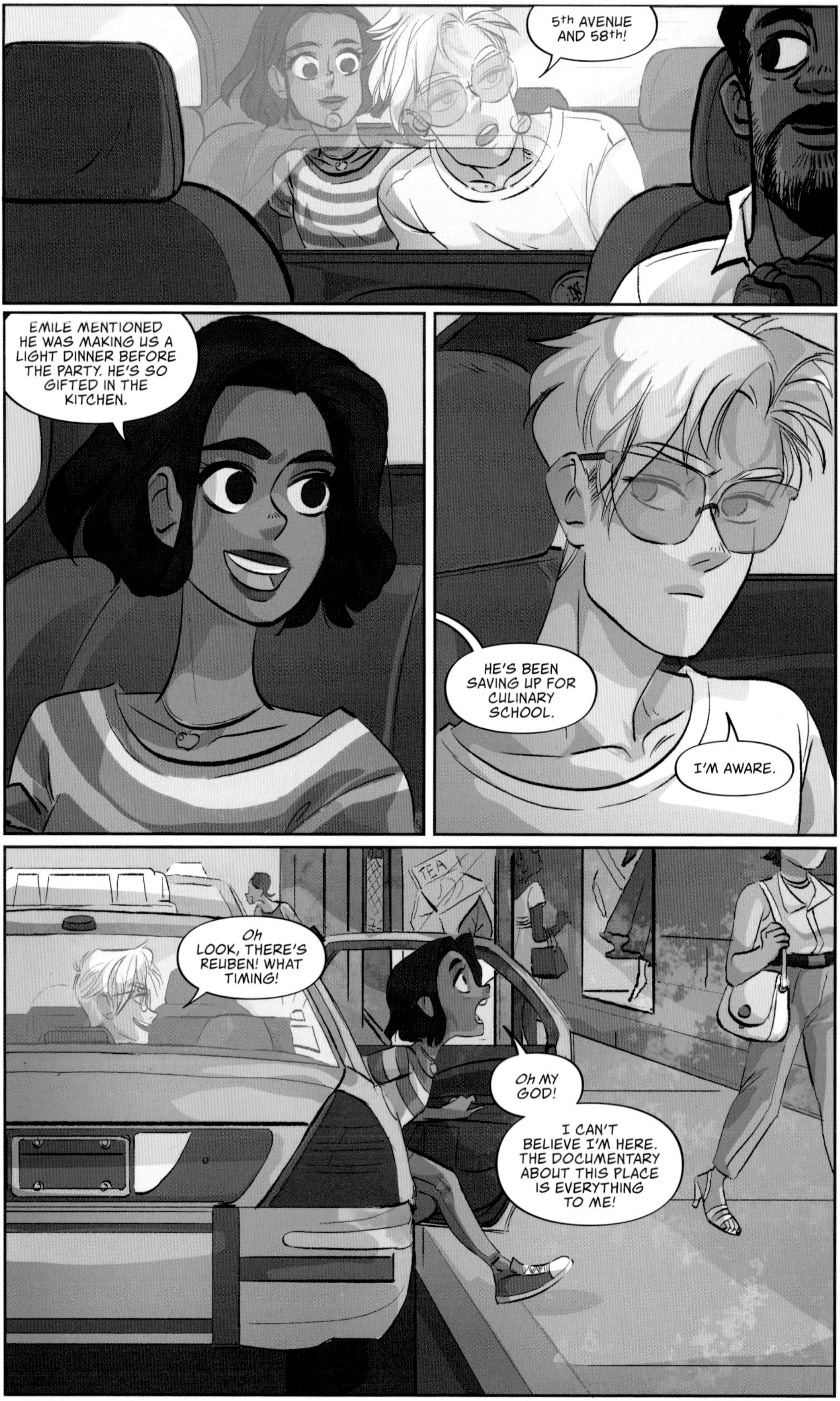
5th AVENUE AND 58th!
EMILE MENTIONED HE WAS MAKING US A LIGHT DINNER BEFORE THE PARTY. HE'S SO GIFTED IN THE KITCHEN.
HE'S BEEN SAVING UP FOR CULINARY SCHOOL.
I'M AWARE.
Oh LOOK, THERE'S REUBEN! WHAT TIMING!
TEA
Oh MY GOD!
I CAN'T BELIEVE I'M HERE. THE DOCUMENTARY ABOUT THIS PLACE IS EVERYTHING TO ME!

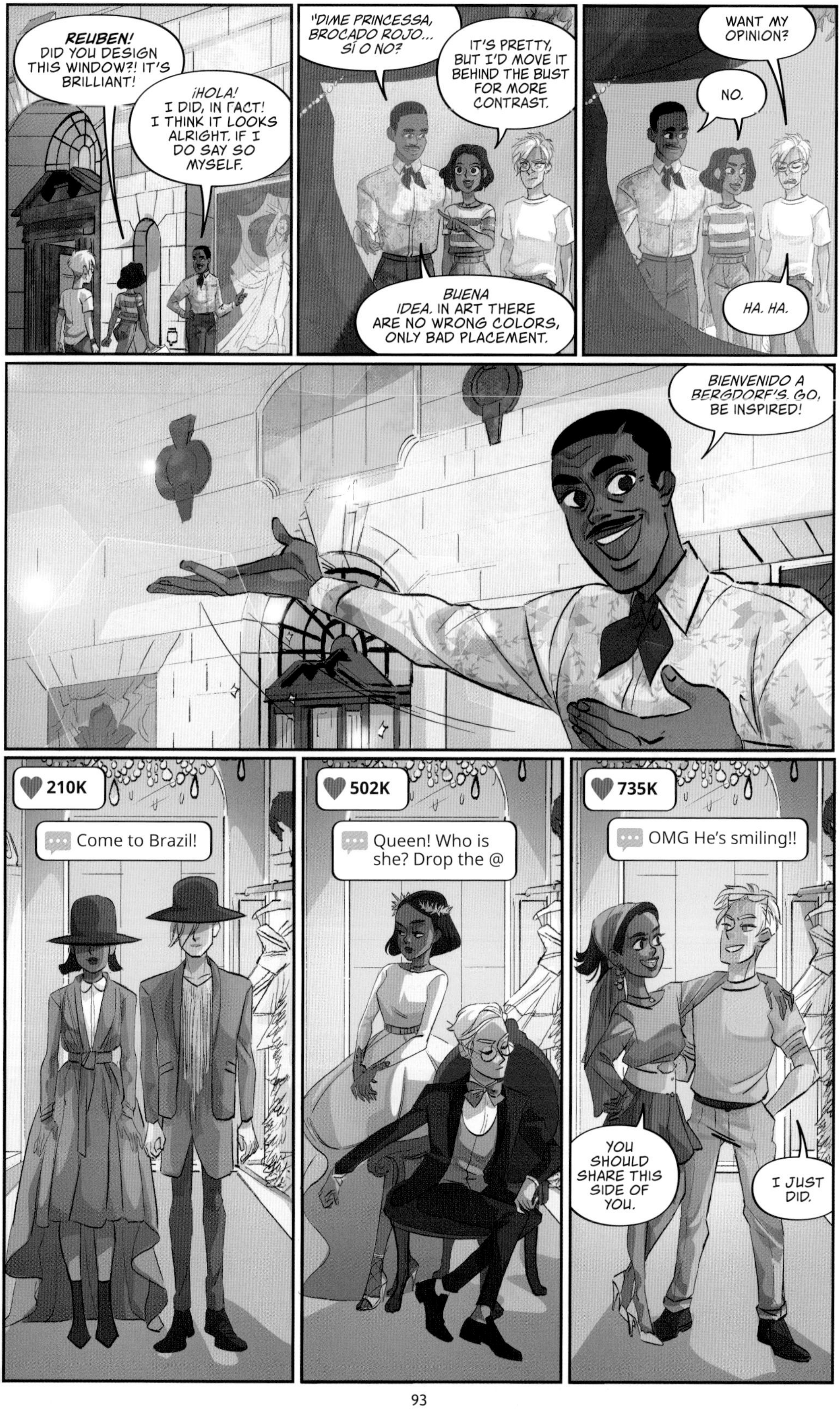
REUBEN! DID YOU DESIGN THIS WINDOW?! IT'S BRILLIANT!
¡HOLA! I DID, IN FACT! I THINK IT LOOKS ALRIGHT. IF I DO SAY SO MYSELF.
"DIME PRINCESSA, BROCADO ROJO... SÍ O NO?
IT'S PRETTY, BUT I'D MOVE IT BEHIND THE BUST FOR MORE CONTRAST.
BUENA IDEA. IN ART THERE ARE NO WRONG COLORS, ONLY BAD PLACEMENT.
WANT MY OPINION?
NO.
HA. HA.
BIENVENIDO A BERGDORF'S. GO, BE INSPIRED!
210K
Come to Brazil!
502K
Queen! Who is she? Drop the @
735K
OMG He's smiling!!
YOU SHOULD SHARE THIS SIDE OF YOU.
I JUST DID.

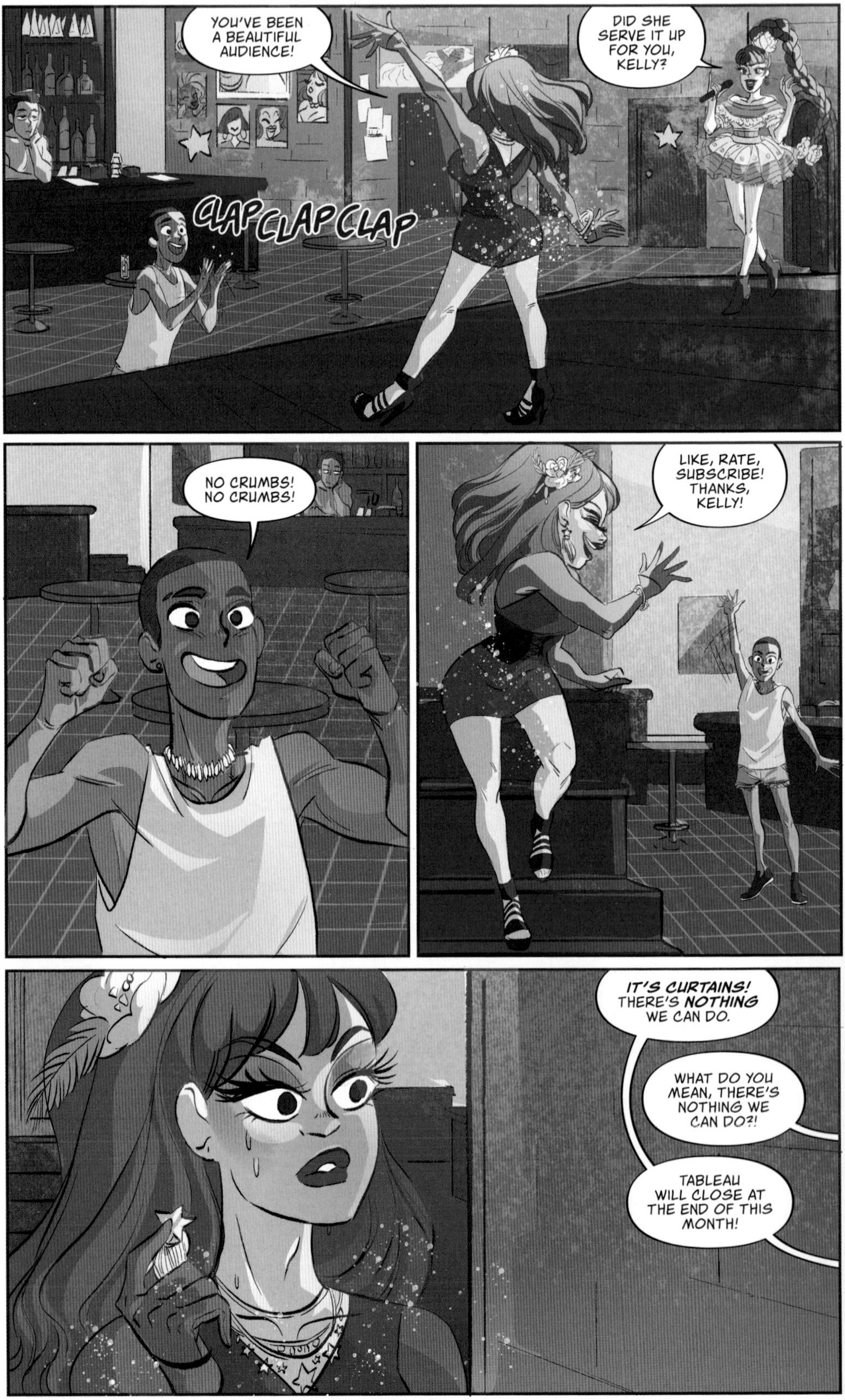

YOU'VE BEEN A BEAUTIFUL AUDIENCE!
DID SHE SERVE IT UP FOR YOU, KELLY?
CLAP CLAP CLAP
NO CRUMBS! NO CRUMBS!
LIKE, RATE, SUBSCRIBE! THANKS, KELLY!
IT'S CURTAINS! THERE'S NOTHING WE CAN DO.
WHAT DO YOU MEAN, THERE'S NOTHING WE CAN DO?!
TABLEAU WILL CLOSE AT THE END OF THIS MONTH!

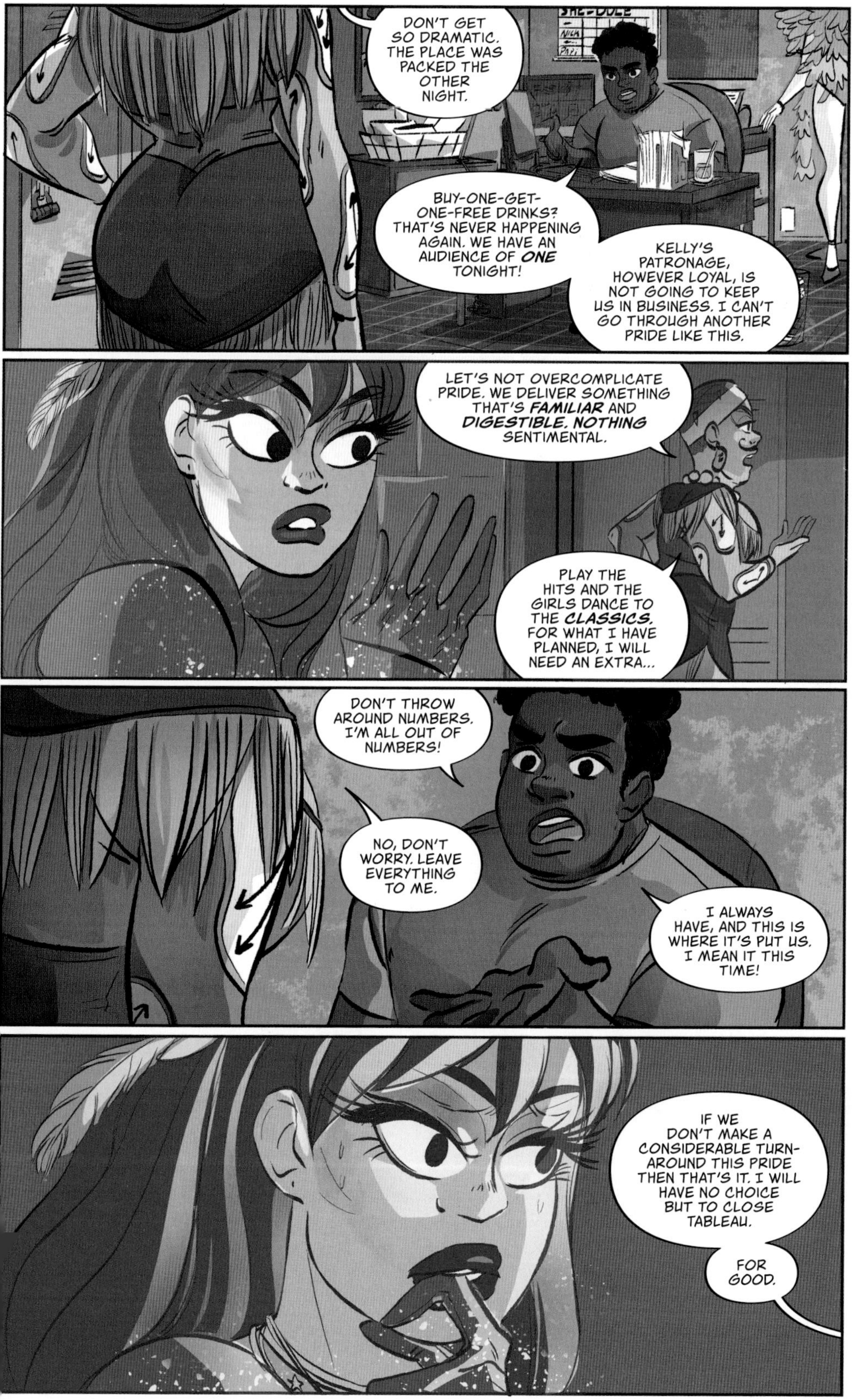
SHE-DULE
NICK
PAPI
DON'T GET SO DRAMATIC. THE PLACE WAS PACKED THE OTHER NIGHT.
BUY-ONE-GET-ONE-FREE DRINKS? THAT'S NEVER HAPPENING AGAIN. WE HAVE AN AUDIENCE OF ***ONE*** TONIGHT!
KELLY'S PATRONAGE, HOWEVER LOYAL, IS NOT GOING TO KEEP US IN BUSINESS. I CAN'T GO THROUGH ANOTHER PRIDE LIKE THIS.
LET'S NOT OVERCOMPLICATE PRIDE. WE DELIVER SOMETHING THAT'S ***FAMILIAR*** AND ***DIGESTIBLE. NOTHING*** SENTIMENTAL.
PLAY THE HITS AND THE GIRLS DANCE TO THE ***CLASSICS.*** FOR WHAT I HAVE PLANNED, I WILL NEED AN EXTRA...
DON'T THROW AROUND NUMBERS. I'M ALL OUT OF NUMBERS!
NO, DON'T WORRY. LEAVE EVERYTHING TO ME.
I ALWAYS HAVE, AND THIS IS WHERE IT'S PUT US. I MEAN IT THIS TIME!
IF WE DON'T MAKE A CONSIDERABLE TURN-AROUND THIS PRIDE THEN THAT'S IT. I WILL HAVE NO CHOICE BUT TO CLOSE TABLEAU.
FOR GOOD.

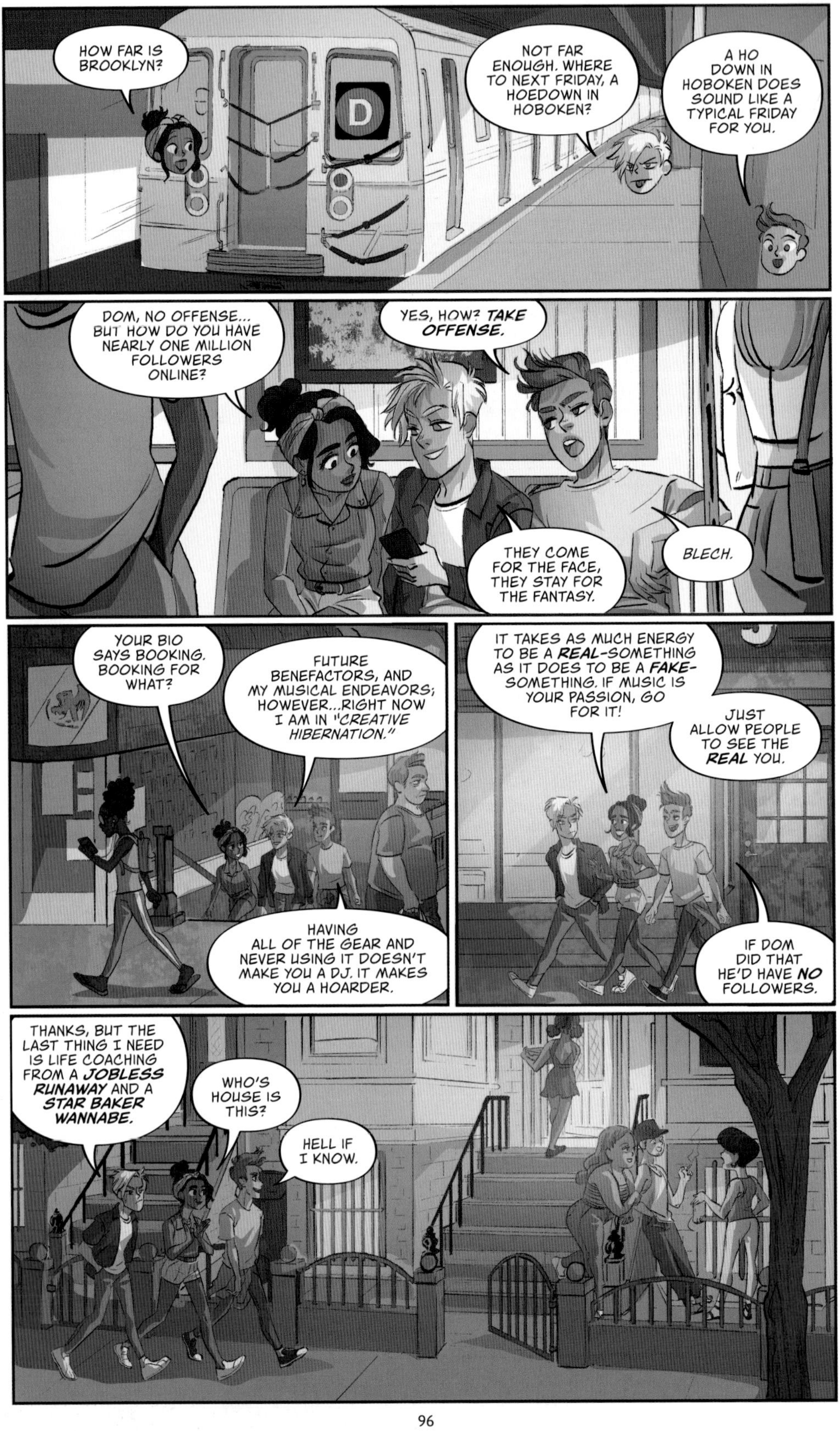
HOW FAR IS BROOKLYN?
NOT FAR ENOUGH. WHERE TO NEXT FRIDAY, A HOEDOWN IN HOBOKEN?
A HO DOWN IN HOBOKEN DOES SOUND LIKE A TYPICAL FRIDAY FOR YOU.
D
DOM, NO OFFENSE... BUT HOW DO YOU HAVE NEARLY ONE MILLION FOLLOWERS ONLINE?
YES, HOW? TAKE OFFENSE.
THEY COME FOR THE FACE, THEY STAY FOR THE FANTASY.
BLECH.
YOUR BIO SAYS BOOKING. BOOKING FOR WHAT?
FUTURE BENEFACTORS, AND MY MUSICAL ENDEAVORS; HOWEVER...RIGHT NOW I AM IN "CREATIVE HIBERNATION."
HAVING ALL OF THE GEAR AND NEVER USING IT DOESN'T MAKE YOU A DJ. IT MAKES YOU A HOARDER.
IT TAKES AS MUCH ENERGY TO BE A REAL-SOMETHING AS IT DOES TO BE A FAKE-SOMETHING. IF MUSIC IS YOUR PASSION, GO FOR IT!
JUST ALLOW PEOPLE TO SEE THE REAL YOU.
IF DOM DID THAT HE'D HAVE NO FOLLOWERS.
THANKS, BUT THE LAST THING I NEED IS LIFE COACHING FROM A JOBLESS RUNAWAY AND A STAR BAKER WANNABE.
WHO'S HOUSE IS THIS?
HELL IF I KNOW.

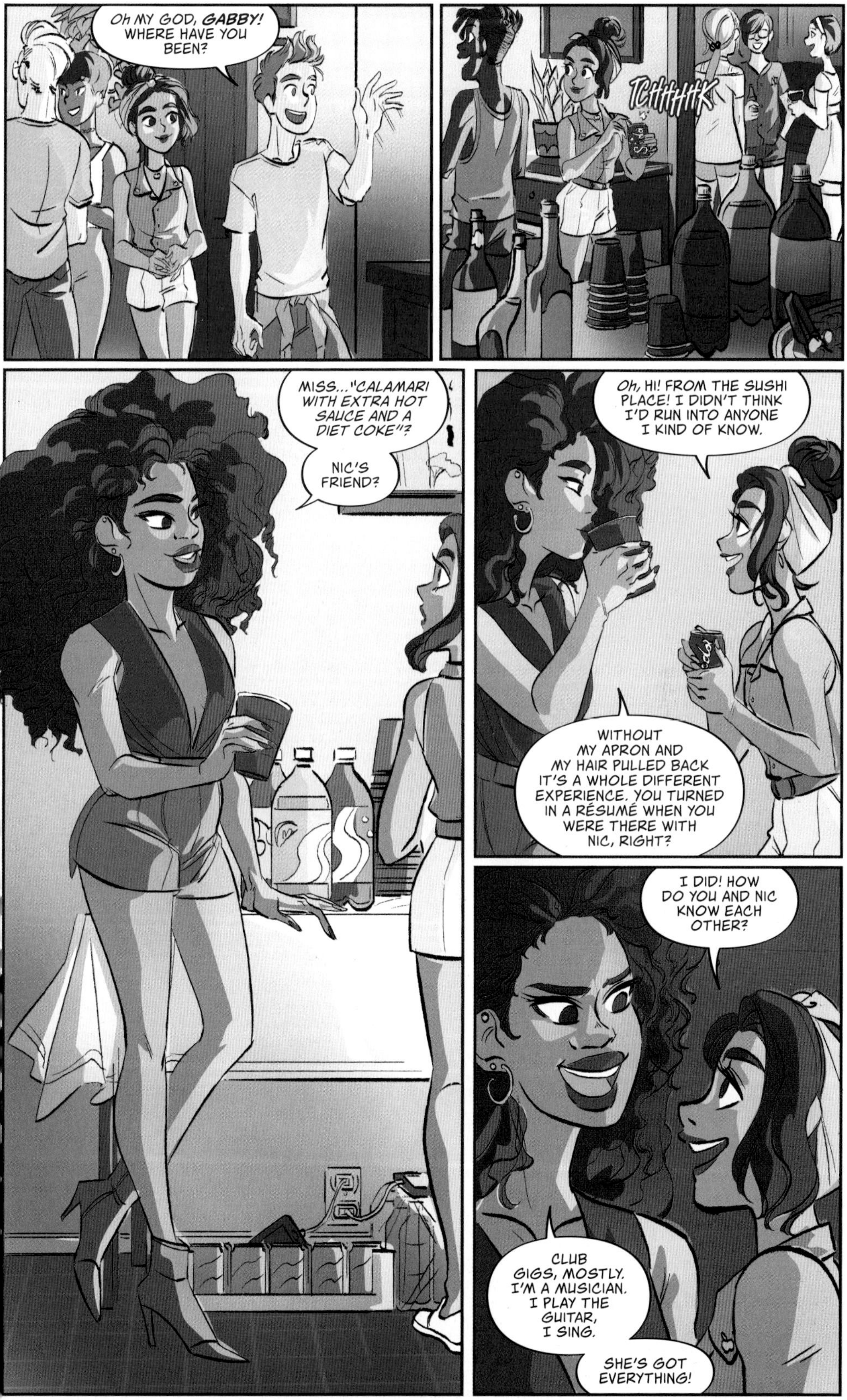
Oh MY GOD, GABBY! WHERE HAVE YOU BEEN?
TCHHHHK
MISS... "CALAMARI WITH EXTRA HOT SAUCE AND A DIET COKE"?
NIC'S FRIEND?
Oh, HI! FROM THE SUSHI PLACE! I DIDN'T THINK I'D RUN INTO ANYONE I KIND OF KNOW.
WITHOUT MY APRON AND MY HAIR PULLED BACK IT'S A WHOLE DIFFERENT EXPERIENCE. YOU TURNED IN A RÉSUMÉ WHEN YOU WERE THERE WITH NIC, RIGHT?
I DID! HOW DO YOU AND NIC KNOW EACH OTHER?
CLUB GIGS, MOSTLY. I'M A MUSICIAN. I PLAY THE GUITAR, I SING.
SHE'S GOT EVERYTHING!

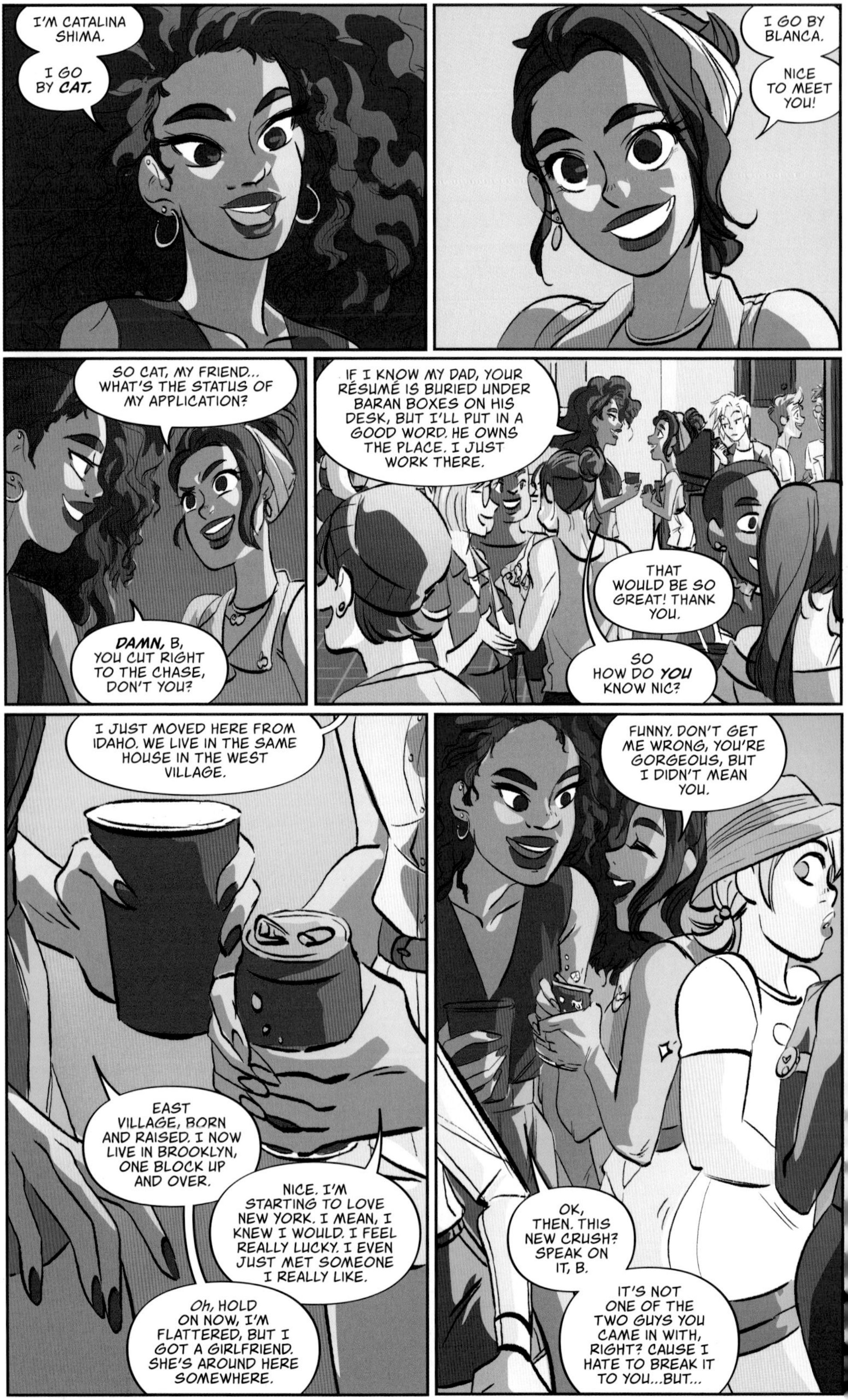
I'M CATALINA SHIMA.
I GO BY *CAT.*
I GO BY BLANCA.
NICE TO MEET YOU!
SO CAT, MY FRIEND... WHAT'S THE STATUS OF MY APPLICATION?
DAMN, B, YOU CUT RIGHT TO THE CHASE, DON'T YOU?
IF I KNOW MY DAD, YOUR RÉSUMÉ IS BURIED UNDER BARAN BOXES ON HIS DESK, BUT I'LL PUT IN A GOOD WORD. HE OWNS THE PLACE. I JUST WORK THERE.
THAT WOULD BE SO GREAT! THANK YOU.
SO HOW DO *YOU* KNOW NIC?
I JUST MOVED HERE FROM IDAHO. WE LIVE IN THE SAME HOUSE IN THE WEST VILLAGE.
EAST VILLAGE, BORN AND RAISED. I NOW LIVE IN BROOKLYN, ONE BLOCK UP AND OVER.
NICE. I'M STARTING TO LOVE NEW YORK. I MEAN, I KNEW I WOULD. I FEEL REALLY LUCKY. I EVEN JUST MET SOMEONE I REALLY LIKE.
Oh, HOLD ON NOW, I'M FLATTERED, BUT I GOT A GIRLFRIEND. SHE'S AROUND HERE SOMEWHERE.
FUNNY. DON'T GET ME WRONG, YOU'RE GORGEOUS, BUT I DIDN'T MEAN YOU.
OK, THEN. THIS NEW CRUSH? SPEAK ON IT, B.
IT'S NOT ONE OF THE TWO GUYS YOU CAME IN WITH, RIGHT? CAUSE I HATE TO BREAK IT TO YOU...BUT...

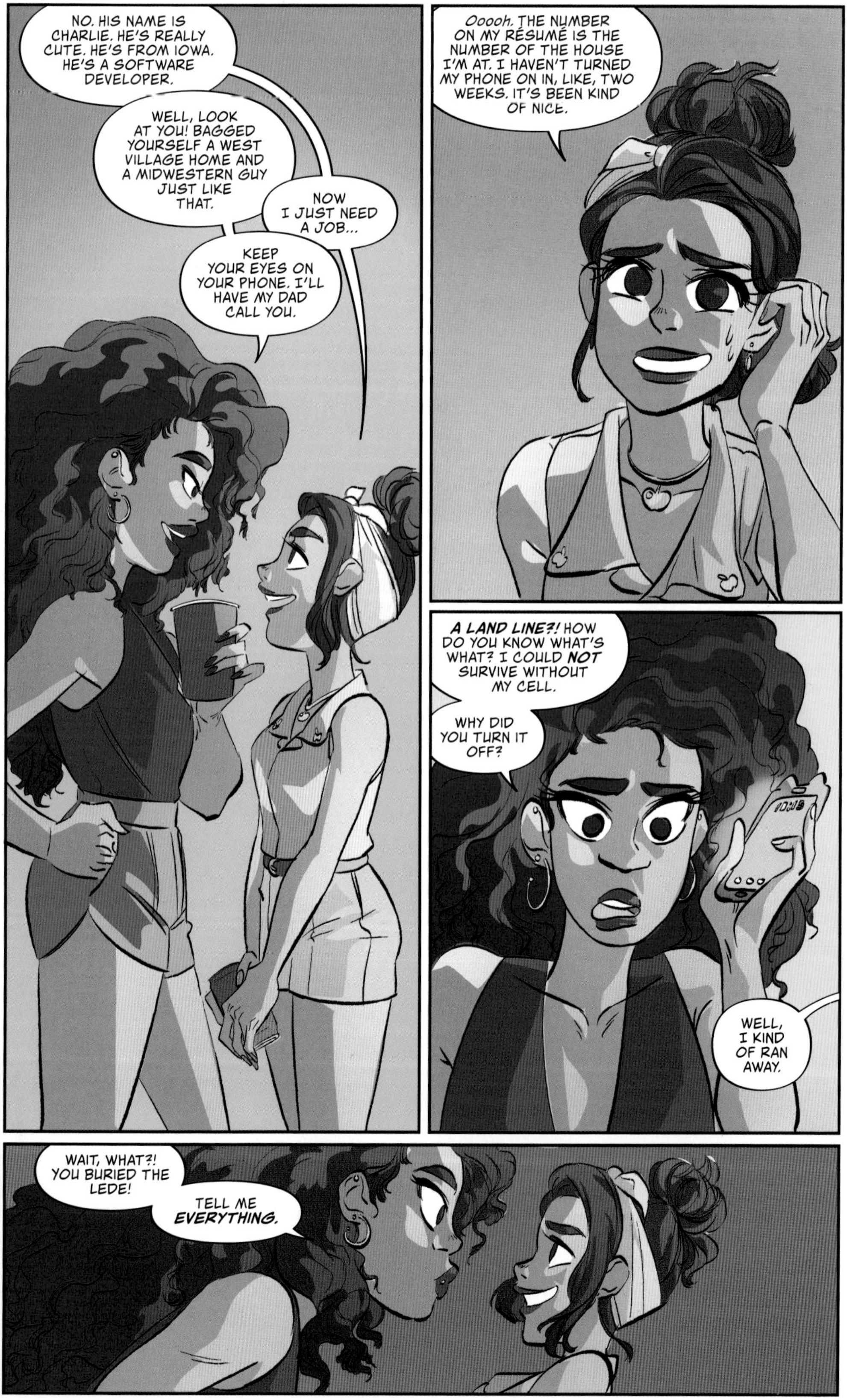
NO. HIS NAME IS CHARLIE. HE'S REALLY CUTE. HE'S FROM IOWA. HE'S A SOFTWARE DEVELOPER.
WELL, LOOK AT YOU! BAGGED YOURSELF A WEST VILLAGE HOME AND A MIDWESTERN GUY JUST LIKE THAT.
NOW I JUST NEED A JOB...
KEEP YOUR EYES ON YOUR PHONE. I'LL HAVE MY DAD CALL YOU.
Ooooh. THE NUMBER ON MY RÉSUMÉ IS THE NUMBER OF THE HOUSE I'M AT. I HAVEN'T TURNED MY PHONE ON IN, LIKE, TWO WEEKS. IT'S BEEN KIND OF NICE.
A LAND LINE?! HOW DO YOU KNOW WHAT'S WHAT? I COULD NOT SURVIVE WITHOUT MY CELL.
WHY DID YOU TURN IT OFF?
WELL, I KIND OF RAN AWAY.
WAIT, WHAT?! YOU BURIED THE LEDE!
TELL ME EVERYTHING.

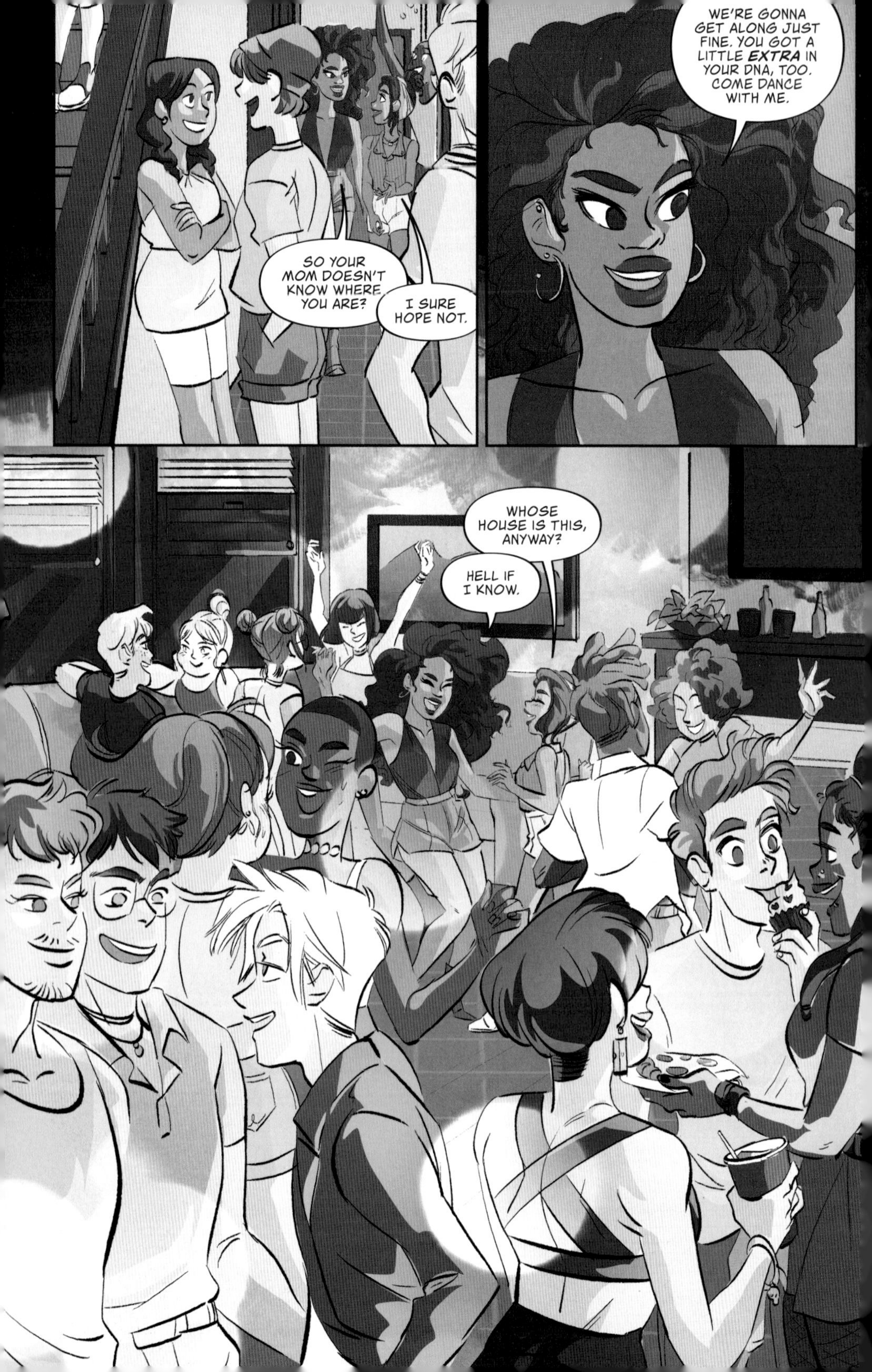
SO YOUR MOM DOESN'T KNOW WHERE YOU ARE?
I SURE HOPE NOT.
WE'RE GONNA GET ALONG JUST FINE. YOU GOT A LITTLE **EXTRA** IN YOUR DNA, TOO. COME DANCE WITH ME.
WHOSE HOUSE IS THIS, ANYWAY?
HELL IF I KNOW.

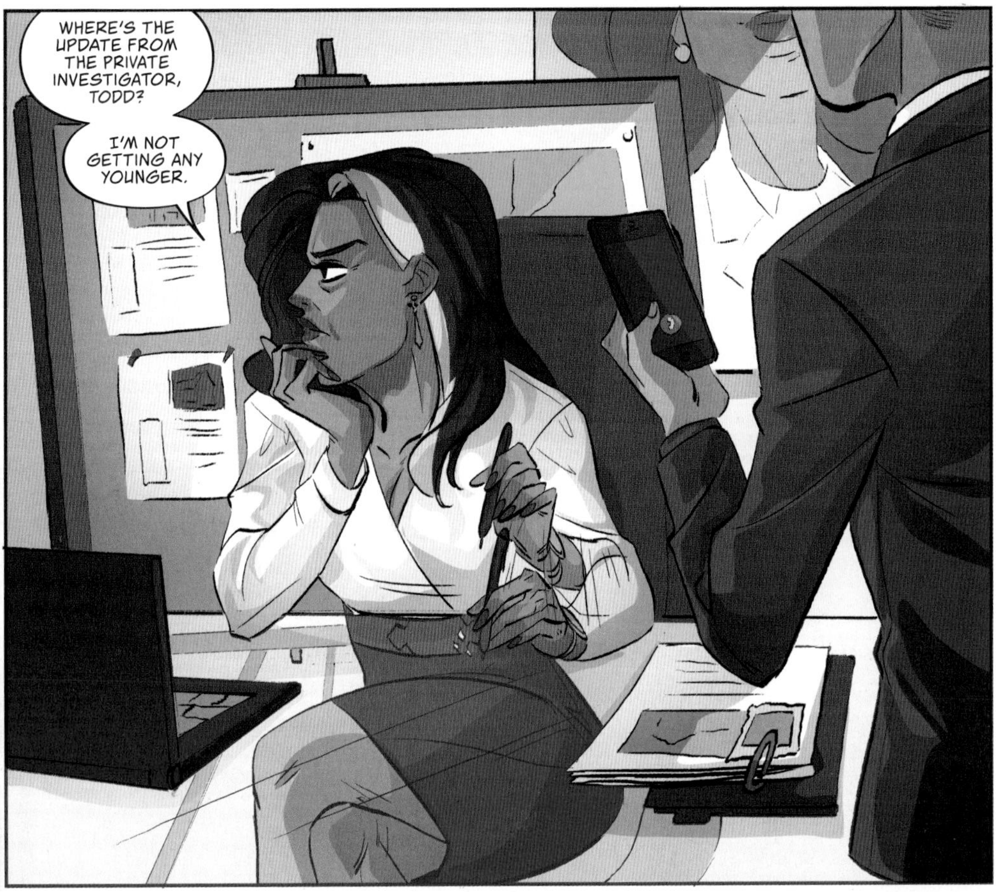
WHERE'S THE UPDATE FROM THE PRIVATE INVESTIGATOR, TODD?
I'M NOT GETTING ANY YOUNGER.

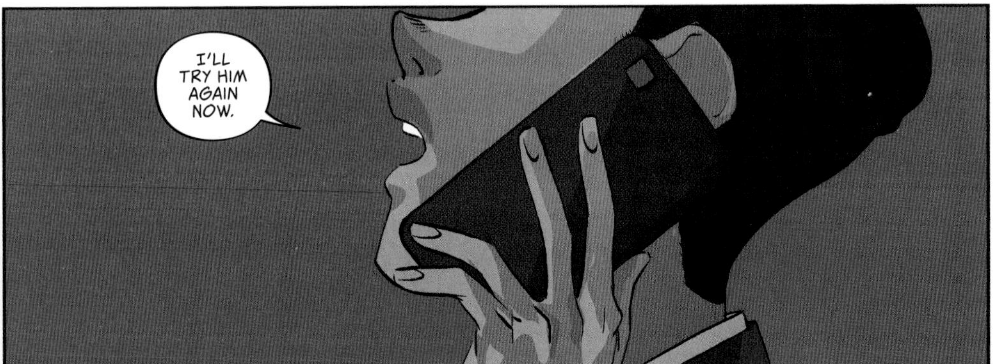
I'LL TRY HIM AGAIN NOW.

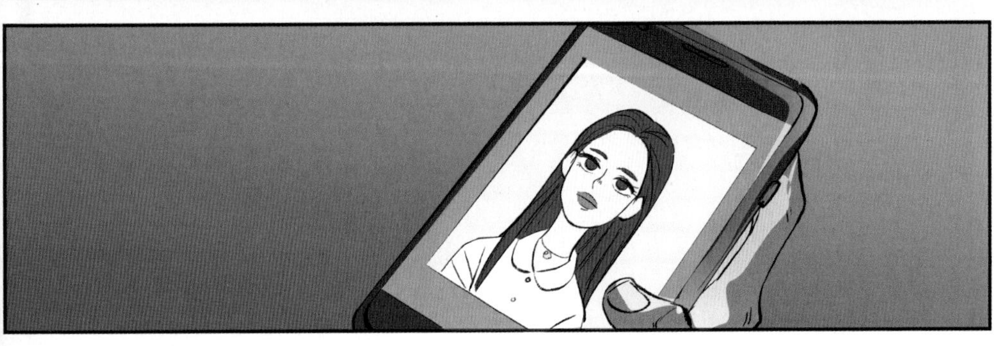

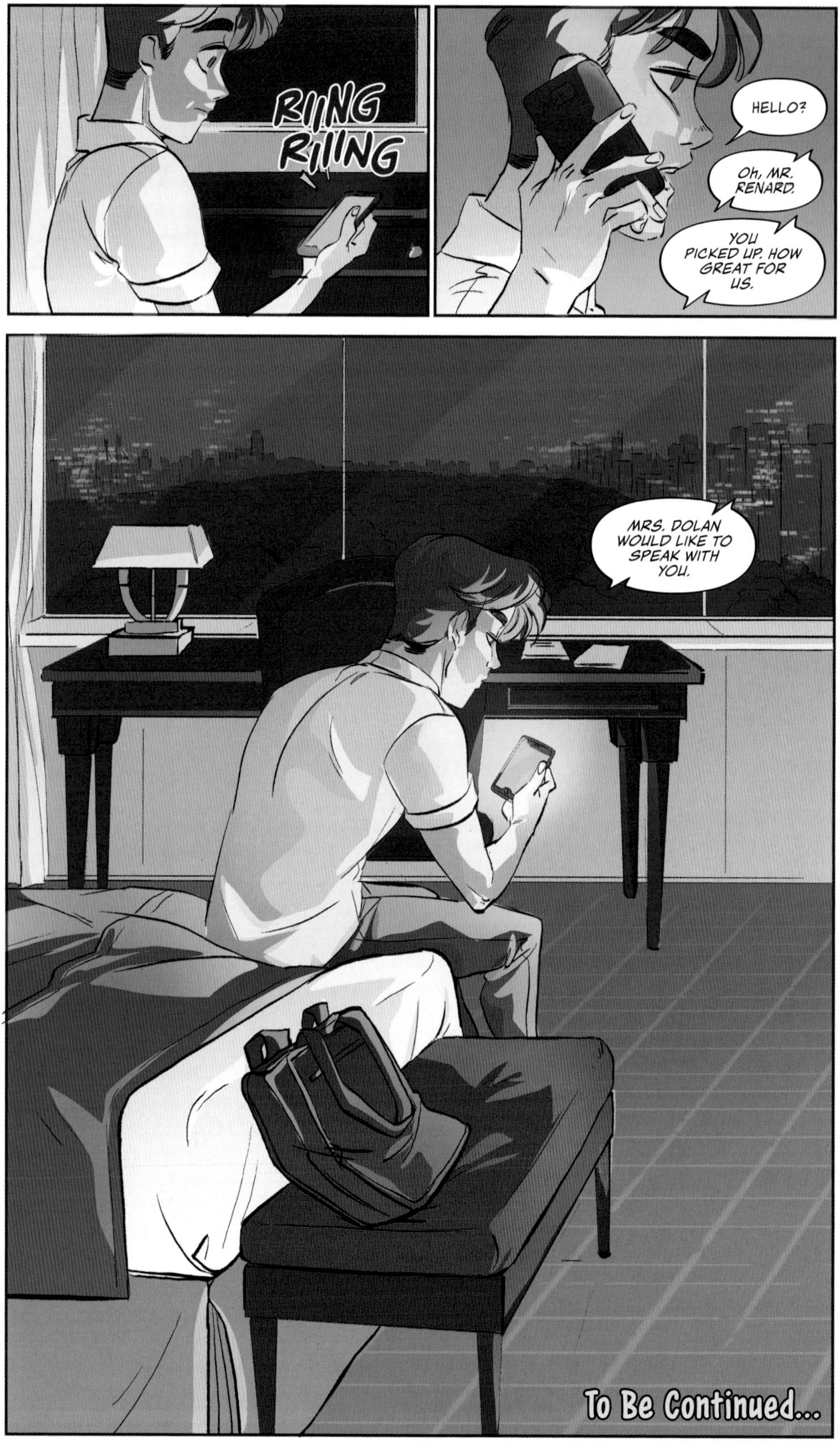
RIING
RIIING
HELLO?
Oh, MR. RENARD.
YOU PICKED UP. HOW GREAT FOR US.
MRS. DOLAN WOULD LIKE TO SPEAK WITH YOU.
To Be Continued...

DEVELOPING THE WORLD OF

Eat Your Heart Out

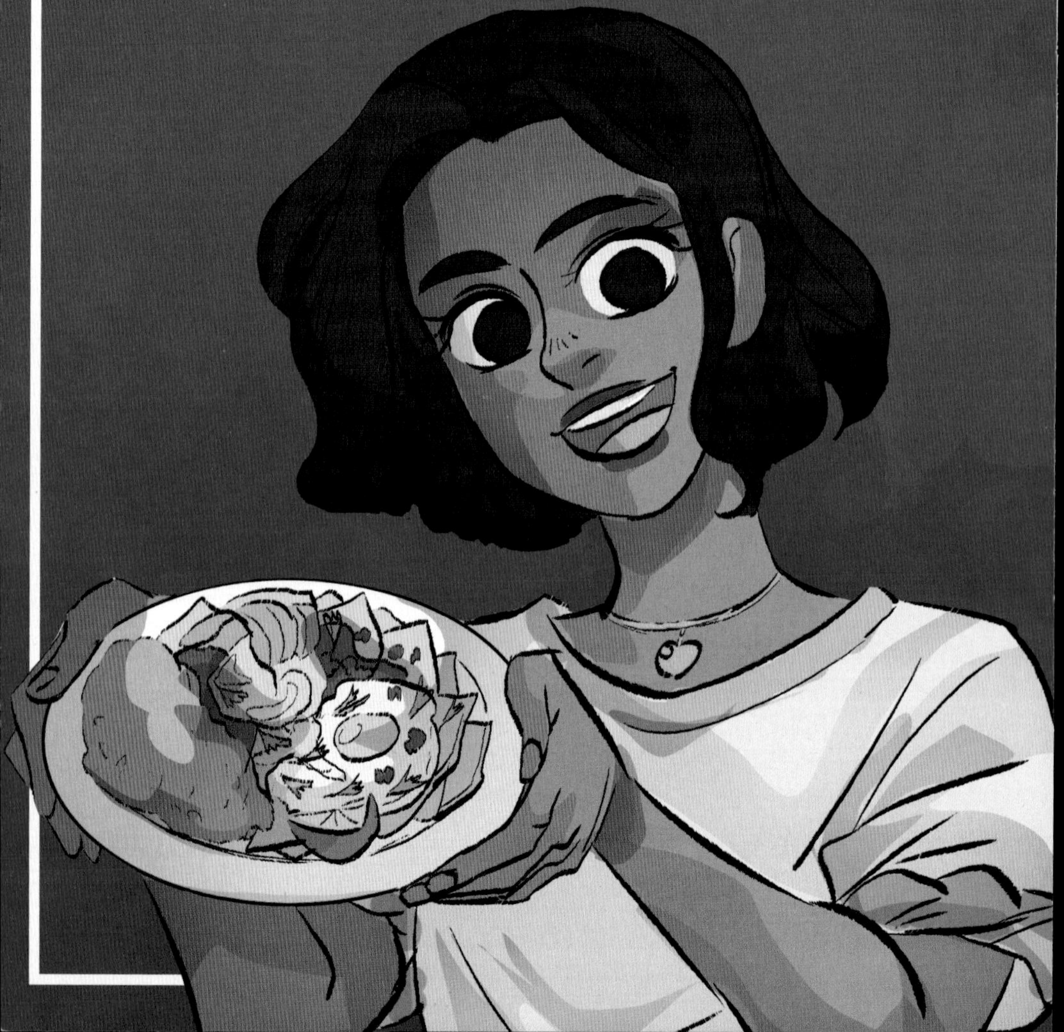

For almost as long as we've been friends, we've had the idea for *Eat Your Heart Out*. We came up with this story in 2005, but we never really took it that seriously. It was just something fun to do.

Many years passed and after Terry's book *Dead Weight* dropped and a career in comics seemed a bit more real, the two of us thought: "Why not give it a try? Why not take the leap and see where it takes us?" In 2016, we wrote up a pitch for *Eat Your Heart Out*, and Oni picked it up.

Terry has always been inspired by fairy tales. *Cinderella*, *The Little Mermaid*, *Snow White*, *The Wizard of Oz* . . . we wanted to bring a little of that magic into a modern story, for people who don't often get to see themselves represented in those tales...that was the goal. We conceptualized this story for many years, continuously revising it to catch up with the times and the mainstreaming of queer culture. To put it in perspective: when we began, *Will and Grace* was in its initial run, there was no *RuPaul's Drag Race*, and the Supreme Court would not make marriage equality legal in the United States for another 10 years. Initially, our protagonist had no exposure to the queer world outside of the fashion designers she idolized; now, virtually everyone in the country has queer culture at their fingertips, and the landscape has begun to shift so queer communities outside of major cities are beginning to find acceptance and thrive. Society was evolving, so our cast of characters evolved as well.

Our main character, Blanca, is a young artist who knows that in order to live the life she wants, she needs to leave home. She has to take that first step into "the scary woods" and escape to an unfamiliar place so she can follow her dreams. Terry did that when he moved to Los Angeles. Matty did that when they moved to Portland. We both found that by taking that leap, it led us to great things, great people, and experiences we'd never have had otherwise. And we wanted that for Blanca.

The New York in our story is a sort of "anyplace." Our Oz, our Wonderland. It's the stand-in for wherever it is someone runs toward in order to be themselves and live a life with purpose. It helped that New York is the fashion capital of the United States; and the farthest away Blanca could get from Idaho. Terry had lived in New York and he wanted the story to reflect and depict the many people of color he knew and loved there who don't often get to see themselves depicted in fantasy. If you look closely, you might find moments inspired by specific fairy tales, stories of women chasing their dreams and running toward something better.

The art in this book is more incredible than we could have ever imagined. Lydia, Claudia, and Gabe brought these characters to life and made them real. They pulled them from the depths of our imaginations and took a leap with us, bringing this project to life. We couldn't have asked for anything better, and we're proud of this story we've made with them.

If you think about a book or a comic or a movie that you love, it's likely because something in it spoke to you, or because you connected with or related to a character's story. You saw yourself in it. In our opinion, this means that seeing yourself reflected back reminds us all that our stories are important, and tells us that we are not alone.

Everyone has it in them to be the person they are meant to be. It was imperative to surround Blanca with a cast of characters who would recognize greatness in each other, and use their talents to help this messed-up world feel more livable. We are hard at work on Volume 2 of *Eat Your Heart Out*, in an election year, where the rights of our queer brothers and sisters, youth and elders, are once again being used as political fodder. We hope to add some levity to the fray. We hope you see yourself somewhere in this first volume and that it serves as a magic mirror who comes to life and tells you, "You're beautiful, you're here, you matter," despite the hurdles you may encounter and the voices trying to silence your dreams from coming true.

—Terry and Matty

BROWNSTONE DEVELOPMENT

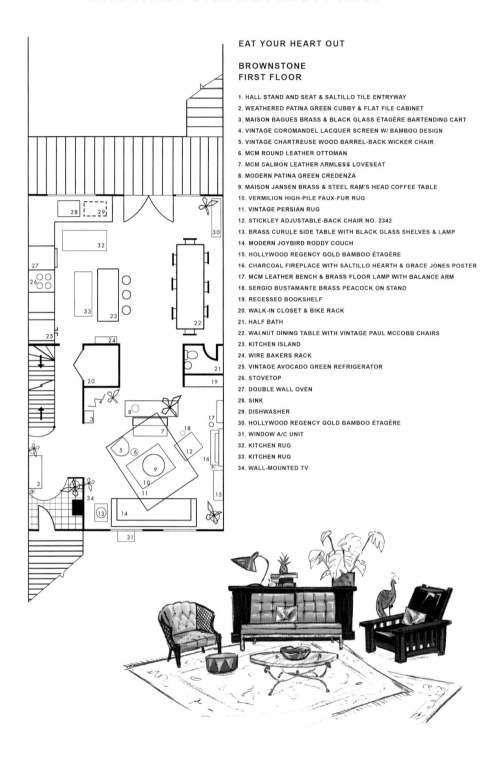

EAT YOUR HEART OUT

BROWNSTONE
FIRST FLOOR

1. HALL STAND AND SEAT & SALTILLO TILE ENTRYWAY
2. WEATHERED PATINA GREEN CUBBY & FLAT FILE CABINET
3. MAISON BAGUES BRASS & BLACK GLASS ÉTAGÈRE BARTENDING CART
4. VINTAGE COROMANDEL LACQUER SCREEN W/ BAMBOO DESIGN
5. VINTAGE CHARTREUSE WOOD BARREL-BACK WICKER CHAIR
6. MCM ROUND LEATHER OTTOMAN
7. MCM SALMON LEATHER ARMLESS LOVESEAT
8. MODERN PATINA GREEN CREDENZA
9. MAISON JANSEN BRASS & STEEL RAM'S HEAD COFFEE TABLE
10. VERMILION HIGH-PILE FAUX-FUR RUG
11. VINTAGE PERSIAN RUG
12. STICKLEY ADJUSTABLE-BACK CHAIR NO. 2342
13. BRASS CURULE SIDE TABLE WITH BLACK GLASS SHELVES & LAMP
14. MODERN JOYBIRD RODDY COUCH
15. HOLLYWOOD REGENCY GOLD BAMBOO ÉTAGÈRE
16. CHARCOAL FIREPLACE WITH SALTILLO HEARTH & GRACE JONES POSTER
17. MCM LEATHER BENCH & BRASS FLOOR LAMP WITH BALANCE ARM
18. SERGIO BUSTAMANTE BRASS PEACOCK ON STAND
19. RECESSED BOOKSHELF
20. WALK-IN CLOSET & BIKE RACK
21. HALF BATH
22. WALNUT DINING TABLE WITH VINTAGE PAUL MCCOBB CHAIRS
23. KITCHEN ISLAND
24. WIRE BAKERS RACK
25. VINTAGE AVOCADO GREEN REFRIGERATOR
26. STOVETOP
27. DOUBLE WALL OVEN
28. SINK
29. DISHWASHER
30. HOLLYWOOD REGENCY GOLD BAMBOO ÉTAGÈRE
31. WINDOW A/C UNIT
32. KITCHEN RUG
33. KITCHEN RUG
34. WALL-MOUNTED TV

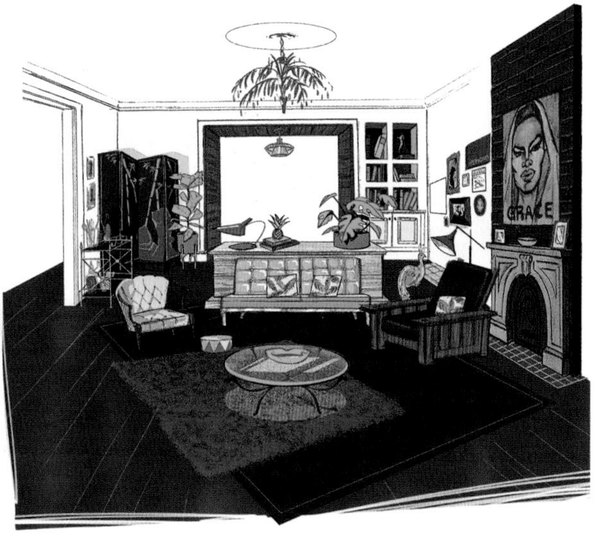
GRACE
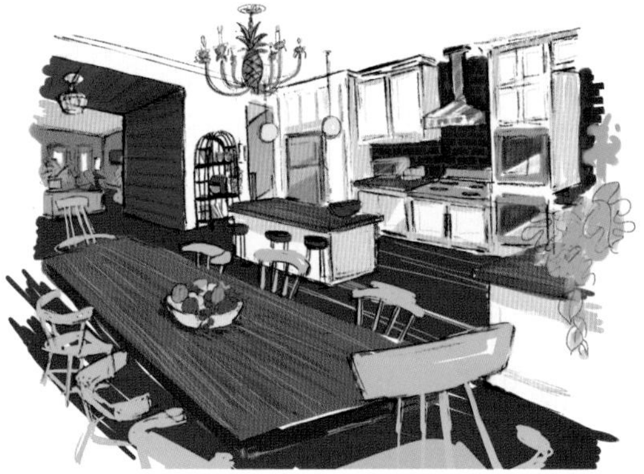
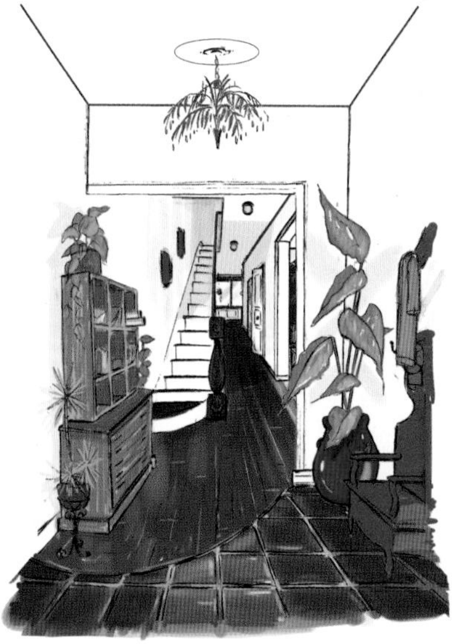
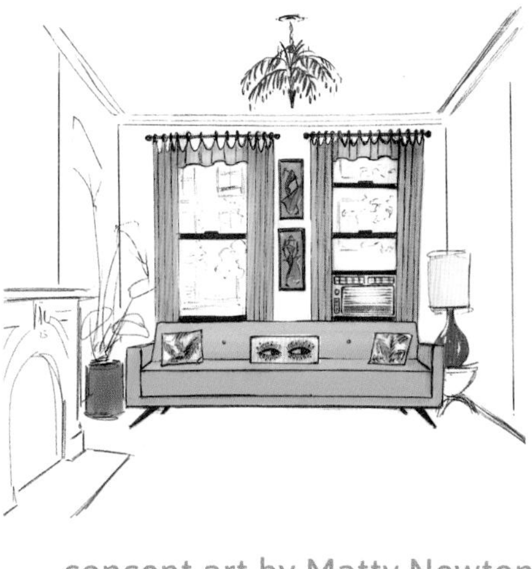

concept art by Matty Newton

CHARACTER DEVELOPMENT

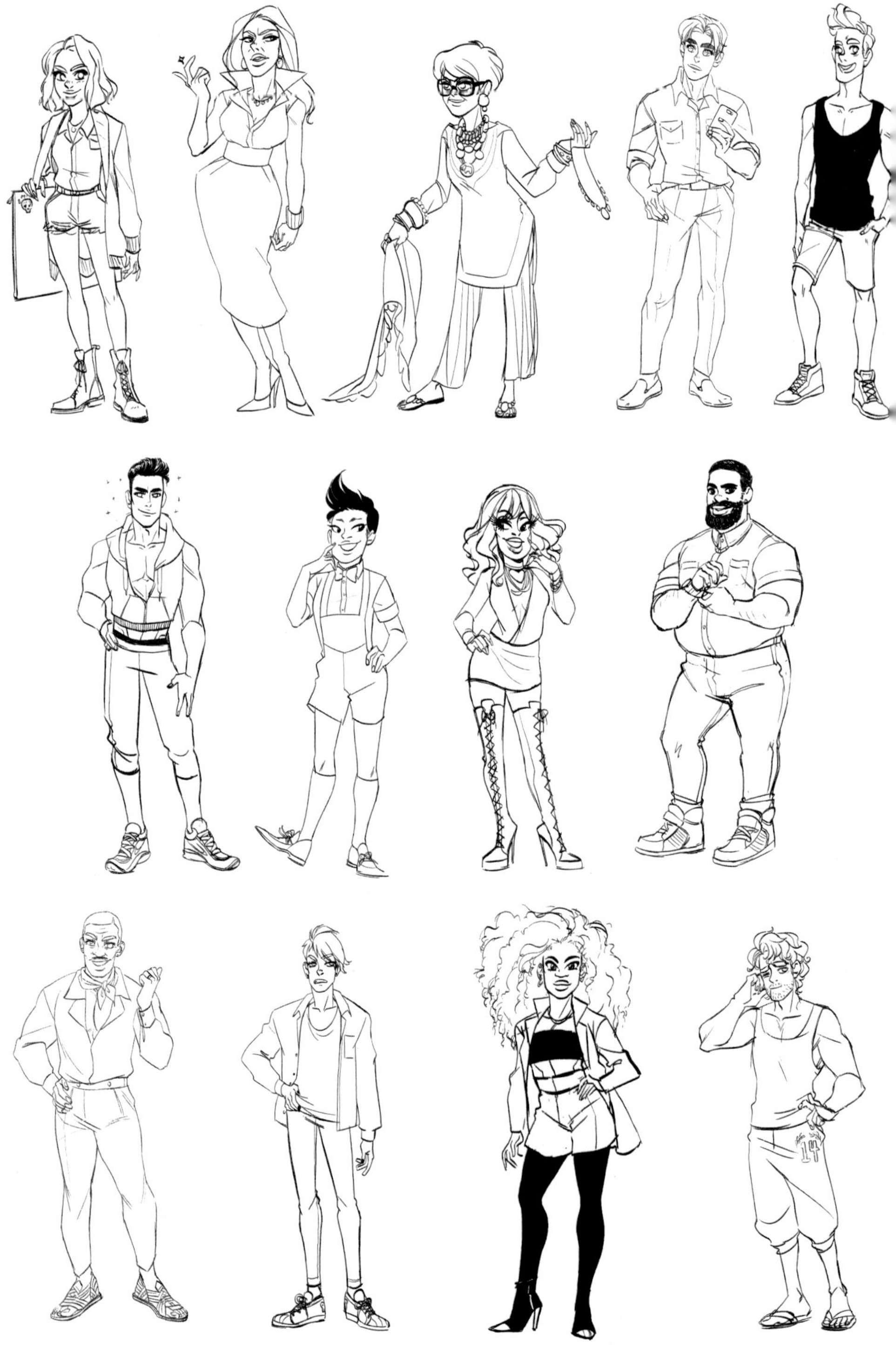

14

COVER DEVELOPMENT

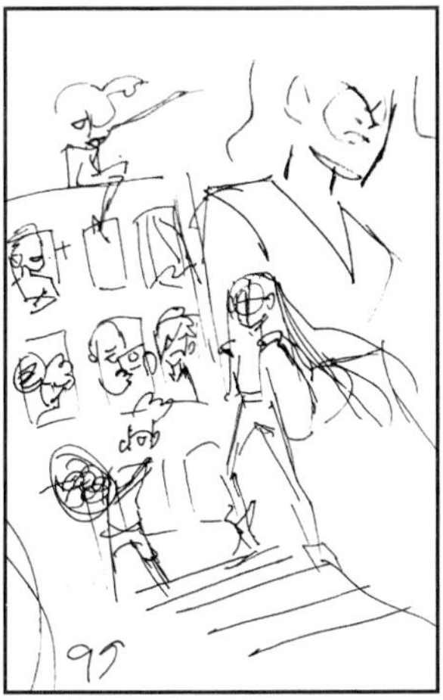

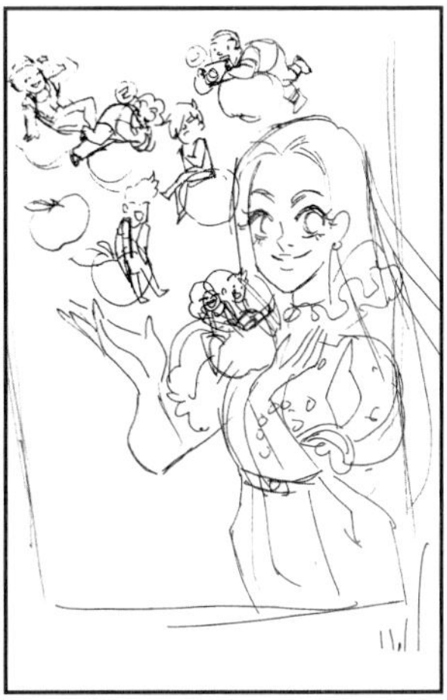

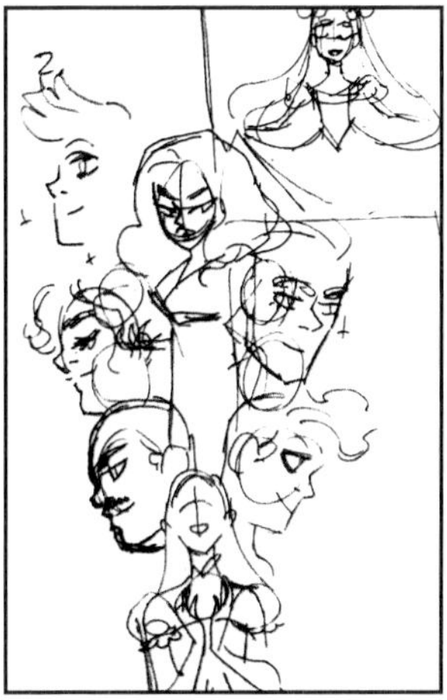

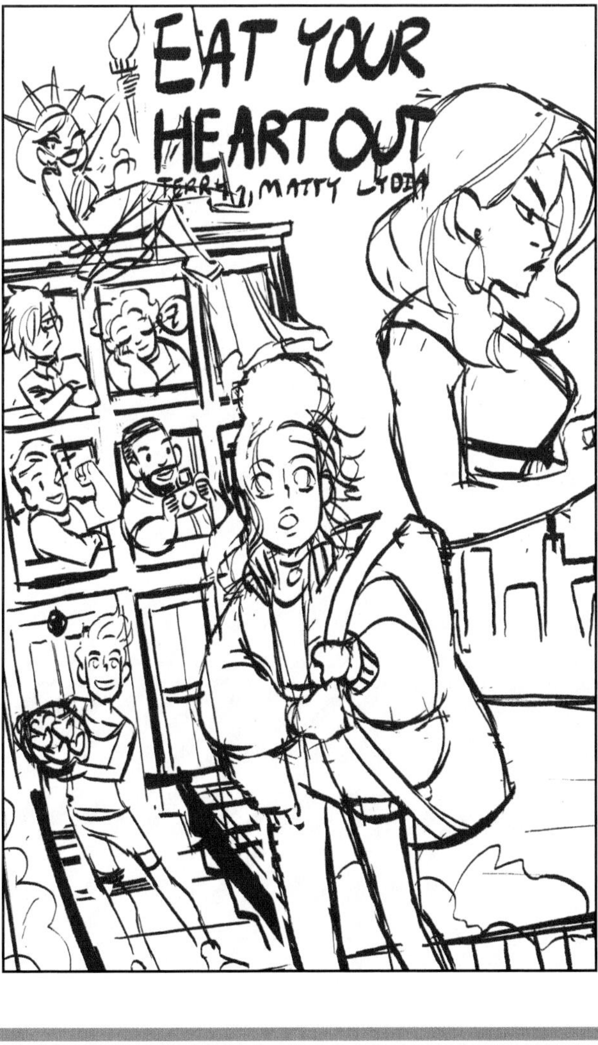
EAT YOUR
HEART OUT
TERRY MATTY LYDIA

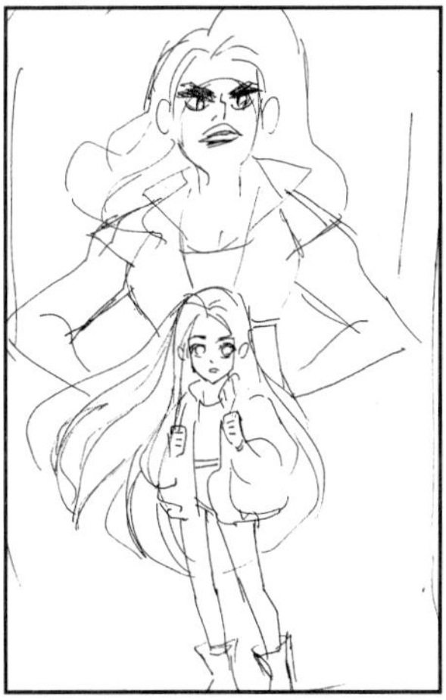

sketches by
Lydia Anslow

TERRY BLAS is the illustrator and writer behind the viral webcomics *You Say Latino and You Say Latinx*. He wrote *Ariana Grande vs. Sergeant Shade and the Clonebot Brigade*, the comic book tie-in for her R.E.M. fragrance. He is also the writer of *Steven Universe* comics for BOOM! Studios, and *Rick and Morty* comics for Oni Press. His original graphic novels are *Dead Weight: Murder at Camp Bloom*, *Hotel Dare*, and *Lifetime Passes*, all of which feature queer and Mexican characters. He has written the Marvel series *Reptil: Brink of Extinction*, *Nova*, and *Runaways*. Terry earned a BFA in illustration from Pacific Northwest College of Art. He lives in Oregon with his husband and their dog.

MATTY NEWTON is an illustrator, writer, and professional hoarder from Southern California. Matty began a career in visual arts as a scenic designer. Previously, Matty worked as a professional blogger for motion pictures at New Line Cinema, and earned a BFA in illustration from Pacific Northwest College of Art. Matty is a monthly contributing artist for *Imbibe* magazine, and has released two book covers published by Penguin Books UK. When Matty is not battling inner turmoils and gluten, they can be found on eBay buying back their childhood and yours, one piece of ephemera at a time.

LYDIA ANSLOW is an Los Angeles–based storyboard artist/revisionist and illustrator who's latest work includes Marvel's *Spider-Man Freshman Year* and Netflix's *Disenchantment*. Lydia helped as a board artist for the short *LUKi and the Lights*, an animated short in support of ALS with Big Grin Productions. Lydia is also a huge fan of manga and anime, her favorites being *One Piece*, *Sailor Moon*, and the *Finder Series* by Ayano Yamane, and she will talk to you at length about all of them.

CLAUDIA AGUIRRE is a Mexican, lesbian comic book artist and writer, GLAAD and Will Eisner Award nominee, and co-founder of Boudika Comics, where she self-publishes comics. Her comic works include *Lost on Planet Earth* with Comixology Originals, *Hotel Dare* with BOOM! Studios, *Firebrand* with Legendary Comics, *Morning in America* with Oni Press, and *Kim & Kim* with Black Mask Studios.